A
Theory
of Full
Employment

A Theory of Full Employment

Second Edition

Y.S. Brenner
and
N. Brenner-Golomb

with a new introduction by the authors

Routledge
Taylor & Francis Group

LONDON AND NEW YORK

Originally published in 1996 by Kluwer Academic Publishers.

Published 2000 by Transaction Publishers

Published 2017 by Routledge
2 Park Square, Milton Park, Abingdon, Oxon OX14 4RN
711 Third Avenue, New York, NY 10017

Routledge is an imprint of the Taylor and Francis Group, an informa business

Second edition copyright © 2000 by Taylor & Francis

Library of Congress Catalog Number: 99-028889

Library of Congress Cataloging-in-Publication Data

Brenner, Y. S.
  A theory of full employment / Y.S. Brenner and N. Brenner-Golomb ; with a new introduction by the authors.—2nd ed.
    p. cm.
  Originally published: Boston, Mass : Kluwer Academic, c1996.
  Includes bibliographical references and index.
  ISBN 0-7658-0608-8 (pbk. : alk. paper)
  1. Empolyment (Economic theory) 2. Labor Economics. 3. Full employment policies. 4. Economic policy. I. Brenner-Golomb, N. II. Title.
HD5701.5.B73 2000
339.5—dc21   99-028889

ISBN 13: 978-0-7658-0608-6 (pbk)

Contents

Introduction to the Second Edition

Three years elapsed since the first printing of *A Theory of Full Employment*. During these years the super-rich have become richer and the poor more numerous and poorer. The rift in society between people with good and well remunerated jobs, and people with little prospects of finding work and decent incomes, widened. Long-term unemployment remained high in Europe and even increased in places. The trickle of takeovers and amalgamation of banks and megacorporations turned into a torrent. The European nations moved closer to economic integration and to adopting a common currency; and the Asian Tigers lost much of their economic credibility. The conservative parties, which traditionally clung to policies designed to keep the system as it is—"because it works"—became protagonists of change, and the traditional Left, the conventional proponents of reform, became the defenders of the status quo—the rearguard of the Welfare State. In several economically powerful countries Social Democrats or Labour Parties were elected to govern or to share in government as major partners, but with a political agenda which is hardly distinguishable from that of the liberal Right. The essentials of true democracy—individual freedom, social equity, societal solidarity, care for the welfare of the majority of people, and the renunciation of violence, have been challenged by an aggressive market-liberalism. Under the guise of "liberty" and "personal responsibility" a new kind of liberalism undermines equity and solidarity, and provides economic success with a moral status that turns the interests of the strongest into the leading universal purpose. And at least in the human sciences the pursuit of truth has been subordinated to expediency, and has been replaced by a new-fangled relativism and mysticism which thwarts the confidence in them.

Facing the onslaught on the fundamentals of progressive democracy, the Left stands empty-handed. It has never been much concerned with solving the problems of the capitalism which it rejects. Competition and free enterprise have never been part of its ideological agenda. Its prime interest has been the political regulation of economic activities, and sometimes the smoothing of capitalism's roughest edges. It never asks whether the new "cures" which capitalism offers are necessary or desirable. It did not, and does not, examine the validity of the arguments given to prop up these "cures." Worst of all, it provides no immediate practicable alternatives to remedy the system's new afflictions. It has not sought new ideas to meet the issues in the center of the current malaise, namely the crisis in the classical labor structure, the growing need for creativity, the new technologies, and the direction of capital and investment. The quintessence of all Leftist politics, the quest for social justice, solidarity and individuals' freedom to develop their talents, still stands. But with no thorough analysis of the recent developments and no new instruments for dealing with them, the Left is allowing society to fall prey to unbridled egoism.

As for the economics profession, it simply went to sleep; and as the gaoler said to Posthumus in Shakespeare's *Cymbeline*: "He that sleeps feels not the toothache." But while it has been dreaming its neoclassical dreams, the social structure of the Welfare State is crumbling. The "Rheinland Model"—the democracy with a market economy and with state intervention to sustain the basic social values without which societal consensus cannot survive—is gradually falling apart.

Contributing to the Left's failure to counteract the new-style "liberalism" is the widespread confusion of economic growth with human progress. Economic growth leads only potentially to the augmentation of people's freedom of choice. *Economic growth* implies the raising of output per unit input of labor and other resources, and thereby to mankind's greater ability to satisfy its material needs more fully and with less effort. There is little freedom without economic security, but economic security depends upon man's mastery of both nature and his social modes of existence. The study of nature is in the domain of the natural sciences, and the study of man's social modes of existence is in the domain of the social sciences, but in their contribution to *human progress* both domains are inextricably interrelated and interdependent. Society's institutional framework determines the direction of its technological advancement, and scientific and technological achievements delimitate the possible forms of social organization. Science and technology govern the effort and labor-time required to satisfy man's material needs, and man's social arrangements determine the nature, diversity, extent, and all but the minimum of these needs, and the techniques adopted and priorities allocated for their satisfaction. With the increasing efficiency of production choice widens. It becomes possible to divide the extra time and effort between a growing variety of purposes. Yet, as the material constraints diminish, production and distribution processes become more complex and cultural constraints proliferate. Mankind enters the bondage of an increasingly sophisticated social environment which it inherits and creates. But the emergence of a society without poverty, a fraternal society which incorporates everyone in a shared moral citizenship without oppression or arbitrariness, is not inscribed into any historic plan.

Human progress is the extension of equal rights to an increasing number of people. The hallmark of a science which is to be applied for the achievement of human progress is the search for what is common to mankind, and for reaction, it is stressing of differences. Ancient Rome regarded slaves as "speaking instruments"; feudal society distinguished people with blue from red blood; early capitalism abolished slavery and "blood" but transformed workers into "labor power"; and early post-war democracy allowed workers to rise on the basis of individual competitive ability but did not provide them with equal opportunities. The liberal democratic capitalism of the Welfare State promoted equal rights for all irrespective of color, religion and sex, though unfortunately they were never fully attained.

The constant progressive element in all of science, and not only in the social sciences, has always been the widening of the likenesses man selects among the facts. Man's observations and experiences are many, perhaps infinite. By dividing them into what he believes matters and what does not, and into what is alike or fitting into a pattern and what is not, he passes judgment on his observations and experiences, and this judgment forms the basis of his beliefs. Newton saw the likeness between the fall of the apple and the swirling of the moon in her orbit round the earth; Einstein saw the unity of space and time, and the identity of energy and mass ($E = Mc^2$). Each of them saw unities, which no one had recognized before, and produced new conceptions of the universe. The point is that "when we discover the wider likeness, whether between space and time or bacillus and crystal, we enlarge the order in the universe; but more than this, we enlarge its unity. And it is this conception of the unity of nature living and dead that determines progress."[1] Early post-war democracy recognized the likeness in all men and arrived at a new conception of mankind. However, unlike Newton's and Einstein's, this conception was threatening too many of the social and economic establishment's vital interests to be universally accepted.

All this has been said before but needs to be restated to remind people that in both the natural and the social sciences it is the shift in the judgment of things regarded alike or unlike that determines our values. When a new likeness is discovered, previously disregarded facts and events assume a new significance, or their earlier significance is reassessed, and value judgments are altered. When society discovers a new likeness, a process of re-evaluation takes place. But the current inclination to regard *pure* self-interest as a unifying principle behind all behavior as if it was a scientifically established fact, and to equate it to individualism, is nonsense. Striving for equality is not antithetical to individuality. Equal *rights* may provide the basis for the opportunity to realize individual aims and desires, but if merely enshrined in the legal system they are insufficient to ensure them in reality. Modern science which searches for the unifying principles behind events makes the distinction between facts and values. Turning economic success into a kind of vindication of almost all means by which it is obtained, deprives it of its progressive content even if in terms of GNP it may from time to time engender economic growth. Economic growth is necessary and desirable, but not all economic growth and not at any price. The growth fetishism offered us these days, which is oblivious to the loss of human values it engenders, and too often even ignores environmental risks, can hardly lead to *human progress*.

New terms entered the political and economic vocabularies: *globalization, privatization, flexibility*, and *political correctness*. *Globalization*, the free movement of work and capital, is presented to the public as an argument for wage-restraint. *Privatization* of public enterprises, and the abolition of institutionalized collective wage-bargaining, are proclaimed the road to greater civil liberty, increasing efficiency, and less bureaucracy. *Flexibility* is extolled as the best means for adjusting supply to demand, and as the panacea for unemployment. And *political correctness*, the discarding of the search for historical truth, is tendered as an antidote against prejudice and discrimination. None of these terms means what they are claimed to signify. *Globalization* does not really mean the spreading of work and welfare over the entire globe. As a rule, and there are exceptions, enterprises do not move to where wages are the lowest. The large multinationals continue to maintain their production and their main offices in the traditional locations and develop their technology close to their customary bases. They find their finance in Europe and North America and invest it near home. Daimler and Chrysler may merge, and Microsoft may force companies to adopt its particular components world-wide, but this signifies a trend toward monopoly and not a shift in the location of employment and production. There has been an increase in Europe of exports and imports, but it is mainly inter-European. Trade with the rest of the world remained no greater than it had been in the 1960s.[2] There has been a tendency toward greater European integration, but this is not *globalization*.[3] Since the collapse of the Soviet Empire several powerful multinational companies began trading with what used to be the Eastern Bloc, but very few businesses have actually transferred their production activities there because of lower wages. Partly this reluctance to move can be explained by the usual reasons, like the absence of a satisfactory infrastructure and the deficiency of close-at-hand auxiliary trades. But there is also another reason, namely lack of confidence. To reduce uncertainty, most multinationals conduct their activities in Eastern Europe, as they have done in the Third World. First they only sell finished goods to traders who collect them from the home base and pay there in hard currencies. Later they make deals with local businesses, "joint ventures," by which they risk no more than the goods they actually send abroad; and only when they have gained confidence in the local partners, or received guarantees and subsidies from their own western governments, they transfer parts of their production lines abroad. Packaging and assembling may serve as examples for such relocations of activities. But this has little to do with low wage rates. More often than not the same work can be mechanized or automatized and done at less cost near base, and although it does create some employment abroad it is done to strengthen the tie with the communities in the new markets or to comply with certain legal obligations. Multinationals only take risks and use costly new technology in poor countries where scarce natural resources can be obtained.

In fact the assumed "trade-off" between wage-rates and the volume of employment is far from being as self-evident as it is claimed to be.[4] The point is that low wages may provide some short-term gains but inhibit a country's long-term competitive capabilities. They delay the replacement of technologically outdated equipment and reduce entrepreneurs' incentives to look for and introduce process innovating new technologies. What has actually happened since the 1970s, and has not changed, is that technological progress has segmented the labour market. It has caused an increasing demand for skilled and a diminishing demand for unskilled labour. Wage restraint in the skilled section of the labour market delays innovation, and in the unskilled sections it has no significant effect on the level of employment. Large multinational enterprises engage workers when they need them, and not because of low wages. Small or middle-size businesses appear initially to gain from lower wages, but as most of them are serving their domestic markets the early advantages are soon thwarted by customers' deficient purchasing power and they are forced to reduce again their output and employment. But this, being a less direct effect, is usually overlooked by the converts to the belief in the self-regulating mechanism of the market system. Essentially, undue wage restraint is no more than a government-initiated subsidy to prop-up the least efficient producers (which in the long-run may have disastrous consequences) and a redistribution of national income in favor of the rich. Since the time that wage-restraint was actually accepted in the Netherlands (1981) the national product rose by approximately 33%. However, the number of poor people increased, the number of people with a middle income decreased, and the rich and best remunerated became richer.[5] By 1994, 10% of the Dutch population owned almost 61.4% of the country's entire wealth.[6] The point is that wage increases below the rate of growth of gross national product (GNP), cannot perceptively reduce the volume of long-term unemployment of poorly skilled and unskilled labour in a highly industrialized country. The truth is that concerning globalization nothing has really changed since the first publication of this book. The economy has not become *globalized*; trade outside the industrialized countries has not significantly increased and wage-restraint, which is still recommended to allow globalization a smooth passage, has not created more jobs for unskilled workers in either the industrialized or in underdeveloped countries. The one thing that has become global is the movement of financial assets.

Privatization is another term bandied about as if it is an indisputable fact that communities are better and cheaper served by privately owned companies than by public enterprises. Again the real meaning of the term is obfuscated and many people are led to confuse profitability with efficiency. They assume that the height of profits reflects efficiency. They forget that some public utilities work very efficiently and show no profit while some private enterprises are inefficient but nonetheless most profitable. They ignore that a large number of essential public enterprises, which are indispensable for sustaining a highly sophisticated economic system, are public because they are unattractive to private investors. Since their privatization, the services of British Rail have worsened, but passenger fares went up; the water supply in parts of the United Kingdom has become erratic while its price to customers increased. In the Netherlands the railways were well run before privatization. To make them profitable, now services to many stations are reduced or abandoned and people are obliged to use other means of transport which are more expensive and less environment-friendly. The National Health Service, which in many European countries has been a public institution which saved sick and old people from financial ruin, has now been partly privatized. Private insurance companies are given the role previously held by the state. This does not only raise the overall cost of health care because its fragmentation causes insurance risks to be spread less widely, but it also engenders the negative effect that to sustain profitability the private companies are reluctant to insure precarious cases or must demand for them high premiums. This means that the poor, but not the poor alone, may soon no longer be able to afford the help they need. In fact privatization cannot improve medical assistance nor can it make it more cost-effective. To become profitable private insurers can only reduce services, refrain from acquiring new equipment, overwork and underpay hospital staff. Without state subsidies they will not modernize. The only consequence will be expensive care for those who can afford it and inferior care for those who cannot. But if in order to prevent this outcome privatized health care will be subsidized it will be as costly as before privatization or even more expensive.

Why then do many European governments now "privatize"? To avoid losing favor with the tax-allergic electorate by raising taxes to meet the ever growing needs, and to obtain money by the sale of public property in order to reduce the National Debt so they can meet the criteria laid down for joining the common European currency. But most important, to shed responsibility—relying on the myth by the use of the new terms, they conceal their managerial incompetence. Consciously or unconsciously the political oligarchy is divesting itself of tasks where managerial ineptitude is directly observable. Whether in commerce and industry or in government, the lords of the new order of industrial feudalism seek power without responsibility.

Another term in vogue is *flexibility*. In industry this means the ability to adjust swiftly to market shifts and new technologies. Many working families with children and with good incomes also welcome flexibility because it affords them the opportunity to work less days per week so that both the husband and the wife can find more time for their family. But more often when applied to work it means greater freedom for employers to dismiss redundant labour than for workers to determine for themselves how many days or hours they wish to work. At first sight this seems a reasonable arrangement. Many employers welcome *flex-work*[7] because it releases them from the pressure of having to organize their businesses in such a manner that employees will not be idle due to delays in the supply of materials and equipment or because of temporary loss of custom for their products. What the public tends to forget is that flexibility also means the retraction of some established institutionalized arrangements to protect their livelihood, such as security of tenure, collective bargaining, minimum wage legislation, and other social security provisions. Again a difference needs to be made between skilled and unskilled labour, and between large and small business enterprises. Skilled workers have little to fear from *flexibility*. Few employers will risk to lay off qualified experienced workers when they are temporarily unable to employ them. *Transaction costs* are much too high for that. Particularly the largest export-orientated firms are well aware of the loss of productivity when new workers need to learn the job, and of the lost experience when workers are replaced. They are wary of the cost involved in finding qualified workers when they need them, and fear the leaking of production secrets to other firms when their former workers seek new employment. With unskilled workers things are very different. For them flexibility does not only mean an end to security of tenure, but loss of income with each recession and depression. As their earnings depend on the number of days, and often of hours, they work, their living standard falls with every economic downturn.

The proponents of flexibility claim that flex-work creates more jobs. In fact it only subsidizes employment in inefficient firms, because it renders some cost advantages to small- and middle-size firms but damages their long-term prospects by reducing the expansion of the domestic effective market-demand upon which most of these businesses depend. The supporters of flex-work also assert that employers, if they are not obliged to enter into long-term contracts with their work-force, are encouraged to experiment with new products and new services; and that under threat of easy dismissal workers become more diligent. The truth is that where flex-work was tried-out it showed no perceptible change in the volume of employment if it is measured in hours worked instead of days. Like piece-work wages, which were quite common before World War II, flex-work impedes technological innovation and shifts the cost of managerial incompetence upon the shoulders of the workers. It makes employers less willing to invest in the schooling of their labour force, reduces workers' loyalty to the firms for which they work, and lessens their motivation and responsibility. Worst of all, it creates a social climate of insecurity and leads to societal polarization, and undermines the one factor to which the success of the so-called "polder model" can be attributed, namely the almost harmonious cooperation between employers' organizations and trade unions.

Not all the arguments in favor of privatization, flexibility, etc., are groundless, and not all the arguments against them are as clear-cut as they appear to be in this introduction, but what the public does not realize is that behind what seems mere technicalities, lurks a reactionary conception of society—a cultural revolution reviving the social and economic pseudo-Darwinism of prewar unregulated capitalism.

Political correctness is a term which belongs to a different genre of modern verbal usage. It was first employed by Stalin's followers to sustain "ideological unanimity" in the Communist party and to silence opposition. In the West it initially appeared to have a liberal progressive connotation. It suggested itself as an antidote to the perseverance of well entrenched prejudices—as a weapon in the struggle against discrimination. In the 1990s it has lost its progressive quality and turned into a divisive force. Disposing of *truth*, the champions of political correctness have adopted an advertisers' stance. Anything which may help "to sell the product," true or false, can be claimed for it. As a result university courses which could have served the advancement of human rights, for example women studies or ethnic studies, have become socially divisive and often their teachings no less bigoted than the establishment's doctrines they intend to dislodge. While the search for truth can promote equality by showing the unifying characteristics of mankind and explain the differences, political correctness in its present usage is in effect denying these unifying characteristics exactly as established power does, both resorting to untruth to bolster up their legitimate or illegitimate objectives. This deprives those struggling against discrimination of their credibility, prevents the making of a common effort by the various groups who are discriminated against, and alienates the many others who are inclined to lend them their support.

At the end of the earlier printing of this book we concluded that our social and economic system is in the process of reorganization and that the final outcome of this reorganization is unpredictable. Since *A Theory of Full Employment* was first published the people of Europe have taken two decisions which will doubtlessly affect this outcome. One decision was to establish a common currency, and the other was to get rid of much of the Thatcherite ideology and vote into office more progressive and humane leaders. In how far these developments signal a new course is still hard to predict. The common European currency may just as well turn out to be a banker's charter which imposes the wishes of a rich oligarchy upon the rest of society, as it may lead to greater prosperity, economic stability, and social progress. The terms formally agreed upon for the introduction of the currency indicate a move in the direction of the first alternative, but the fact that in several member states of the European Community the New Left obtained political power may give this tendency another twist. The New Left has declared employment to be at the top of its agenda, but in fact it has developed few promising new initiatives to solve the unemployment problem. Unlike the previous governments the new ones admit that education and training are the key to the solution of the problem, but they continue cutting the funding of universities and other educational institutions. They speak of solidarity, the need for social services, but do not end the sale of public assets and privatization. They acknowledge the decline in citizens' domestic security, but do not appreciably increase the budget for paying more policemen on the streets. They perceive that the rich are becoming richer and that the number of the poor increases but they do not raise taxes in order to finance the revival of full employment and the positive social arrangements of the Welfare State which they continue to dismantle.

The future is still in the balance, it will neither be like the past nor entirely unlike it. The measure in which the citizens of Europe will recognize the opportunities the demise of the Thatcherite ideology offers them will influence whether the future will be ruled by selfishness and unbridled egoism, or by the endeavour to build a society without poverty, arbitrariness and oppression.

Notes

1. See Bronowski, J. [1951] *The Common Sense of Science*. Harmondsworth, Penguin Books Ltd (reprinted 1968) p.134; and concerning the political widening of unity see Ginsberg M. [1946] *Sociology* OUP.

2. For example, the volume of Dutch trade with the rest of the world, except for one year in 1985, was the same as by the end of the 1960s.
Vide Kleinknecht A.H. [1998] *Mythen in de polder*. Delft, Technische Universiteit Delft. p.3 Table 1.

3. *Vide* Kleinknecht A. and J. ter Wengel [1997] "The myth of economic globalisation,"*Cambridge Journal of Economics*.

4. In Italy exports increased when wages rose and decreased when they fell. And in the Netherlands, a country which is crucially dependent on its export, during the decades of wage restraint GNP rose by more than the European average from 1982 to 1986 and from 1989 to 1993, but fell below the average from 1986 to 1989 and from 1994 to 1996. Kleinknecht A.H. [1998] *op.cit.* p.7, and Deelsen L. & De Jong E. [1997] "Het wankele mirakel" in *Economisch Statistische Berichten*, Vol.81, pp.324–327

5. *Vide* van Eijck S.R.A. [1998] "Verrijking en de belastingplannen Zalm-Vermeend" in Albeda W. de Gaay Fortman and Goudzwaard (eds) *De rijke kant van Nederland* Van Gennep, Amsterdam. pp.223–225

6. Data from Dutch Central Office of Statistics *(CBS)*.

7. The term *flex-work* may not be familiar to American readers because in the USA employers can usually fire workers at will and without compensation. This is not the case in most European welfare states (where minimum wages are imposed by law and employers are legally obliged to contribute to their employees pension funds and health insurance premiums). To evade the legal obligations, and to dodge the agreements with the trade unions, and be able to employ workers part-

time, for example in super-markets only during the short number of hours when they are most crowded, employers can now take advantage of private labour exchanges, which are businesses that hire out "their" workers for hours or days with no duty by the actual employers to abide by the legal obligations. Often these workers are young people who work for the minimum youth-wage, and who are dismissed as soon as they reach the age at which they must be paid adult wages. The advantage governments gain from this is that statistically it reduces the level of unemployment. During the last years the system of flex-work has become fairly widespread in the Netherlands but was prevented from being adopted in Germany by the trade union resistance.

Foreword to the 1996 Edition

This book has three purposes. First, to convince professional economists who study the behavior of the economic system as a whole that they must re-examine some of the assumptions behind the reigning economic theories. Second, to explain to the general public why the currently fashionable economic policies cannot solve the problem of massive long term unemployment. Third, to show that if people's political engagement is revived there is hope for escaping from the economic morass and moral wasteland into which, ever since the 1970s, the fashionable policies have been leading us.

To elucidate the theoretical problem the authors pass in review several recent structural developments and consider their effect on the economy. To encourage renewed public political engagement they draw attention to the risks involved in allowing things to drift on in the present direction.

The avowed purpose of the book imposes the need to present it in a manner accessible at once to professional macroeconomists and to a wider public of people concerned about today's malaise, politicians, sociologists or philosophers and others. This imposes the need not to encumber readers with the customary glut of academic references in the text, and to refer only to the best known and politically most influential theories and to authors who are also widely known to people who are not professional economists. However to reassure readers who may have doubts about the appropriate interpretation of these authors' views, a list of cited literature is appended to the text which should enable them to find the book or article from which the quotation or the attributed opinions were gleaned. In addition a glossary of terms is also appended so that those who are not familiar with economic or philosophical terminology can find the meaning of the terms we use without resort to special dictionaries.

Although several suggestions are made as to how economic theory must be restructured to suit the new circumstances, and what action should be taken to escape the wasteland of the spirit into which the fashionable policies are leading us, the authors do not presume to offer easy answers. All they can do is indicate why, if people will abandon outworn "habits of thought" and think about alternatives, and renew their political engagement, there is hope to find useful employment for all who are able and willing to work and to put an end to the fear of destitution.

The authors wish to thank Dr. Eric Clavering, as well as the members of the department of social economics of Utrecht University, for the helpful comments on the various early drafts of the book, and Mrs. Maiumi Sadler-Hamada for the time she spent preparing it for publication.

1

Introduction

For more than a thousand years the world of the *Almagest* ruled supreme. Ptolemy's perception of a finite world contained in the sphere of the fixed stars, with the earth stationary at its center, and the sun and other heavenly bodies revolving about it in their orbits like "jewels in their fixed mountings," remained unshaken. In spite of the continual need to modify this perception of the universe to fit the calendar it was not abandoned. It seemed self-evident and was confirmed by the Holy Scriptures. The earth was stationary in the center of the universe. Apples landed beneath their trees, not way behind them as they would have done if the earth was moving; and there was no perpetual storm constantly blowing from the east. It made no difference that people saw that objects falling from the top of the mast of moving ship landed at the foot of the mast on deck and not in the ship's wake. Such is the power of "received beliefs." The most ingenious ideas were advanced to modify Ptolemy's model, but the alternative, a rotating earth revolving around the sun, was plainly too far-fetched to be considered.

When early in the 16th century Copernicus dared to suggest that the sun and not the earth is at the center of the solar system, his hypothesis was suppressed for thirty years and published only a year after his death. When Galileo made Copernicus's heliocentric theory plausible he was banned by the Church authorities and made to recant and placed under house arrest for the last years of his life. One could improve and supplement the Ptolemaic system, not challenge its essential "truth."

Like the astronomers of old who kept on "improving" the Ptolemaic system, Paul Samuelson, Robert Solow and others tried to bring the economic orthodoxy closer to reality. Ingeniously they lumped together indigenous self-adjusting elements into proxy variables, such as "real national income per head" or "capital-labour ratio," and made them part of formulae for predicting the effects of exogenous factors on these fictitious variables representing the equilibrating economic system. Sir John Hicks transformed Keynes's critique into a "special case" of sticky wages which originate outside the economic order and do not form an inherent part of it. Dissent from the economics mainstream dogma was either internalized or marginalized by the establishment.

1

Arthur Cecil Pigou, in derision, called Keynes "a new Galileo" because he denied the validity of some major tenets of the ruling doctrine. More recent critics are either not published at all or published in journals and books which are seldom read by anyone but the converted.

The point is that while scientists' philosophical background seldom influences their answers it does determine their questions, and the final outcome can depend on this. Economists educated in the neoclassical mechanistic paradigm are ill equipped to ask questions about the organic long-term dynamic process of our complex economic life. To obtain rigor by quantification they leave out of their models the so-called exogenous variables. They admit that such variables as technological innovation, changes in social conduct, the emancipation of women, the increasing alertness to environmental hazards, may influence the economic system, but they pretend that these factors are not themselves also influenced by the economic system. They assume a one-way traffic and ignore that most of the forces labelled exogenous do not develop in an economic vacuum. They simply disregard the mutual influence of social and economic factors by introducing unrealistic assumptions such as "ceteris paribus." These assumptions may be expedient for the prediction of short-run microeconomic processes, but are a travesty where long-term macroeconomic processes are concerned. They transform Economics into scholastics—calculating how many angels can simultaneously dance on the point of one pin.

Professor Milton Friedman tells us that he is less concerned whether an economic theory is true or not than whether or not his recommendations obtain the expected results. There is of course nothing wrong with pragmatic predictions, but they are poor substitute for fundamental science. Donald McCloskey believes that economics and other sciences must be read as rhetoric. Pragmatic decisions and rhetoric are important because they are politically effective, but expediency is the hallmark of the bureaucrat, not of the scientist. The scientist's hallmark is the search for truth.

In his Nobel Lecture Professor Friedman claimed that there is little difference between economics and the natural sciences because "in both there is no certain substantive knowledge." He is wrong; there is a fundamental difference. Individuals and entire societies learn from experience: molecules do not. The reason why neoclassical economics makes proselytes is therefore not its superior scientific status but the illusion of objectivity it conveys. It answers scientists' deep-rooted urge to obtain precision by quantification. But as Ray Marshall, the US Secretary of Labour in the Carter Administration, once said: "it is better to be approximately right than rigorously wrong."

There may be different perceptions of the universe and various ways of explaining how it functions, but the universe is "given" while social institutions and individuals' modes of conduct are transient. They are the historical product of societies. Man cannot change the fact that apples fall down and not up, but by formulating a law of gravity he can calculate the required initial velocity for sending a rocket to the moon. Yet man's reaching the moon does not invalidate gravitation. But institutional changes can make nonsense of the behavioral assumptions upon which our economic theories are founded. The notion of a rational utility-maximizing individual is absurd in a Feudal context, or in an environment in which greed constitutes a mortal sin unless utility includes the expectation of reward in a life hereafter.

Unlike neoclassical economics, modern science recognizes the two-way traffic between disciplines. Classical physics never produced a comprehensive theory of matter. It described the behavior of mechanisms taking some material constants (such as density, elasticity etc.) as given. But with the knowledge gained in chemistry many questions, like *why* copper melts at 1083 centigrade, which were not discussed in classical physics, could be answered. This does not mean that the laws of classical physics were overthrown by physical chemistry. But it does show the limitations of earlier classical theories. It is the same with economics; until its reciprocal relationship with other social sciences is established it will remain debilitated. It must sweep some of the most important questions under the carpet. It must proclaim unemployment voluntary or define it into obscurity. Professor Friedman does this by introducing the term *natural unemployment*. This he defines as the level of unemployment "that would be ground out by the Walrasian system of general equilibrium equations provided there is embedded in them the actual structural characteristics of labour and commodity markets, including market imperfections, stochastic variability in demands and supplies, the cost of gathering information about job vacancies and labour availabilities, the cost of mobility and so on." In other words, natural unemployment is all the unemployment which equilibrium economics cannot account for because its sources impinge upon the neoclassical system from outside. Like Pontius Pilatus, neoclassical economics washes the curse of unemployment from its hands, creating the impression that mankind was on earth to serve the economy and not economic science to serve the needs of man.

Similarly mainstream economic theory cannot reconcile short-term with long-run expectations when they run in opposite directions, nor solve the problems which arise when private and public interests are in conflict. Neoclassical economics either ignores such questions or denies their actuality. The one it declares none of its business because "proper economics" is only concerned with short term problems; the other it proclaims solved because an "invisible hand" leads people pursuing their own interest to promote that of society more effectively than when they intend to do so. In essence, therefore, neoclassical economics endows *rationality* with a short-run individualistic subjective value-laden meaning which makes economic theory scientifically untenable. It presents laws of limited validity in a manner which gives the impression that they are of universal applicability—as if the adding up of micro events produces a true reflection of macro reality. This is the same as concluding that our earth is flat from the observation that the oceans are not drained of water, and liquids flow off uneven surfaces.

It is perfectly rational for a profit-maximizing entrepreneur to expand production when demand for his produce is increasing. Should his competitors be doing the same the combined output may exceed demand and his profit expectations will be thwarted. This is an information problem which can perhaps be solved. But what when the maximizing entrepreneur experiences a fall in demand? Competition will make it rational for him to reduce prices if he can, and if the business rivals do the same, to scale down his volume of production. In fact, given a competitive market, he is left with no other alternative and his competitors are forced to do the same. But scaling down the volume of output implies laying off labour. With this the problem shifts from the micro to the macro level. The question becomes whether the *income effect* of falling prices, or lower interest rates, and perhaps the demand for labour to produce new cost-reducing equipment, is sufficiently powerful to make good the diminution in consumers' demand. If it is powerful enough then before long surplus stocks will be depleted and the higher *real wages* of those who are still employed will usher in recovery. But what if the loss in incomes caused by unemployment is larger than the gain in *real earnings* due to the lower prices? Then the entrepreneur is facing a dilemma because in the long run the revival of his profits requires an upturn in employment. In the short run, individually in a competitive market, he has no alternative but to dismiss redundant labour, but terminating the depression demands overall employment to be sustained. In other words, contingent necessity imposes on the individual producer the need to act contrary to his best advantage in the long-run.

This contradiction between what is rational and indeed unavoidable for an individual entrepreneur, and what is rational from a wider and long-term point of view, is by no means hypothetical. It was the reality of the 1930s when neither poor wages nor low interest rates led to a restoration of entrepreneurs' profit expectations, investment and recovery. It is true that when entrepreneurs believe the recession to be short—part of the familiar business cycle—low costs may well encourage them to invest even though the immediate returns may not be very profitable. But this will hardly happen once they lose faith in imminent revival. Once this faith is lost, only an independent agent, who is free from the short-term rationale of the market place, can offer solace. In Post-War *Regulated Capitalism* this role was assigned to the state. Not fettered by the rationality of the individual profit-maximizing entrepreneur, but guided by another kind of logic, the state became a corrective agent. Its task was to intervene where individual self-interest comes into conflict with the common good. What was not sufficiently recognized was that the state is also no free agent and that it functions in a dynamic cultural environment, that its policies reflect power structures. As Professor Gellner observed, an egalitarian society which incorporates everyone in a shared moral citizenship and high culture, without poverty, oppression or arbitrariness, and with perpetual economic and cognitive growth, is not inscribed into any historical plan. A stored surplus needs to be guarded and its distribution enforced and no principle of distribution is either self-validating or self-enforcing. Conflict is inevitable, and the victors have no interest in permitting a return match. Herein lies the root cause of political coercion.

In essence the utilitarian individualism underlying Neoclassical economics resembles a Newtonian system. Like particles individuals are endowed with some kind of self-centered materialistic gravitation and driven by competition to constant motion, while the entire system is held together by their relative positioning. This is a mechanistic and not an organic perception. It excludes all variables which are not subject to the self-adjusting mechanism ascribed to competition. Collective hazards, such as nuclear disaster, water and air pollution and the prospect of long-term mass unemployment, are seen as forces which originate outside the economic system whose control is assigned to the pragmatic, "exogenous," intervention of the state. The multiplicity of these corrections, and the growth of a large state-controlled economic sector, which is not primarily informed by profit maximization, gave rise to many useful modifications in neoclassical models but the belief in the soundness of the conception as a whole persevered. Like Ptolemaic astronomers, neoclassical economists "corrected" the system but refused to examine its overall validity. They took and continue to take the results of institutional and social changes as data without asking in how far the economy itself precipitated them. They ignore the dynamics of socialization processes but calculate their volume and cost. Postulating that long-term massive unemployment or the proliferation of crime originate *outside* the "proper" economic system, they relegate the one to the progress of technology, trade union power, population accretion, or the legacy of the Welfare State, and the other to the realm of psychology and sociology. In most other modern sciences such a mechanistic "isolationist" approach is a stage long passed.

Sombart was of the opinion that the economic philosophy behind the Free Market is dominated by three principles: acquisition, competition and rationality. The purpose of all endeavors is acquisition, the means to this end competition, and the methods employed strictly rational. He believed that the spirit of acquisition seizes not only upon all phenomena within the economic realm but reaches over into the entire cultural sphere, including social relations, and tends to establish the supremacy of business interests over all other values. "Distinct from the purposes of its owner the capitalistic enterprise takes on a separate intelligence—it becomes the locus of economic rationality which is quite independent of the personality of the owner and the staff." As a result of this the system imposes on society a purely utilitarian valuation of people, objects and events. The motives of entrepreneurs can be many: the desire for power, the craving for acclaim, the impulsion to serve the common good and the simple urge to action, but by virtue of an inner necessity they all become subordinate to profit-making, because without economic success these desires cannot be attained.

This is a fairly accurate description of pre-war Capitalism. Behind all this there was the constant fear of destitution: employers were afraid of being driven out of business and reduced to the ranks of the proletariat, and workers feared destitution and starvation. It can therefore be said that the dynamic element in old-style capitalism was a two-pronged mechanism of competition—competition between entrepreneurs for their respective shares of the market, and competition between employers and workers for their share in the fruits of production. Fearful of being driven out of business by more efficient competitors, entrepreneurs were inexorably driven to search for and introduce superior technological and organizational methods of production, and facing an increasingly well-organized and powerful labour force they were pressed to introduce improvements which could help them raise output per worker sufficiently to maintain the necessary profit to finance the innovations and to compensate them for the rising wages. Though it was not the exclusive driving force, this dual mechanism was not only the dynamic but also the progressive element in old-style capitalism—the element which increased mankind's ascendancy over nature and gave it the power to produce the material affluence which the citizens of the technologically-advanced countries in a considerable measure still enjoy. But the fuel which kept this economic growth-producing mechanism functioning was fear. Take out fear and the entire mechanism falters. It should be obvious that it is not the intention of the authors of this book to recommend the reinstatement of this mechanism.

2

The New Feudalism: Managerial Oligarchy

The growing affluence in the first decades of the post-war era provided employers and the middle class with enough financial reserves not to be fearful of the worst, and gave workers the feeling that they were sufficiently protected by Labour Unions, social legislation, and their power at the ballot box not to be inordinately concerned about their future. Before long the "dual mechanism" driving force began to weaken; *greed* was taking the place of fear and *complicity* the place of solidarity. But greed is not like fear, it is a different kind of fuel, and when the ownership of means of production becomes divorced from their management it affects the economic mechanisms in another way.

The Free Market system allows individuals to find their places in society on the basis of competitive ability. At least in theory this means that the most able rise to the top and are therefore worthy of esteem. Consequently, unless most flagrant transgressions against the ruling moral code are brought to public knowledge, success becomes a symbol of distinction—of being good. This gradually shifts the emphasis in what is proper conduct away from an internalized moral code toward an externally imposed set of legal rules. The various Biblical dictates, which were transmitted from one generation to the next by the demeanor of elders in a moralizing setting and by oral admonitions and literature until they seemed to be *"human nature"* lose power. The "Thou shalt" and "Thou shalt not" reduce to "Thou shalt not be caught."

At first sight this seems of little consequence for economic theory. Greed, well circumscribed by legal constraints, may appear to be just as good a fuel to keep competition going as fear did in the past. This is an illusion. The complexity of modern economy, and the degree of specialization which is associated with this, allows no part of the system to function in separation from most others. Without the performance of all tasks with care and on time the system grinds to a halt. But when the ownership of the most important business conglomerates is separated from their management, greed is less certain to keep the clockwork adequately functioning than fear because there is no reason why the satisfaction of owners' "expectation of plenty" and managers' personal aspirations must always fully coincide.

7

The old *"Captains of Industry"* were owner-managers. They operated with their own money, or with borrowed funds for which they staked their good name. Their wealth determined their position in the social hierarchy. It reflected what was taken to be evidence for their economic sagacity. The new *"Captains"* of large enterprises are managers whose personal wealth and attainment is less directly tied to their businesses profitability than that of the owner-managers. Shareholders, the *owners* of the enterprises, are of course interested in profit, but they have only indirect control over the businesses in which they hold their shares, and they compete in a quite different market from the managers'. More often than not managers' positions are determined by their education (and the particular institution where they received it) and by their social background. They may or may not have economic acumen, but this is not the most decisive factor which determines their rewards. But their rewards, their salaries and perks, determine their position in the social hierarchy. Business success will enhance their prestige and earning capacity, but failure need not signal their ruin. Unlike the owner-managers, they can abandon a failing enterprise and become directors in another. Such managers form a new stratum of society which has more in common with a feudal estate than with a capitalist class. They exercise *power* over people, but do not hold this power by wealth but by virtue of position. This vests status with a new significance. Status becomes a rival to wealth in a competitive scramble for distinction.

Controlling large funds which are not their own, the members of this new élite are less careful than their forebears to avoid unnecessary costs when this can strengthen their personal prestige. Provided such expenditures can be correctly booked as business costs and if possible are tax-deductible they will be incurred regardless of whether or not they are really necessary for the business. Wealth continues to bestow numerous advantages on those who own it, and company profits remain an indispensable necessity, but the role of salaries and profits is reversed. Not current business profits but the height of his personal remuneration reflects the manager's social status. This means that the new utility-maximizing "Captain of Industry" is no longer Adam Smith's business-profit-seeking entrepreneur who is willy-nilly promoting efficiency, but an individual who constantly weighs his own against the enterprise's best advantage. With this the concept *utility*, as it is conventionally applied in economics, becomes too narrow to reflect conflict between personal and corporation interests, and if it is extended to include craving for status it is too broad to sustain the causal mechanisms at the root of neoclassical theory. The narrow definition of *utility* no longer reflects economic reality, and a broader definition undermines the premiss that competition is a self-sustaining economic growth-promoting mechanism.

In the 1950s and 1960s top management was mainly recruited on the basis of the candidates' prior scientific, technological, or otherwise professional capability. This was the Galbraithian *technostructure*. The more recent managerial oligarchy in most countries has risen from the ranks, inherited its positions, or received its education in schools of management which provide useful social contacts. Without going into the question whether or not such schools equip their graduates with much learning that is really functional for the efficient management of enterprises, it is obvious that unlike the Galbraithian members of the technostructure the new managers can seldom show prior evidence of competence in any sphere, not to mention professional capability. Once holding managerial position their true ability can also hardly be assessed because the test of business perspicacity is in its practical application where success or failure depends on a great variety of circumstances from which the role of management can seldom be disentangled. Naturally, even today there are some very competent managers, but unlike the owner-managers of the past, the least competent are less likely to be weeded out by business competition.

The *"Feudalisation"* of the modern economic system does not affect top management alone. It penetrates the entire structure of most large scale corporations in both the public and the private sectors. As the vertical and horizontal integration of businesses progresses and more and more firms amalgamate to achieve greater economies of scale and market control, their management becomes increasingly bureaucratized and hierarchical. Top managers delegate tasks and responsibilities to sub-managers, to heads of branches, departments and sections. Each of these strata is assigned its own responsibilities and status. Beside its appropriate wage or salary, the holder of each rank is also given its specific privileges—expense accounts, official or business vehicles, housing allowances, etc. The higher the rank the greater the perks. This is a natural concomitant of the growing size of corporations. But the newfangled type of competition, the scramble for position and status, introduces an economically debilitating element. With personal status the object of attainment each head of department or section becomes more interested in his own part of the organization than in the achievements of the business as a whole. This comes to light, for example, in the constant squabble between the heads of sales departments and research divisions in large enterprises. Moreover, within each department or section, the worth of an employee is more often measured by his contribution to the activities of his particular department than by his value to the profitability of the organization as a whole. Sometimes it is not even the employee's actual efficacy which determines his employment and position but the impression that his particular section is functioning without a hitch. In this way promotion becomes less a reward of good performance and more of acquiescence, obedience, and personal relations between inferior and superior members of the organization. Criticism which does not suit the personal interests of the direct superiors upon whom an employees personal advancement depends is muted. Step by step not capability but the quasi-feudal nexus, "who one knows and who one serves," becomes the overriding factor for personal advancement. In this way a new vertical relationship is forged by which the whole hierarchy is held together. The lower ranks protect the higher since their positions depend upon their superiors' standing, the higher ranks protect the ones below, since by holding higher responsibility any mistakes made by their inferiors eventually come to rest on their own doorstep. As each member of the hierarchy has little personally to gain by questioning the value and efficiency of his organization but good reason to fear jeopardizing his chances for promotion by it, and as all members of the organization will be adversely affected by outside criticism, little is left to stimulate commitment and efficiency.

The position of the scientific and technological research units in the large enterprises is somewhat different. Scientists are motivated by curiosity and peer appreciation. They are therefore less keen than administrators to obtain the kind of status which comes from power and control of people. Often their successes and failures are immediately visible and can be tested by experiments. Their status is linked to their achievements. Therefore, unlike administrators whose status is determined by their level of remuneration, scientists' and technologists' remuneration only *reflects* their status which is in fact determined by their and their assistants' genuine achievements. It is this special position of Research and Development which permits economic growth in spite of managerial inefficiency and rising unemployment.

The decline of managerial sagacity is however not the only debilitating factor which disturbs the efficient functioning of the Free Market system. The growing size of enterprises makes "bookkeeping supervision" almost the only means of financial control. This provides many opportunities for dubious practices, particularly in the production, purchase and sale of public goods such as military equipment or space technology which are shrouded in secrecy. The funds involved in most such transactions are not the property of those who disburse them and it is hard to ascertain whether they are well spent or not. All that can be checked is if the receipts match the claimed expenses. Consequently not only individuals but firms fall prey to temptation, and corruption undermines the confidence which used to be a fundamental constituent of traditional Capitalism. It can of course be argued that by any moral standard, except by that of the capitalist system itself, the system has always been unethical, but this is beside the point. It is true that many old-style capitalists were hardly noted for their honesty, but unlike their modern peers they were at least aware of it. When they transgressed against the unwritten rules of their society they did their best to hide it. To be found out meant social disgrace and often economic ruin. The reason for this was that the entire system rested on trust and confidence. 'My word is my bond' was the slogan of the Stock Exchange; 'The Bank of England promises...' was printed on the British currency and made it acceptable as a medium of exchange. In short, confidence was an essential ingredient of transactions. The demise of this ingredient is therefore not only a moral matter but a real threat to the proper functioning of the economic system. The point is not that traditional capitalists never indulged in shady practices, or that present-day managers are all corrupt, but that the opportunities for engaging in dubious practices under traditional capitalism were more circumscribed, and that few self-respecting capitalists would ever have admitted to having given or received a bribe. This is no longer so. When the US agency Business International questioned the managers of 55 multinationals about their experiences with bribery it was told that bribes are taken practically everywhere. When a study group to investigate corruption was organized by the United Nations Social and Economic Council (ECOSOC) and the American delegation suggested that all payments to persons involved in the arrangement of contracts should be made public to avoid corrupt practices, this suggestion met with the strongest opposition.

Classical capitalism had always made a clear-cut distinction between legitimate and illegitimate means of acquiring wealth. Thieves, swindlers, embezzlers, hold-up men, forgers, extortionists, and the rest of that ilk were excluded from free enterprise society. This is still so. The press, for example *The Independent* of February 4, 1995, still reports with derision that four peers as well as several MPs received substantial sums from private citizens to act on their behalf. But the frontiers of social disapprobation have receded and the modus operandi has changed. In their new guise these transgressions have become less easy to prosecute and more socially admissible. Respectable businessmen regard tax evasion as a peccadillo and even brag of it in their circles; workers take undue advantage of the state and their employers' property without compunction. Nor does anyone prosecute the garage owner who submits a bill for four hours labour time for a job which, but for his mechanic's mistakes, would have taken only one hour. Doctors prescribe unnecessary medicines and treatments for which either the patient or the National Health Service is made to pay. People receive unemployment benefit who are employed. "Moonlighters" obtain an income and demand social security benefit, and employers engaging them save money by not having to pay value added tax and all other impositions. The weight of evidence of the spreading of corruptions in all strata of society is overwhelming. The effect is disastrous because while the Free Market system may well endure occasional corrupt practices it cannot survive a general loss of moral inhibitions.

At one time or another everybody comes face to face with these malpractices, with the result that among decent people the feeling is spreading that they are made fools of by the rest of their society. Their resentment against taxes and national insurance contributions rises, and their incentive to work responsibly and honestly for normal wages plummets; the old sense of propriety is lost. But without reasonable prospects for advancement, without the fears associated with job loss, and without the sense of propriety making working-men feel responsible for the jobs they do, there is little left to keep the intricate clockwork of modern industry running efficiently enough to uphold the present living standards. Again, dishonesty is not a new phenomenon; there have always been corrupt individuals, but the blurring of the boundaries between what is and what is not socially acceptable is new. Coming at a time when the old efficiency-promoting mechanisms wane, this threatens not only the economic but the entire moral fabric of society, and the behavioral assumptions which were the tacit underpinnings of the Free Market's economic theory. Adam Smith believed that man does things or refrains from doing them because of his desire for the approval of his fellow men. In his *Theory of Moral Sentiments* "the rich man glories in his riches because he feels that they naturally draw upon him the attention of the world." But if success by itself, irrespective of the means by which it is attained, becomes the final arbiter of *good*, neither the system nor the theory of Free Enterprise can be sustained.

3

The New Market Structure: Globalization

Another problem which has plagued markets and mainstream economic theory is *Monopoly* or *Oligopoly*. In practice, though with only limited success, monopoly has been subjected to a great volume of corrective legislation. One difficulty was how to distinguish between *natural* and *administered* monopoly, and another how to deal with firms which, though they are acting independently, are aware of their mutual interdependence of sales, production, investment and even advertising plans, and arrive at their decisions on the basis of the expected behavior of their rivals. These problems were recognized and some neoclassical models were designed to take account of them and even of extreme situations when rivalry is replaced by co-operation and collusion. It can therefore not be said that neoclassical price theory ignored *monopoly* and *oligopoly*, but it treated them as the exception, not the rule. In reality however, oligopoly is no longer an anomaly.

Although price competition continues to play an important role particularly in wholesale and retail trade, its influence on large-scale producers has been waning. The enormous and continually rising costs of breaking into markets makes prospective entrepreneurs shy away from competition with established businesses even when they are very profitable. Shared profit where initial outlay is high makes such investments unattractive. The greater the cost of innovating the more the large producers tend to concentrate on what they consider to be their *core* activities. Rather than competing, they prefer to co-operate, amalgamate, or buy up each other's shares.

The power of monster conglomerates is too well known to need much elaboration. In the 1970s, five Dutch conglomerates directly employed 18 per cent of the working population, and indirectly many more. These five controlled electronics, metallurgy, food processing, chemicals and oil. In Germany, some 2000 businesses employed about 50 per cent of the total labour force. In the USA some 2000 corporations controlled about 80 percent of all resources used in manufacturing. By 1994, their share in employment had fallen more steeply than the fall in overall employment, but their grip on all other resources had increased. Globalization had added an entirely new dimension to the familiar problem of economic concentration.

While there was little new in the tendency toward monopoly, the stimulus it received in the 1980s from technological developments was different. The new type of globalized monopoly exorcised the odium of malpractice and illegality from a great many monopolistic and oligopolistic practices. In fact, corporations manufacturing production technology, but not they alone, ushered in a *new market structure*. The process was triggered by three developments in the production sphere: 1) in computer-aided manufacturing (CAM), flexible manufacturing systems (FMS) and robotics; 2) in computer-aided design (CAD) and paperless knowledge work; and 3) in the increased understanding of physical phenomena. The combination of all three provided the basis for computer-integrated manufacturing (CIM). Together with the concurrent changes in the world economy CIM caused a revision of large corporations' market strategy. From being companies in many countries, important *multinationals* became *global* concerns. Their new managerial watchword became *globalization*.

The most obvious reasons for this change are the growing capital-intensity of manufacture; the accelerating momentum of technologies; the emergence of a growing body of universal users; and the spreading of neoprotectionist pressures. As early as 1989 André Manders observed that the pursuit of economies of scale was inordinately increasing the capital-intensity of manufacturing. In his opinion this was, and will probably continue to be, a major source of "globalization" in spite of the spreading of flexible manufacturing systems (FMS) which provide cheap short production runs. The accelerating pace at which new technologies are discovered and applied makes R&D costs soar, while the diffusion of new technology through the industrialized countries is quickening so rapidly that it has become increasingly difficult to sustain technological advantage. This forces companies planning to penetrate Japanese, American and European markets with new products to invade the entire zone simultaneously rather than gradually, country by country, as they used to do. Finally the emergence of an unprecedented massive body of universal users is also pushing companies in this direction.

Coalition-forming is the specific type of cooperation which accompanies globalization. It has become *the* new strategy of large enterprises. Coalitions differ from mergers and takeovers because they allow participants to retain relative independence. Their *raison d'être* is that they provide the opportunity for establishing positions in strategic markets. They have a "synergistic" effect by recruiting partners to fill gaps in each other's operations and to increase the possibility for exploiting economies of scale. They lead to cost and risk spreading and, last but not least, help to arrive at new standards. Kenichi Ohmae listed several examples for this type of cooperation. In *aero engines:* General Electric and Rolls Royce; Pratt and Whitney-Kawasaki-Rolls-Royce. In *motor vehicles* (components and assembly): GM and Toyota; Chrysler and Mitsubishi; Volkswagen and Nissan; Volvo and Renault. In *consumer elec-*

tronics: Matsushita and Kodak; JVC and Telefunken and Thorn, Philips and Sony. In *computers,* AT&T and Olivetti; Hitachi and Hewlett and Packard; Fujitsu and Amdahl and Siemens and ICL; IBM and Matsushita.

In The Netherlands, Philips cooperates with Sony in the field of compact-disc players and with Matsushita and Yamaha in efforts to establish a standard for interactive CD and in seeking a standard for CD-video. A detailed study of the technological alliances into which Philips had entered by 1989, and of the multiplicity of relationships with other companies working with it in tandem (with five or more cooperation agreements) lists 27 agreements with Siemens, 11 with Thomson, 10 with Matshushita, 8 with Bull, Olivetti and Sony, 7 with AT&T and Bosch, 6 with DEC and Nixdorf, 5 with Alcatel (CGE), Hewlett-Packard and STC (+ICL). Of the listed inter-company agreements, 43% were finalized between 1986 and 1988. During the same period the proportion of alliances in professional products and in the systems sector (including production automation) rose from ten percent prior to 1986, to more than thirteen percent in 1989.

This type of alliances and coalitions, especially favored by capital-intensive industries with high R&D costs and a broad technological basis, practically dominate production in aviation, electronics and increasingly also motor vehicles. Even the largest enterprises feel that they can no longer afford the independence which previously they had been jealously protecting. The choice of coalition partners depends on the companies' *core activities.* To maintain international standards large enterprises need to specialize in order to reduce the cost associated with the increasing complexity of their operations. They must avoid the risk of destroying competency by diversification, or from engaging prematurely in activities outside the technological and market paradigms with which they are familiar. This concentration on core activity, globalization and coalition-forming, is the salient feature of new strategic planning. It introduces a new *market structure* dominated by something close to what used to be known as *natural monopolies.*

The new market structure implies the presence of a near monopoly in certain semi-finished goods and in particular production processes. It facilitates the determination of prices in line with investment plans with little regard for market competition. Consequently variations in the volume of demand do not influence prices but determine the volume of production. With this the whole idea of the self-correcting economic mechanism falls into disarray. Effective demand remains the final arbiter of production, but instead of influencing prices it determines the volume of employment. If in a number of important industries a new investment produces a greater output than an equivalent investment did before, and oligopolistic structures prevent prices from falling, then irrespective of rising or falling interest rates, unemployment will increase. Moreover, if sticky producer prices prevent consumer prices from falling, then consumer demand cannot increase in line with rising productivity, and profits can no longer be made in the market place. The result is that producers turn to *process innovation* because in an inert or shrinking market the way to preserve or increase profitability is to reduce production costs. With this, competition shifts from markets to innovation. The most efficient process innovator makes the highest profit. As process innovation usually involves high R&D expenditure and costly new equipment, the new structure replaces familiar market competition by a scramble for investment funds. And so, since *process innovation* is normally associated with a reduced demand for labour (and an increased demand for funds) the final outcome is growing unemployment and rising rates of interest.

With this becomes questionable the entire theory by which prices, wages and the rates of interest, regulate the economic system. If prices are determined by investment plans, then the latter determine the volume of demand, and income effects thwart price effects. Whether this has always been the case because, as Post-Keynesians believe, production antecedes sales, and producers only learn ex-post from the movement of prices if their estimations of the markets were correct, or if this is a new phenomenon, is here irrelevant. The point is that the new market structure practically forces large producers to adjust their volume of output to demand and not their prices; and that it obliges them to increase expenditure on technological innovation even more when markets are stagnating or reducing than when they are expanding. As a result of this, inflation, rates of interest and economic growth can all be rising simultaneously while the volume of employment dwindles. In other words, the *new market structure* allows or practically compels large enterprises not to pass on to consumers in lower prices the advantages of innovation. If this is true then the entire full employment equilibrium-restoring mechanism at the root of neoclassical economic thought becomes a travesty.

Earlier in this discussion Capitalism was characterized as a system dominated by the spirit of *acquisition, competition* and *rationality*. In this context the concept of *utility*, receives an almost purely materialistic connotation, namely the pursuit of wealth. The separation of the management from the ownership of enterprises transformed this perception of *utility*. It added to the quest for wealth a new type of pursuit of Status. A similar fate befell competition. Competition continues to play a crucial role but the role is no longer the same it was before. Competition may be brisk, indeed cut-throat, but the floor under which prices cannot fall is increasingly determined by the investment plans, and financial requirements to implement them, of a small number of corporations. Irrespective of whether markets are expanding or contracting, these corporations cannot avoid investing heavily to preserve their technological primacy in their core activities. All they can do is adjust output to the volume of demand, but not their prices. This determines for all other enterprises purchasing their inputs from these corporations the floor below which their prices cannot fall. As a result a kind of "cost-push" inflation is embedded in the new type of competition. But cost-push inflation not matched by rising wages implies a negative income effect, and consumer good suppliers are confronted with stagnant or reducing markets. They are forced either to cut profit margins or innovate themselves. But, again, for innovation, more often than not, they are dependent on the output of the firms specializing, and thereby monopolizing, the produce of their core activities. This means that competition may well be intense without inducing the income effect which neoclassical theory, and in particular Pigou, assigned to it.

In the past when productive efficiency in agriculture increased, when within several decades the proportion of farm labour diminished from about one in three of the working population to less than one in eighteen, market competition led to an equivalent fall in the real prices of agricultural produce. The fall in food prices and of raw materials produced by agriculture raised real incomes. Consequently people were able to spend more of their earnings on industrial goods and the share of consumer income spent on industrial products increased in both absolute and relative terms. As a result the demand for labour in industry made good the loss of jobs in agriculture. When efficiency in industry also rose, and the demand for labour in this sector began to flag, competition reduced the prices of industrial products and raised real incomes even further. A growing demand for services ensued and made up for the loss of jobs in industry. In short, as long as competition passed on the benefits of technological progress to consumers, incomes rose, and the diminution of the demand for labour in one sector of the economy gave rise to an increasing demand in other sectors.

In this manner, well into the 1970s, the loss of jobs in agriculture and industry was matched by an increasing demand for labour in the service sector. The process was not always smooth or undisturbed by the familiar business cycle and by stochastic shocks, but the long-term trend is fairly evident. In the USA the share of the working population engaged in the provision of services rose from 55 per cent in 1948 to 67 per cent in 1974; in France it rose from 20 per cent in 1950 to 44 per cent in 1970; and in West Germany from 28 per cent in 1950 to 42 per cent in 1968. This shift was the result of an impressive rise in productivity in the goods-producing sectors. Nowhere did the "loss" of labour engaged in the production of tangible goods cause shortages of agricultural and industrial products. On the contrary, markets in rich countries showed distinct signs of approaching saturation.

The conscious promotion of what Herbert Marcuse called *"false wants,"* and the growing interest in Third World markets, were at least in part manifestations of an approaching glut. The industrial countries' technological capability to produce far more than necessary for providing all citizens with the food and comforts normally expected by the middle-class was obvious in spite of the relative decline in the number of people employed and the shorter working week in agriculture and in industry. The reason why some people in the rich countries could not obtain the goods they needed was not the inability to provide them but the inequity of income distribution. As affluence increased and people were able to purchase the goods they wanted and still had money to spare, they began spending more on other comforts. The relative share of people's income spent on consumer goods diminished and the share spent on housing and services increased, though it should be added that in some countries people were practically driven by their governments to purchase houses.

This suggested to a number of social scientists that the future of full employment lay in the continued expansion of the service sector. Since several services can hardly be improved by time-saving innovations this did not seem unreasonable. Particularly activities requiring the simultaneous attendance of the recipient and the provider of the service (doctors and patients, teachers and pupils, waiters and patrons of a restaurant) seemed to lend credence to the thought that once again the *invisible hand* was leading the economy toward full employment equilibrium. It did not happen. What those who placed their trust in services could not see was that the new technology would also reduce labour requirements in many services; that the rise in productivity in an increasing number of key manufacturing industries was increasingly attended by oligopolistic practices; and that some services are intrinsically cost-inflating.

In summary: since the late 1970s the emphasis in investment shifted in many key industries from *product innovation* to *process innovation*. As old equipment was being replaced by more advanced technology the cost of R&D increased. The volume of employment in the capital goods producing sector remained more or less the same as had previously been employed in capital *replacement*. The share of labour cost in corporate expenditure diminished and the share of material cost increased. By 1986 a manager of Philips was able to proclaim that "to lower costs, we need not search for the solution in employing fewer people; a more judicious use of materials often saves more money than the scrapping of a few jobs." At that time material costs (including energy) amounted at Philips to 70 percent, and added value (including labour cost, depreciation and overheads etc.) to 30 percent of total outlay.

As the labour previously engaged in the production of the *additional* capital stock to meet the *growing* demand for goods and services became redundant, and labour to produce consumption goods was replaced by more efficient technology, consumers' aggregate real income ceased to rise at its former pace. This, together with the increasing complexity of the new technologies, imposed on several major producers the need to monopolize their core activities. As a result cost reductions were no longer passed on to consumers in full, and the demand for consumer goods and services stagnated and sometimes even fell. For a time the effect of these processes on aggregate demand was delayed in spite of growing unemployment. In part the lag was due to the fact that for almost a decade Trade Unions remained sufficiently powerful to raise wages in line with, and sometimes even in excess of, productivity and rising prices, and in part because Social Security and other state expenditure filled the gap left open in consumer demand by the increasing unemployment. But as tax revenue from employment decreased and corporations were discovering new ways of avoiding taxes, and learned to exploit the fear of unemployment to obtain government subsidies, state deficits swelled. Consequently, governments became increasingly inclined to reduce expenditure and to use their political powers to reduce wages. With this the distribution of the national income between consumers and investors deviated further and further from the path at which demand would have matched supply at full employment. In the 1980s effective consumer demand no longer sufficed to sustain the earlier volume of production and employment, and efforts to contain inflation by "tight" money made things worse. These put an extra burden on small enterprises with little liquid reserves and forced them to abandon whatever plans for product innovation they might have had, and obliged trading firms to reduce stocks to a minimum and to maintain prices which would cover the high cost of borrowing. Recession turned into depression and unemployment became chronic. The obvious solution would have been for governments to create more employment in the *service* sector but there were too many forces lined up against it, not least among them the economics establishment which tenaciously held on to its trust in the neoclassical self-restoring full-employment mechanism.

4

The New Significance of Services

Services are activities for which there is a demand and price: they are intangible goods usually "consumed" at the point of their production. They are not transferable, which means that they cannot be bought and later sold at another price. The reason why economists showed little interest in the study of services can perhaps be explained by a bias, dating back to Adam Smith, that mechanization, which is the key to productivity, had little or no role to play in them. Another reason may be that as economic theory focused on the competitive market-place and many services are anchored in the public rather than the private sector, it was thought that they have little to contribute to the understanding of the economic system. This was what Eli Ginzberg believed in 1982. But this alone can hardly account for the "oversight" after 1982, when services were invaded by the new communication technology. Therefore there must have been more weighty reasons for the relative neglect of services by the economics profession. The likely reasons, in addition to Ginzberg's, are the difficulty of incorporating the service sector into the neoclassical paradigm, and perhaps the recognition that its positioning in the economic system has important political implications. If it is admitted that services are no less productive than the other sectors, then the contribution of the public sector (approximately one third of employment and a quarter of GNP) which is mostly in services, must also be acknowledged. But then, *public expenditure* can hardly be written off as money "wasted," and the entire indomitable campaign against "excessive" taxes loses its veneer of common sense.

Essentially all labour is service except in that some services do not provide, and other services do provide, a *tangible* product, that some produce direct and others indirect *utility*. In the National Accounts both types of remunerated work contribute to GNP. It follows that statistically economic growth reflects equally an increase in goods production and in the provision of services. The difference is therefore rooted in attitude rather than in substance. For generations most of humanity lived in poverty. In the early days of Capitalism many were even deprived of the limited security they had enjoyed in former ages from the social and economic safeguards of a rural way of life. This was the time when Capitalism was performing its technological miracle but had not yet reached a sufficient level of technological efficiency to provide enough to be shared by everyone. A more equitable distribution of the fruits of production would have meant little more than a wider spreading of poverty. It was the time when the fears of imaginary ghosts and demons which had plagued people's mind throughout the Middle Ages were replaced by the real nightmare of unemployment, destitution and starvation. As a result the motor driving the technological progress which was to give humanity the *potential* power to banish hunger and destitution, namely Capitalism's competitive individualism, made *acquisition* a necessity for providing households against adversity. But gradually the pursuit of wealth became an objective in itself. It became less and less an inescapable necessity and more and more a socially approved mode of conduct, something like an inseparable constituent of human nature. Earlier status symbols, such as aristocratic and academic titles, yielded primacy of place to the all-pervasive power of wealth, and property became the yardstick by which an individual's position in society was measured. Young people were encouraged by mentors and elders to distinguish themselves *individually* in the pursuit of property. The ownership of *goods* became not only a means to secure the comforts they render but a confirmation of their owner's status in society. In this way a distinction in people's attitude toward goods and toward services became immanent, and even more so a differentiation between private and collective ownership.

Services add to their purchaser's comfort but do not necessarily contribute to his sense of property. With some exceptions (such as employing a butler) services are less suitable than tangible goods, or the legal claim to tangible property, for confirming their proprietor's prestige. Like the physiocrats in the eighteenth century, who regarded manufacturing as a *sterile* occupation because it merely transforms one thing into another without adding a tangible quantity to the nation's volume of output, many people today feel that services are an economic burden rather than an asset. In fact, at least in England, the working class also felt very strongly until fairly recently, *production* to be noble and *service* to be degrading, whether domestic ("lackeys") or military—"going for a soldier" a last resort of the starving. That this is nonsense needs little elaboration. No sophisticated economic system can function without a large variety of services because the proliferation of services is inherent in the progress of technology. When subsistence farming is replaced by market production the surplus must be processed, stored, graded, packed, transported and distributed for sale, and banking facilities, schools, and a whole range of other ancillary occupations become necessary. The same goes for manufacturing and industry. For this reason increasing productivity in a *properly functioning* Free Enterprise economy does not cause unemployment. In fact, whether technological progress was fast or slow, the ratio of the number of persons producing the national output to the number of people sharing in it remained fairly stable throughout the entire era of industrialization, and the share of the *inactive*, that is of children, old people and other non-working or work-seeking persons, had most of the time been about 65 per cent of the total population.

Why then are the misconceptions about the role of services so tenacious? In essence the answer lies in the earlier mentioned psychological legacy of the shortages endured during the many ages before high productivity and adequate storage facilities practically banished scarcity of food and other material necessities from the industrialized countries. But there is more: many modern services are prospective, impersonal and collective. Few people are "happy" to pay an insurance premium which at some future date they may or may not have occasion to call upon; and few people feel "happy" to pay rates and taxes even when they are aware of the advantages they receive in return from the services provided by their local authority or the state. The link between the payment of rates and taxes and the advantages is too remote, too roundabout, and often too impersonal, to be readily accepted. People who can afford it are frequently prepared to pay much more for private education, private security guards, private medical care, etc. than they would have to pay in taxes to receive the same services from the state. This is true even when private and state services are of equal quality. Moreover, socialized into the individualistic culture of the Free Market, people tend to feel that they have insufficient control and supervision over the money paid to local authorities and to the state. Their resentment against the fact that other people are handling *their* money leads them to magnify beyond reason each disclosure of inefficiency in the use of public funds. They notice each case of mismanagement in the public sector, but remain unimpressed by the evidence of the inefficiency in the private sector reflected in the multiplicity of business failures. They disregard the large profits earned by public corporations, and from activities in which the state participates, and forget the fact that many of the public sector's loss-making operations are only undertaken because they are insufficiently profitable to attract private investment, were never intended to maximize profits, and render indispensable services to the community. In short, many people confuse efficiency with profitability and forget the vital role public services play in the proper functioning of an industrial society.

There is, however, one way in which the increasing share of services can and does effect efficiency. In the era of mechanical production, of the conveyer-belt, the machine determined the efficiency of factory labour; in the era of automation, of the chip-controlled robot, a much larger share of the employment is in office work where the worker is more able to determine his own speed. Consequently bad management becomes a much greater hindrance to efficiency than it had been before.

Neither Adam Smith nor John Stuart Mill believed that the pursuit of profit alone could meet all the communal wants. For them it seemed self-evident that things like national security and education must be provided out of public funds. What they could not foresee was the tremendous increase in the need for public spending. It is of course untrue that the rising share of government in national expenditure is due only to inefficient use of public funds, though occasionally it may be a contributing factor. The real cause of the rising cost of government is in the great structural changes in industrial society. For example, the dissolution of the traditional family in western Europe transferred the responsibility for supporting the aged from the household to the state, the progress of technology increased the cost of education and transferred it from the private and local to the national budget, and the growing complexity of economic and social relations increased the need for a network of national motorways which is too costly to be built with private funds and whose cost of maintenance rises with the growth, proliferation and specialization of modern industry. Finally the cost of protecting the public from epidemic diseases and from air and water pollution must also mainly be borne collectively.

Even assuming that these and other wants could be met by private enterprise, and that private enterprise could do this more efficiently, the share of the national income to satisfy them would still be high and rising. The aged and infirm would still have to be housed and fed, teachers paid, roads constructed and maintained, and epidemics and pollution prevented. That most of these activities involve a large component of the type of services which require the simultaneous presence of the provider and receiver, and that much work for which the state or local authorities must pay cannot be readily reduced by technological innovations, are complicating factors. While the labour-time required to produce a given volume of output in the goods-producing sector is reducing, the labour time required to meet many of the services provided by the state remains the same or, when the services are improved, is lengthening. This means that relative to the labour cost involved in goods production many labour services become increasingly costly. Given that precisely the services which require the simultaneous presence of provider and receiver and which cannot be substituted by technology are taking up a large share in public employment, the rising cost of government is practically built in into the modern state. This being the case the real problem of the public services is the distribution of income between different strata of society, and as such has no place in neoclassical economics.

Neoclassical theory has little if anything to say about the distribution of the national income between the private and the public sector. It differentiates between *functional* and *personal* income distribution, between the distribution of the national income among factors of production and the distribution of income between individuals, families and households regardless of the factor from which it is derived. In *functional distribution* theories the rewards of the factors of production are related to supply and demand. In some such theories market imperfections and wage bargaining are taken into account, but essentially *marginal productivity* remains the crucial determinant. In *personal distribution* theories relative shares are associated with technical and social factors. But neoclassical doctrine has no mechanism for distributing the national income between the public and the private sector. The public sector does not follow market rules and therefore can simply not be incorporated into the neoclassical system.

To a certain extent the same is true for Marxist analyses of the Free Market structure. Marxists relate distribution to class struggle, technological innovation, population accretion, the degree of labour's organization and the extension of capitalist production. They either regard the public sector as of only marginal importance in the capitalist economy or entirely ignore it. Keynes and the champions of the neoclassical synthesis who followed him recognized the importance of the distribution of the National Income between consumption and investment as well as the role of the public sector for sustaining stability and full-employment. But what neither Samuelson nor Hicks nor the many other neo-Keynesians were ready to perceive was that the public sector was an economic factor by itself, with economic interests and an economic logic of its own. Never entirely abandoning the thought that in final analysis and with no sticky wages the economy naturally tends toward full-employment equilibrium, they assigned to the state a merely marginal corrective role, namely to increase or to reduce expenditure when necessary. What they did not fully appreciate was that the public sector, being neither "individualistic," nor profit-maximizing, nor subject to the conventional rules of market competition, but dominating a major share of employment and GNP, introduces a completely alien element into their economic system.

A point too often overlooked is that although government officials are expected to pursue national objectives, and business executives are obliged to maximize company profits, they normally share the same background and mentality. They enjoy a comparable life-style, have similar powers of control over their employees, and consequently cause the new feudalism to spill over from private business to government service and from government service to private enterprise. Successful business executives do not find it very difficult to secure important government appointments and top government bureaucrats to obtain prominent positions in private enterprises—this is what the British term "sleaze." The director of the Dutch National Bank became an executive with Shell; the former Minister of Social Affairs of the Netherlands became an executive with the multinational OGEM; the Minister of Education became chairman of the employers' association, and a former Minister of Finance became a director with RABO bank and returned to public service when the post at the head of the Dutch State Bank fell vacant. It is simply taken for granted that someone who is good for business must also be good for the state. As a result a microeconomic conception is imposed on efforts to solve macroeconomic problems. If prime emphasis on technological education is good for a firm then, ipso facto, it must also be good for the country. In this way many public services become a kind of "unprofitable appendix" to private enterprise, an unavoidable expenditure which ought to be kept at a politically sustainable minimum. No one asks how large the public sector must be to allow the economy to grow with full employment, but everyone is concerned with how much the private sector is ready or able to pay to sustain government expenditure.

At first sight this seems a fairly reasonable question. Scared of accelerating inflation and misled by the simplistic analogy between government expenditure and household budgeting, it does not seem illogical to "cut the coat to fit the cloth." In the guise of macroeconomic truths the old *wage-fund* and *marginal productivity* theories even provide this perception with a kind of scientific justification. Money spent on public services "crowds out" private investment, and increasing employment in the public sector raises wages and "crowds out" employment in the private sector. The fact that the idea of a fixed wages-fund was shown to be a fallacy, and that the marginal productivity doctrine is a purely microeconomic phenomenon hedged in by an unrealistic *ceteris paribus*, is forgotten. But the mass media adopts such managerial points of view and turns them into "received science." As Professor Galbraith says: "high social business, and academic position gives access to television, radio, and the press, and the voice of economic advantage, being louder, regularly gets mistaken for the voice of the masses." The media picks up and broadcasts these ideas and the new élite listens and is confirmed in its opinions.

But the analogy is false. The state is no private household and all microeconomic truths need not be valid in macroeconomics. Recent fears about the height of the *National Debt* can serve as an example. The point is that even a private corporation can spend more than its current receipts from sales without negative implications, provided of course that the money is spent to acquire profitable assets. Building a new factory which costs more than the business's annual turnover is no *loss* but an investment. It creates a debt, but as long as the asset is maintained and the bond holders are paid their annual interest, the debt can stand forever. In 1929 EXXON (or more precisely its predecessors) borrowed $170 million to finance a new location. By 1975 the debt had increased to $3500 million, but EXXON was better off, not worse. It is not debts which cause sleepless nights for company directors but the question whether the assets bought with borrowed money are sufficiently profitable to cover the expected returns of the lenders. The sale of any debenture or share creates a debt, but unlike households debts, such company debts are assets. The *returns* of a government are taxes which rise and fall with the volume of economic activity. The problem of the debt is therefore not its height but the volume of economic activity it generates.

In the war the national debt of the United States rose enormously but the USA survived. Deficit financing, the spending of money borrowed from the public against the sale of interest-yielding bonds, must not be likened to household borrowing for consumption. What is important is that in the long run the borrowed money is well spent, that it will sufficiently increase employment and hence tax revenues to cover the interest payable to bond holders after the tax on bond earnings has been deducted. There are of course also real problems: the issuing of bonds affects the rate of interest, the distribution of the national income and the balance of payments. But these effects and the necessity to provide and sustain an expanding service superstructure for the distant future are seldom mentioned in the public debate. Taxes and the spending of money in the public sector is unpopular, and therefore rather than carefully explicating these difficulties and becoming involved in a sensitive polemic about social priorities most politicians prefer to conjure up the false analogy of the indebted household. As a result the public is deprived of the ability to make educated judgments and democracy ceases to be *meaningful.*

It is, however, not their ideological background and ignorance alone which determine the attitude to public services of top politicians and establishment economists. Politicians, like managers in large private corporations, are subjected to the strains of hierarchical juggling for position. They are constantly beset by colleagues vying for their post and impelled to take account of their electorate. The director of a private corporation has to satisfy shareholders' expectations of profit, but as long as he keeps within the law their social inclinations do not concern him and have little influence on his decisions. This is not true for a politician who is incessantly subjected to the scrutiny of his party membership. He is constantly obliged to parry the machinations of his colleagues and to be wary of the immediate wishes of the particular group of people who voted for his party for a large variety of reasons not necessarily consistent with each other.

This last restraint particularly inhibits the politician's freedom of action. He must remain popular and his popularity depends on immediate measures rather than on long-term achievements materializing in the future. It is therefore irrelevant whether he does or does not recognize the necessity to expand the public services to meet the challenges of future developments, because if their expansion runs contrary to the immediate needs or wishes of his electorate he cannot act accordingly. Therefore it is also less relevant for him to know whether more government spending on public services can or cannot reduce unemployment than to decide whether his electorate is or is not prepared to allow him to raise taxes to finance expansion.

In this light many of the nonsensical government measures taken in recent years become "logical." In 1982 a Minister in the Center-Right coalition of the Netherlands decided to dismiss several thousand nurses from the National Health Service to reduce the government's deficit. At the same time the Minister of Labour and Social Affairs made plans to allocate almost the same sum of money to provide a smaller number of new jobs for other people. From a restricted point of view both these decisions are logical. The Minister of Health and the Minister of Labour and Social Affairs did what their electorates wanted: less state expenditure and more employment. But sacking the nurses deprived the state of their tax contributions, and the human capital invested in their training and experience. It reduced overall time worked in the country because of longer waiting lists in hospitals, and impaired the nation's standard of health in general.

The real problem is neither the rising share of government in the national income nor its cost. The crux of the matter is progressive taxation: the rich pay more taxes than the poor while the advantages accruing to the poor from the services provided by the state are more directly visible. Although few rich would remain rich without a large and expanding public sector keeping the modern economic system moving, their advantage is less immediately obvious. Therefore, in simple language, the vocal condemnation of increasing public spending is a reflection of the rich wishing the poor to pay a greater share of the bill for maintaining the latter in comfort, and all the rest is more or less sophisticated eyewash. This does not mean that there is no room for great improvements in the public sector, nor that government leaders are intent on grinding the faces of the poor, but it does tell something about the company they keep.

Politicians and high government officials are simply overwhelmed by the opinions of the social oligarchy and do not dare to swim against the stream of public opinion. Mostly they are simply too busy solving immediate problems to consider deeper and long-term consequences. The rush to "privatization" is a case in point. Nobody denies that the collective services provided by the public enterprises are necessary, but their *privatization* was thought to make them more efficient and less costly. Experience has shown that this is seldom true. Initially after privatization some public utilities have indeed become a little more "consumer friendly," but this was mainly due to the general fear of unemployment and not to changes in ownership. An alteration of the rules regulating tenure in the public sector would have had the same effect. As for cost, the prices of services supplied by private enterprise have also, usually after a short initial interval of price restraint, increased rather than lessened. On the whole private enterprise took over profitable public services and for unprofitable received considerable compensation. For maintaining a bus service to a small remote village private operators demanded and normally received subsidies. In short, the *cost* of services does not depend on who supplies them, but who supplies them does affect the distribution of the national income between the strata of society. Supposing that in the Netherlands *Social Security* and *Public Health* were abolished, workers' take-home pay would increase and they would have to pay for pensions and for health insurance. The minimum total cost of providing for retirement and health, which now when necessary is supplemented out of taxes, would still remain the same, but the distribution of the burden would be different. The higher contributions presently collected from the rich would be cancelled and the expenditure of the lower income groups would rise. Instead of having the choice of living on their own in council houses many old people would have to live with their families. The cost would be the same and the "active" would still have to pay for sustaining the "inactive" but the sharing of the expense would differ. In short the question of privatization is not a matter of cost but of income distribution between classes. It is not a question of economics but of ideology, of the norms by which a society chooses to live. Seen in this light *"back to basics"* (the slogan of Prime Minister Major which was hastily dropped in the wake of the sex scandals in his government) is hardly a summons to revive an idealized family life, but a call to relieve the higher income groups from supporting the "inactive" members of less affluent households.

In conclusion: modern industrial society requires a growing number of collective services, and whether they are privatized or not they take a major share in national income. The cost of many of them cannot be reduced by technological innovation, but being collective and seldom subject to market rules, they are not easily integrated into the neoclassical model. They impose the need for a radical revision of the reigning economic model or for its replacement by another which makes the public sector, instead of individualistic competition, the motor of full employment and responsible economic growth. That in a recession or depression this may involve a good deal of deficit financing and that there are substantive reasons for not allowing deficit financing to run out of control is true. But these reasons must be regarded as by-products of sound economic management. They require serious attention but they must not be taken as the kingpin of economic policy. The main object of economic policy must be sustained full-employment growth, and finding ways to reduce or eliminate inflation and avoiding balance of payment difficulties must begin from there. To fight inflation in the hope of regaining full employment is to put the cart before the horse; perhaps God did not create mankind to serve the economy. Economics is supposed to serve the needs of Man, not Man to serve any particular social and economic paradigm.

In theory there is no reason why a government should not create employment by issuing more money or by borrowing. The former is rejected because relative to the volume of goods and services offered in the market it increases the money circulation and generates inflation; the latter is spurned because it is thought to reduce the volume of savings with which private investors finance their activities. In fact there can be little doubt that in a state of full-employment equilibrium additions to the money supply in excess of the growth of the volume of economic activities is at least initially likely to engender rising prices. But this is not the point. What needs to be realized is that once full employment becomes the prime objective of economic policy, and not the stabilization of the currency, attention will focus on new ways by which inflation can be neutralized. It will be appreciated that the money supply is not the *only* cause of price hikes and that other causes can effectively be tackled. There is no need for price controls or legally regulated wages to curb inflation, neither of which can be easily enforced. Simpler expedients can go a long way to do the trick. For example, if "representation costs" (expense accounts) cease to be tax-deductible, the prices charged in expensive restaurants and hotels and other similar businesses would soon fall, and with them their knock-on effect on the general price level. People would still frequent such establishments, but the places vacated by business executives would be filled by customers who previously were unable to afford them. The same is true for many other perks—company cars, interest-free housing loans, subsidized meals, etc. As the height of perks is usually directly related to the hierarchical status of the person who enjoys them they are in effect disguised untaxed (but production-cost increasing) extra incomes for the best remunerated. A judicious review of all such tax exemptions may well raise government revenue enough to make superfluous the creation of *new* money for investment. Similarly not allowing tax relief for maintaining private "security guards" would pay for better state policing and reduce the cost of overheads. All this entails conflict between the economic and political élites because it involves changes in *income distribution* and *institutional rectifications,* which neoclassical economics declared exogenous. It would involve a re-examination of the validity of the role neoclassical economics assigns to money and to foreign trade, a re-consideration of social and economic priorities, and a revival of *informed* democracy. Many countries, including the Netherlands, have the necessary institutions (like the Dutch Central Planning Office CPB) to calculate the likely economic consequences of such changes, but these are not questions they are asked. Again, it is not economic scientists' answers but the questions which are asked, and upon which the final outcome does depend, which are inadequate.

5

The Failure of the Neoclassical Synthesis

Keynes and the protagonists of *Regulated Capitalism* where not unaware of the role of government, but underrated its function when more and more collective services became necessary to sustain the increasingly complex economic structure, and they overrated its powers to exercise control over an economy which was rapidly becoming internationalized. Their models visualized something like a closed economy, a system with a large measure of autarchy topped up by imports and exports that tend to equilibrate through monetary fluctuations which, under extreme circumstances, could perhaps be adjusted by currency devaluations or revaluations. They believed that on the whole the system inclines toward equilibrium either with or without full employment. Keynes himself was of the opinion that real wages and not money wages determine the volume of employment, that the level of national income and not the rate of interest determines investment and employment, that profit expectations and not the current rate of interest is the prime cause of investment, and that the equality of savings and investment does not imply that the economic system can only be in equilibrium when there is full employment. His followers were more skeptical than he was about the last point, but accepted that "exogenous" forces, such as Union-administered "sticky wages," could prevent the inherently equilibrating mechanism of the system from restoring full employment. But neither Keynes, nor his followers who dominated economic thought in the period of regulation, appreciated that with the proliferation of the public services provided by the state and with the internationalization of the world economy new powerful forces were coming upon the stage, of which the former is not subject to the mechanisms governing the market and the latter deprives the state of adequate power for their regulation.

Not abandoning their belief in the self-adjusting forces of the system, the neo-Keynesian "regulationists" believed that all that was necessary to sustain growth, stability and full employment was to find a method for determining the precise measure and timing of state intervention, and to add the financial sector to the *real* elements of the Keynesian model. The former was attempted by Samuelson, Harrod and Domar, and the latter by Hicks and Hansen. Samuelson examined the mutual dependence of changes in consumption and investment, the interaction between the *Multiplier* and the *Principle of Acceleration*, and Harrod and Domar examined whether economic growth with full employment was possible, and if so what the warranted rate of growth should be. Hicks and Hansen provided a diagram detailing the simultaneous determination of equilibrium values of the interest rate and the level of national income as a result of conditions in the goods and money markets, the *ISLM* model. Given all this it appeared credible that governments are indeed able to regulate the economic systems of their countries. It seemed that *fine tuning*, raising or reducing effective demand as necessary, by fiscal or monetary instruments could sustain full-employment stability and growth.

For two decades the system worked reasonably well. There was impressive economic growth, business cycles were dampened and there was little if any unemployment. But there were forces at work which gradually deprived governments of their powers of controlling the economy. Not least among them was the proliferation of multinational corporations. One may define a multinational as a corporation which derives a substantial proportion of its income from activities in foreign countries. Usually such enterprises are large and have a home base and several wholly or partially-owned subsidiaries in other countries. They expand internationally to take advantage of vertical and horizontal economies of scale and to obtain a near monopoly status in the sphere of their activities. The arguments against them are that they "export" jobs, transfer technology to foreign affiliates, retard economic growth in their base country, alter the distribution of the national income away from labor towards capital, erode the bargaining power of trade unions, draw off revenue from the national government, involve the state in the internal politics of other countries, manipulate foreign exchange markets and destabilize their currencies, and when it suits their purpose subvert governments both in their home country and abroad. In favor of multinationals it is argued that foreign direct investment creates jobs, that they stimulate exports, help the balance of payments, promote foreign policy, foster economic development and contribute considerably to the state revenues and therefore help to sustain social security in the mother countries where they are based.

All this may or may not be true, but one thing is certain: multinationals introduce a break in the direct link between domestic saving and investment, and thereby sever the tie upon which both Keynesian and non-Keynesian economic theories depend. Multinationals can accumulate savings in one country and invest them in another. At best this may give rise to new income by way of international trade; at worst it promotes the growth of competitive industries in low labour cost or low tax countries and causes domestic industry to falter. But whatever the outcome, multinationals can introduce an inequality between savings and investment. This makes nonsense of economic theories founded in *Say's Law* or based upon the assumption that with the *multiplier* all investment generates domestic employment and hence domestic savings. It also makes inane the belief that it is in the power of national governments to regulate their countries' economies by fiscal fine-tuning or monetary measures.

At the end of the 1970s the president of the Royal Shell Group defended his organization against criticism by claiming that the *only* power his multinational possessed is to decide *if* to invest, and *where* to do so. But this is no small power. It means that with little regard for where the savings come from multinationals can invest when and where it suits them. While the Dutch government was pressing for wage restraint to allow enterprises to accumulate the savings deemed necessary to revive domestic investment and employment, capital exports from the Netherlands increased at an unprecedented rate. They almost equalled the "missing share" of GNP which was thought necessary for revival. In spite of rising unemployment in the Netherlands, in 1976 Holland became the largest investor in the United States with $850 million. This was close to one-third of all European investments there taken together. Kenneth C. Crowe's list of foreign investors in the United States in this period is headed by three multinationals, namely Royal Dutch Shell, Unilever and Philips. The most obvious reason for this expansion was the low exchange rate of the US dollar. For the transfer of Dutch savings to several other countries the reasons were wage differentials and the wish to establish bases for future growth. At the time Grundig Electronics was paying DM 0,40 per minute to its workers in Germany, but only DM 0,33 in Austria, DM 0,28 in England, DM 0,18 in Portugal and DM 0,06 in Taiwan. Shipbuilders paid DM 18.50 per hour in Germany, DM 11 in Japan and DM 2 in Korea. In metallurgy, wages in Korea, Taiwan, Singapore and Hong Kong were respectively 17, 20, 21 and 26 per cent of those paid in Japan. In other words, international exchange rates and wage differentials, rather than the volume of domestic savings, played the decisive role in many countries' level of investment and employment.

These examples illustrate why the power of multinationals to invest when and where it suits them leaves little room for trust in the assumed automatic equilibrating mechanism, or in the Keynesian and monetarist instruments of state control. Since the mid-eighties *globalization* has transformed the character of multinationals but their power of circumventing national governments' economic regulation has increased rather than diminished. The conclusion is that a Free Market would require Dutch wages to fall below those of Korea and Taiwan, and a "Keynesian" approach would require economic autarchy which even if it were practicable would make the "solution" worse than the disease. In other words, the trust in automatic mechanisms is best abandoned and the Keynesian and neo-Keynesian approaches to be useful need first to be drastically amended to suit the new structure of the economic system.

Earlier in this discussion the decline in producers' *price competition* and the scramble for funds was related to *globalization*. The term "producers" was used advisedly because in spite of the fact that there are also large trading corporations which have successfully restricted price competition the role of producers is decisive. They determine the floor below which prices cannot fall. The great international grain merchants and the European traders in fertilizer can and do restrict competition and cause prices to be unnecessarily high. The governments united in the European Community can perhaps solve this problem if they really wish to do so, but they cannot prevent the negative consequences of globalization of production.

Some researchers deny or belittle the impact of the price-fixing powers of giant corporations. They point to the relatively small and since the 1970s declining *formal* share of multinationals in the total number of registered corporations, and to their diminished volume of employment. Other researchers see evidence of the lasting dominance of competition in the price "wars" in the retail trade, and in the tariff between conflicts between Japan, the United States and Europe. They are deluded. Certainly for a while some Japanese manufacturers were vying with their equals in other countries and several are continuing to do so, but the major global producers show a clear tendency to specialize and cooperate rather than compete. Producers, unlike traders who are compelled to reduce their profit margins to maintain their market shares, determine their costs and prices by their investment requirements to sustain their leading position in their core activities, and this leaves little room for the revival of employment. It is therefore less the size of the share monopolists or oligopolists hold in the market that determines their influence than the nature of the resources or products they control. And it is in the supply of resources which are crucial for other industries, such as energy, electronics and machine-tools, that the oligopolistic control is strongest. This means that even if statistics are modified by behavioral evidence, measuring market shares and concentration is not enough to determine the strength of monopolistic influences.

The fact that there are several suppliers of chemical fertilizer trading in Europe, and that there is no evidence of collusion or formal price agreements between them, may support the notion of surviving competition. But how can one explain the fact that in spite of open frontiers fertilizer prices differ considerably from one European country to the next? How does one determine the degree of competition in the market for farm produce where the degree of producer concentration (which is the conventionally employed measure for assessing the degree of monopoly) is low but the number of wholesale distributors is minute? Market control is a matter of power and as such cannot be gauged by counting units of production. Perhaps it can be measured by long-term profit margins but these are hardly ever readily available in a manner which is helpful for this purpose. Sometimes tax-audited losses in one country reappear as profits in another, and book-debts and book-values are recorded in a way which cannot be untangled by outsiders. Moreover, market power often depends on such elusive intangible factors as "good connections."

While shedding crocodile tears over the loss of jobs because of cut-throat foreign competition, many multinationals cooperate with their competitors and integrate them into their markets. This may be seen as a kind of international share-swapping. It is not unusual for giant corporations in Britain, Germany, Japan and the USA to combine their own interests with those of similar corporations in other countries by offering them their domestic services and local expertise in exchange for certain partnership arrangements. As a result jobs are lost in the mother country but not profits. If more Japanese cars are sold in the USA, American labour in the automobile industry may become redundant but it need not cause loss of profit to the American shareholders, at least not in the short run. If American interests in the American automobile industry are exchanged for an equally profitable share in the Japanese automobile industry it makes little difference for the American shareholders whether Americans drive Fords or Toyotas, but it *does* make a difference for the American labour force. Already in the 1970s British Leyland was cooperating with Honda of Japan, and Germany's Volkswagen with Nissan, while Italy's Fiat joined forces with Japan's Honda to build a Yamaha motor factory in the United States.

At the same time, however, Renault of France threatened Belgium that unless it imposed restrictions on Japanese car imports it would close down its assembly works near Brussels and 4000 Belgian jobs would be lost. In the Netherlands six cigarette manufacturing firms were fined f 3,848,059 in 1982 for entering into illegal price agreements. In West Germany the twenty enterprises supplying the market with bottles evaded competition by agreeing on production quotas and forcing retailers not to sell foreign-made bottles below a price specified by them.

No less important for the demise of traditional capitalist competitiveness than these types of machination, and symptomatic for the new climate in which economic policy is made by monster corporations and the state, is the intangible factor of "personal connections." By the mid-1970s out of the eighty-six largest enterprises operating in the Netherlands, eighty-four were either directly or indirectly connected with each other through the multiplicity of functions of several of the members of their boards of directors. Eighty of the 86 corporations had similar personal links with the government, mostly through the advisory functions of their executives.

These examples, and there are too many to be cited here, indicate that neither neoclassical orthodoxy nor the old type of Keynesian regulation can provide guidance for conducting the economy back to full-employment growth. The shortcomings of the neoclassical theory are obvious: their underlying assumptions simply do not accord with present day reality. The Keynesian approach depends too much on the effectiveness of educated democracy and the power of national governments. It cannot be said that Keynes was unaware of the problems of internationalization, but he underrated the rise international trade was soon to take. He, and the theoreticians of *Regulated Capitalism*, believed that states were less dependent on foreign supply and demand than they turned out to be.

In 1944, at Bretton Woods, Keynes suggested the establishment of an international means of payment, and a clearing union from which countries with a balance of payment deficit could obtain "bancors" to settle international debts. His suggestions were not accepted and Harry D. White's plan was adopted instead. The *White Plan* did not provide for the establishment of a new international means of payment nor for the extension of credit facilities. It endorsed a system by which member countries contribute currencies and gold to a central reserve fund to help finance *short-term* balance of payments deficits. It also did not furnish automatic American credits to countries experiencing persistent balance of payments shortages. Eventually, IMF practice came somewhat closer to the Keynesian proposal but the underlying thought remained that in the *long run* international trade and balance of payments tend toward equilibrium. Even the enormous debt run up by the developing countries did not shake this figment of the neoclassical imagination.

Another debilitating factor with which the Neo-Keynesian regulationists did not reckon was that governments are run by politicians who often allow electoral and other short-sighted considerations to take precedence over long-term economic necessity. In a paper published in 1988, J.P.G. Reijnders showed how in the Netherlands, after the early phase of post-war reconstruction in which the Dutch government played an important active role, the State became reluctant to interfere with private enterprise, did not know how and when to stimulate and when to restrain the economic flow, and took what with respect to the long-run trend turned out to be "pro-cyclical" decisions.

The conclusion from all this is that only judicious politically-determined investment can revive employment, but not in the manner proposed by Keynes and his followers of the *neoclassical synthesis*. Creating effective demand by government expenditure and hoping that this alone will entice domestic investment and employment is not enough. International trade and international money movements, as well as the structural changes in production and employment, must be taken into account and this entails long-term government economic planning, not short-term regulation. It requires the recognition and acceptance of the fact that only part of the system is subject to competition and that the distribution of the national income between consumption and investment cannot be left to market forces alone but must be regulated with an eye on long-term needs. It is true that "in the long-run we are all dead," but some of us have children and grandchildren who we want to live in reasonable security and affluence. What is necessary for the revival of full employment and responsible economic growth is a judicious politically-determined policy; and this involves several distribution problems. In the first place it involves *the distribution of the national income between investment and consumption*; secondly, *the distribution of the national income between the various strata of society*; and thirdly, *the distribution of national income and employment between services and the production of tangible goods*, and *between state expenditure and private enterprise.*

6

The Distribution of National Income between Investment and Consumption

In real terms everything that is produced is either intended for direct consumption or for helping to produce what is wanted for direct consumption more efficiently. When the fruits of production satisfy a human need directly they are termed *consumer goods* and when their contribution is indirect they are termed *capital*. A tractor is a capital good because it only helps to produce bread with greater efficiency. Capital can therefore be defined as a factor of production representing produced goods which are used as factor inputs for further production. This means that the entire output of a society is the sum of all the consumer goods and capital goods produced by it. As the efficiency of production, that is productivity, greatly depends on the availability and quality of the supply of capital goods, the accumulation and improvement of capital is a crucial determinant of a society's material affluence. But as with the given resources the production of capital can only increase at the expense of less production of consumer goods it always reflects a choice between the satisfaction of present wants and the better satisfaction of these and additional wants in the future. This can be compared to a household's decision whether to spend the entire monthly family earnings on good living or to save part of it and invest it in an asset, say a lorry or good education for the children, to increase the family earnings at some future time.

Classical economists, Ricardo in particular, were aware of this distinction and related it to the division of society into social classes. One class, the Capitalists, earn profits and the other class, the laboring poor, earn wages. The Capitalists use part of their profits to gratify their personal wants and the other part to purchase the resources required to keep their business going and improving. The laboring poor spend their wages on consumption. As nothing is produced without work, and few hold idle cash balances, all earnings whether they are profits or wages are spent on either consumption or investment. Hence national income is equal to profits and wages, and national expenditure to consumption and investment. Given that investment is the source of productivity, the more it is increased the richer the society becomes. But the riches need not be shared equally between capitalists and workers. If the accretion of population is greater than the growth of the demand for labour required to serve the growing industry, competition among workers for the vacant jobs will cause wages to stagnate or fall. But even when labour increases at the same rate as the opportunities for its employment, the rich as a class may still become richer while wages remain scanty. Competition equalizes the rate of profit earned from the various employments of capital, but it does not equalize the accumulation of wealth from profit with the wages the working class is receiving for its labour. Wages are determined outside the economic system, namely by population growth and custom, and therefore have a "natural rate." Notwithstanding the tendency of wages to conform to this natural rate, "their market rate may, in an improving society, for an indefinite period, be constantly above it; for no sooner may the impulse which an increased capital gives to new demand for labour be obeyed, than another increase of capital may produce the same effect." Indeed, Ricardo observes, "many of the conveniences now enjoyed in an English cottage would have been thought luxuries at an earlier period." But then he is not certain if this must always be the case and whether the application of machinery would merely be accompanied by the inconvenience which generally attends the removal of capital and labour from one employment to another. If the capitalists receive the same income as before thanks to the application of labour-saving machinery they would benefit from the reduction in the prices of some of the commodities on which they spend their money. The same applies to the labour class. It too would gain from the use of machinery, as they would have the means of buying more commodities with the same wages, which would not be reduced because the capitalist would wish to employ the same quantity of labour as before, although it might be in the production of new, or at any rate different commodities. But, and Ricardo stresses this point, it is also possible that the substitution of machinery for human labour may be "very injurious" to the interest of the working class because there are no grounds to suppose that whenever the net income of society increases, its gross income would also increase. "The one fund from which landlords and capitalists derive their revenue, may increase, while the other, that upon which the labouring class mainly depend, may diminish, and therefore follows that the same cause which may increase the net revenue of the country may at the same time render the population redundant, and deteriorate the condition of the labourer." In other words, unless the improvements in mechanical production are powerful enough to absorb continually the newly redundant labour, "the use of machinery may be attended with a diminution of the gross produce, and whenever that is the case, it will be injurious to the labouring class." Therefore, Ricardo concludes that "the labouring class have no small interest in the manner in which the net income of the country is expended..." But given all this, he hoped that his statements will not lead to the inference that machinery should not be encouraged. He only raised the problem to elucidate what could happen in principle if improved machinery is suddenly and extensively applied. But he supposed that in fact discoveries are gradual, and rather operate in determining the employment of the capital which is saved and accumulated, than in diverting capital from its actual employment. "The consequence of a rise of food will be a rise of wages, and every rise of wages will have a tendency to determine the saved capital in a greater proportion than before to the employment of machinery. Machinery and labour are in constant competition, and the former can frequently not be employed until labour rises."

Although Ricardo did not consider such a possibility, the same will also happen if the rising productivity accompanying new investment is not accompanied by a sufficiently powerful competition in domestic markets to pass on to consumers in reduced prices the benefits of innovation. This can be illustrated by the following example. Let it be assumed that the entire capitalist class is one entrepreneur who produces all consumer and investment goods, and the entire work force consists of 100 workers, each earning $10 which they expend on their necessities of life. Total capitalist income and outlay will be 100 x $10, that is $1.000. Without changes in the shares the entrepreneur allocates to spend on consumption and on investment this situation can continue more or less indefinitely. But if the entrepreneur decides to spend a much greater part of his money than before on investment, the consequences will be very different. If half the working force were then to be employed in capital production, and only half in the production of consumer goods, the capitalist would earn back his outlay of $1000 because all workers would still have to buy from him the necessities he sells, but at a higher price. As half of the work force is engaged in producing investment goods and only half the number of workers remains available for the production of necessities, the output of necessities will be diminished by half, but the demand for them will have remained the same as it had been before, namely $500 from the workers who earned their income from the production of consumer goods, and $500 earned from the production of capital goods. In this event workers will be vying with each other for the reduced volume of consumer goods and their prices will rise until the entire workers' income is absorbed. Workers' living standard will deteriorate, but the capitalist will have recovered his initial outlay of $1000 and in addition he will own new capital equivalent to the $500 wages he paid for its construction, less the cost of the depreciated capital. The same would be true if the capitalist decided to increase not his investment but his consumption. He would make a greater demand on consumption goods and force workers to buy less for all the money they received collectively. In short, whatever the capitalist decides to do, whether to increase his consumption or expand his investment, his income will remain the same, but if he decides to invest rather than consume his wealth will grow. And so, with the passage of time, the rich become richer while the poor do not obtain an equal share in the growing affluence.

Naturally all this applies to capitalists and workers as a class and not as individuals. An individual capitalist may well engage in the production of unwanted goods and therefore lose his wealth, but his loss will be another capitalist's gain. The same goes for workers' savings. To the extent that a worker earns income from his savings, it becomes part of the volume of capitalist earnings and in the aggregate it takes the place by which his "not spending" reduces pure capitalist earnings. These, in a nutshell, are the ideas behind the Ricardian "wages fund," and Marx's conception of the antagonistic relationship between capital and labour. Both believed that sooner or later the process of Capitalist growth would discontinue. Ricardo thought that capital accumulation will end as it becomes subject to diminishing returns, and Marx when the system is either transformed from within by the concentration and accumulation of wealth, or violently overthrown by the working class. Both recognized the existence of a compensating element, namely that as investment tends to raise productivity, that in the illustration above the 50 workers engaged in the production of consumer goods could be able with the new investment to produce an output in excess of what 100 workers were previously able to produce, and that consequently prices might fall and real incomes rise. But Ricardo saw this merely as a solution to the short-term problems of the system which in the long run is thwarted by population growth, dwindling natural resources and diminishing returns. Marx was unclear about this point. In some of his work he actually wrote about the increasing "pauperization" of the working class while the general tenor of his *Das Kapital* also allows for a reformist abolition of the inequity of distribution.

Except during the era of Mercantilism, this division of societies' aggregate product between *consumption* and *investment* was seldom consciously promoted by the capitalist states. It grew organically, with labour for a long time paying the full price for the accumulation of the resources whose investment eventually provided the high living standard we presently enjoy. For many generations fear of unemployment and destitution kept wages lower than they could have been had the fruits of technological progress been equitably distributed. This allowed capitalists to accumulate resources and provided the enterprising among them with the incentive to invest. The result was rapid technological progress driven by competition among entrepreneurs for their relative shares in markets and between capitalists and organized labour for the division of the fruits of production. Eventually this dual mechanism produced the type of distribution which bore the positive fruit which the era of classical capitalism bequeathed to modern industrial society.

After the Russian Revolution the Soviets tried to accelerate economic growth by deliberate policies to raise the share of investment, in the hope that within a decade it would increase productive efficiency sufficiently to boost consumption to the level already attained in the most advanced capitalist countries by several centuries of "organic" economic growth.

Believing that the Soviet Union was facing the "ruthlessly severe alternative of either to perish or economically to overtake and outstrip the advanced countries," Lenin tried to turn the State into an independent agent of development. Setting Marx's organic growth theory on its head, he allocated to the State the function of autonomous investor. He recognized that investment was the key to productivity, and determined that the State was to invest as large a part of national income as was possible in productive capital assets. The capacity of the basic industries was to be increased in order to raise the output of both producer and consumer goods. The production of consumer goods and the production of capital goods were to be treated as two distinct and separate sectors. The former was concerned with the satisfaction of consumers' needs at the current level of productivity, and the latter with the refurbishment of depreciated capital, its augmentation and the replacement of technologically outdated equipment.

The implementation of this policy immediately raised the problem how it should be financed. Economists like Shanin, Bazarov and Groman argued that because of its low capital/output ratios and farmers' relatively low consumption rate, employment and net savings in the agrarian sector were the largest. Hence, if assisted by government financial support, returns from this sector could be channelled toward industrial development. In time economies of scale in industry would reduce the cost of manufactured goods and the lower prices would raise the farmers' and workers' real incomes and demand. Other economists, supported by Bukharin, favored an investment equally balanced between agriculture and industry. They argued that because agriculture was by far the largest sector in terms of population, and because it depended on industry for equipment, and industry on agriculture for food, raw materials and human resources, it should be given either priority or no less investment than industry. A third group of economists, led by Preobrazhenskii and supported by Trotzky, maintained that the prime objective of economic policy must be the rapid modernization and expansion of industry, which ought to be financed by agriculture through taxation and price fixing. They thought that rigorous pricing and taxing would force farmers to produce more and consume less and thus provide the savings for industrial investment.

In the end, for political rather than economic reasons, and because productivity in agriculture turned out to be too low to sustain the growing industry, Preobrazhenskii's "super-industrialism" prevailed and massive investment in industry at the cost of low consumption became the official strategy. In 1928 Stalin declared that "a fast rate of development of industry and the production of the means of production in particular is the basis and key to the industrialization and development of the economy as a whole." The ensuing shortages of consumer goods were presented as a *temporary* necessity on the way to greater affluence. In Russian textbooks, for example in *Fundamentals of Marxism-Leninism*, the formulation went as follows: "The creation of modern industry requires huge material and financial outlays, therefore the national income previously devoted to the parasitical consumption of the exploiting classes is used for socialist accumulation. The peasantry is released from paying mortgage debts and land rents and this increases the possibility of enlisting the financial assistance of the countryside for industrial development. The revenue of state enterprises, foreign and domestic trade, and banks, is also used for industrialization."

In line with these principles the division of the economy into two distinct sectors deepened. With little regard for actual market demand, industrial investment was made to increase with the progress of technology. Agriculture was more or less neglected and expected to progress through the application of technologically improved equipment, better organization (collectivization) and the fall in the prices of industrial products. The only restrictions which were recognized were the availability of input resources, and in the short run, the prevailing socio-economic relations in the Soviet Union, and in the long run opportunity costs, which is the value of missed gains from taking alternative actions. In 1926 P. Popov attempted to quantify the material restrictions in his *"The volume and structure of the output which flows into the national economy of the Soviet Union from its individual branches and its distribution among the separate branches and classes of society,"* but his work was not taken seriously. In the words of Strumulin, "the accuracy upon which strict science insists is by no means necessary for practical purposes." This statement did in fact typify the pragmatic muddle which passed as "scientific planning" under Stalin.

The fact that the system failed needs today no reiteration. But the reasons why it failed in spite of its inherent economic logic, which rightly regarded investment as the key to economic growth and consumption as the limiting constraint, are interesting. One reason was that it ignored socio-psychological factors and assumed that *fear* alone, without the close prospect of personal advantage, is a sufficiently powerful incentive for diligent commitment. Another reason was that it ignored the self-interest of the class of administrators who were to run and supervise the system. In *The State and Revolution* Lenin declared that "accounting and control" are the main requirements for a smooth working communist society, but he did not consider the sociological and psychological processes affecting the persons by whom this should be done. To convince people returning from war, and having made a revolution to better their standard of living, that they must tighten their belts even further in order to have greater affluence at some future date, is something different from explaining to a class of affluent students of economics why in the long-run investment is preferable to consumption. This almost impossible task of explaining to the uneducated majority of people the need to forgo the present for a better future and to convince them to agree to it, together with the strongly autocratic Russian traditions, practically steered the Russian leadership toward the application of undemocratic means to gain their ends. It was to no avail. Good accounting and adequate supervision require the freedom and ability to criticize and valid criticism can only flourish in *genuine* democracy.

Some western Communists had been aware of this and warned the Soviet leadership but their opinions were ignored. More than three quarters of a century ago, Rosa Luxemburg predicted that "without unrestricted freedom of press and assembly, without a free struggle of opinions, life dies out in every public institution, becomes a mere semblance of life, in which only the bureaucracy remains the active element... only a dozen outstanding heads do the leading and an élite of the working class is invited from time to time to meetings where they are to applaud the speeches of the leaders, and to approve proposed resolutions unanimously—at bottom then—a clique affair—a dictatorship to be sure, not however of the proletariat but only of a handful of politicians..." History proved her right. But what was true for Soviet Communism may well also be true for other systems. Tinbergen once wrote about the convergence of the western and the Soviet economic systems. Had he not only written about the similarities directly related to the economic structures, but considered social and political reality as well, his words might have been a timely warning to the west. There the separation of ownership from management of capital had precipitated similar conditions, and a new managerial "class" of bureaucrats, closely resembling the Russian *"nomenklatura"* was rapidly rising, and democracy was being flooded by a deluge of irrelevant and misleading information.

7

Overproduction, Underconsumption, and the Business Cycle

The mechanisms by which the national income is distributed between consumption and investment in the Free Enterprise system is competition. Taking for granted that the incentive to invest in the private sector is the expectation of profit, and that capitalists are rational people, it is clear that sustained investment requires that effective demand must eventually suffice to satisfy this expectation. This means that, allowing for some time-lags, full employment requires effective demand for consumption and investment to match or exceed the rate of accretion of the labour force and the rate at which technological innovation is increasing productivity. Under *perfect competition* an excess of labour would reduce wages and an excess of produce would reduce prices. Lower prices would increase *real incomes* and spending, and the ensuing greater velocity of money circulation would cause prices to rise again and revive investment and employment. This, in a nutshell, is the *Real-Balance or Pigou effect*. Without going into the question whether this would really be the sequence of events or if it would only happen when banks have reached the limit of their lending capacity, one thing is fairly certain, namely that it can only apply to an idealized and not to a actual Free Market system. In reality, when consumer demand continues for a lengthy period to fall below producers' output, incentives to invest and to employ more labour will diminish; and if demand exceeds output, prices rise and inflation may be leading toward economic entropy. As profit expectations are prospective they may or may not be influenced by past and current experience, but usually an experienced rise in demand for goods and services tends to induce investment, and economic stagnation or falling demand to discourage it. Normally, if potential investors assume that the stagnation or diminution in demand is transient they may wish to take advantage of the lower interest rates and reduced cost of other resources to renew or supplement their stock. If they suspect that the recession will be lasting they will hold back, and the accent in technological improvements will shift from *product innovation* toward labour cost or other costs reducing *process innovation*. The only exception is the case when a potential investor has

47

some completely new invention of a product in hand which is not merely replacing another but opens up a novel market.

On the whole both types of innovation usually have gone together, but when the demand for consumer goods was buoyant and expanding, the emphasis in *Research and Development* tended toward the former type of innovation, and when the demand for consumer goods dwindled and the recession appeared to be long-lasting firms felt that cost reduction was essential and the emphasis tended toward the other type of innovation. The one was dominant in the 1960s and 1970, in the era of "false wants" when electric toothbrushes and Silly-Putty were invented, the other has been dominant since the 1980s, when silicon chips and robots flooded manufacturing and services like water from a burst dam.

In the past, when market competition between producers was reasonably lively, both types of innovation had similar effects. When Henry Ford introduced his inexpensive standardized car it not only created jobs in the motor industry and in the industries directly involved in automobile production, but also raised the demand for labour to provide machine tools, in oil extraction, oil refining, construction of roads and garages and in the services required to keep the new vehicles in good repair. The same was true for *process innovation*. For as long as market competition was brisk it reduced prices, raised real incomes and increased effective demand for other goods and services. But lately, since powerful producers tend not to reduce prices but adjust their output and try to sustain profits by reducing costs when demand is shrinking, this type of innovation tends to protract and deepen recession rather than alleviate it. The fruits of innovation are not passed on in lower prices to consumers and interest rates do not fall, because efforts to finance the introduction of the new technologies, without which specializing companies cannot sustain the international primacy in their core activities, send more and more firms scurrying for investment funds. Consequently, real incomes and effective demand do not rise, and in spite of unemployment and recession interest rates are high and mounting. At the same time the financial problem is exacerbated by increasing state borrowing to meet the mounting cost of the social services, which rises with growing unemployment, while tax revenue diminishes.

Throughout the era of *regulated capitalism* there was a good deal of learned controversy about the required division of the national income between investment and consumption. Keynes did not believe that the system could only be in equilibrium with full employment. In his opinion full employment was only one of many situations at which the system could come to rest. He rejected Say's postulate that supply always creates its own demand, and that unemployment cannot be the result of insufficient demand. He believed that consumption depends on investment, but that investment is exogenously determined; that investment depends on the decisions of one group of people, and saving on another group; and that if consumption depends on the decision of thousands of people who can at any time determine how much of their income they wish to spend and how much to save, the problem is even more complicated. He agreed that (ex-post) the amount actually invested is always equal to what actually is saved; but that this need not be the same as what (ex-ante) people want to invest and wish to save. However, for equilibrium (which is something other than equality), what people want to invest must also be equal to what people wish to save. If desired investment falls short of desired saving, or if the desire to invest exceeds available savings, this will effect the National Income. National Income will fall or rise until what investors want to invest is equal to what savers want to save.

In other words, Keynes asserted that an inequality between planned investment and planned savings is adjusted by way of changes in the level of output and employment; and that the equality of savings and investment is reached by way of changes in the level of aggregate demand and not (as his colleagues in the economics profession claimed) by changes in the rates of interest. This recursive process involves the *Marginal Propensity to Consume* and the *Multiplier*.

The term *Marginal propensity to Consume* means the change in consumption resulting from a unit change in income. The term *Multiplier* stands for the ratio of change in total income to the initial change in expenditure that brought it about. Keynes granted "that the propensity to consume is a fairly stable function so that, as a rule, the amount of aggregate consumption mainly depends on the amount of aggregate income. People are disposed "to increase their consumption as their income increases, but not by as much as the increase in their income... For a man's habitual standard of life usually has the first claim on his income, and he is apt to save the difference which discovers itself between his actual income and the expense of his habitual standard; or, if he does adjust his expenditure to changes in his income, he will over short periods do so imperfectly. Thus a rising income will often be accompanied by increased saving, and a falling income by decreased saving, on a greater scale at first than subsequently... This means that, if employment and hence aggregate income increase, *not all* the additional employment will be required to satisfy the needs of additional consumption." The same will be true in the opposite direction if incomes decrease as a result of falling employment. However, as changes in the volume of employment depend on changes in the propensity to consume it is necessary to define the ratio between consumption and investment expenditure and aggregate employment. This is what R.F. Kahn did in 1931 in his article on "The Relation of Home Investment to Unemployment." Though differently formulated, the basic idea of Kahn, which Keynes adopted, was as follows: Let it be assumed that people save one tenth of their income and "*l'oncle d'Amérique*" injects $100 extra into the system to build a factory. The builders will then spend $90 extra on consumption, and save an extra $10. But here the matter does not rest. Those who receive the extra $90 will also spend 9/10 of their new income and save 1/10. Hence total incomes and savings will increase again. Total expenditure at this point will have become $100 + $90, that is $190, and total savings $10. But those who receive the $90 will also spend 9/10 and save 1/10. They will spend $81 and save $9. So after this round of spending and saving total spending or income will be $100 + $90 + $81, that is $271, and savings $10 + $9, that is $19. This process of spending and saving will go on until so much of the initial injection of $100 has leaked out into the savings that what is left over to spend is no longer worth mentioning. In other words the process of spending will end when the entire sum of $100 has disappeared (as savings) and none of it is left to circulate as earnings and expenditure. Now, if indeed each group of recipients divides its earnings in the assumed manner, 9/10 for consumption and 1/10 for saving, the total flow of income generated by the American Uncle's injection can be predicted with the help of the formula of a geometric series:

$$S = A \frac{1}{1-r}$$

Where A is the first term in the series (here $100) and r the ratio by which each subsequent term is multiplied (9/10) namely the *marginal propensity to consume*. In other words, following Kahn, Keynes distinguished between *stocks* and *flows*. The money injected by the "American uncle" is a stock which remains as savings throughout the entire proces, while the money-income received and spent by each successive group of earners generates a flow which, depending on the strength of the marginal propensity to consume, increases and in sum becomes more than the original investment.

Naturally the process works both ways. If for one reason or another $100 should be "lost" rather than gained, the sign in front, the A in the formula, becomes negative and in the given example total income would be reduced by $1000. Similarly, if the r in the formula (which is the *marginal propensity to consume*) should only be, say, 5/10, the multiplier would raise (or reduce) spending by no more than $200; and if the r is 5/100 than the multiplier would raise spending to no more than $105.26.

A point important to note is that at any stage in the sequence of income-generation by the multiplier savings are exactly equal to the original amount injected. In the example of the uncle's $100, if the flow of spending and saving was stopped after the third group received its income but before it could spend it, total savings would still be $100. This is so because the first group saved $10, the second $9, and the third, which has not yet spent its money and therefore is still holding (saving) it, has $81. It means that while savings are always equal to investment this does not imply that *savings* determine *investment* but investment determines savings.

The conclusion is that the total amount of savings is determined by the rate of investment alone, but the propensity to save is determined by psychological factors such as the way in which people regard the future. The *propensity to save* does not determine the overall volume of savings but it does determine the level of income associated with any given rate of investment. Investment determines the level of incomes but the propensity to save (or to consume) influences the decisions of potential investors whether to hold on to savings or invest them, and this finally determines the level of income and employment.

This seems to introduce a paradox, namely that on the one hand increasing consumption induces investment and on the other it reduces saving. But in fact increasing investment creates new incomes, and (if earners' propensity to consume remains unchanged) new savings. In other words investment is the crux of the matter; it generates employment and income and at the same time savings. But desired investment, which needs not necessarily be equal to savings, depends on the growth of demand, that is on the growth of income which in turn depends on the level of employment. This makes *effective demand* the key to investment and employment. However, if savings need not be equal to desired investment then there is no necessity for an "American uncle" to provide the required resources for the new investment. If savings can or cannot be invested then it is anticipated profit which either does or does not cause the $100 to be injected which set the *Multiplier* going.

What remained to be explored was how the working of the multiplier *interacts* with the changes in aggregate demand. Paul Samuelson did this in 1939 in an article entitled "Interactions between the Multiplier Analysis and the Principle of Acceleration." The essential idea of the *acceleration principle* is that the level of aggregate net investment depends on the expected change in the required output. Assuming that entrepreneurs attempt to maintain a fixed ratio of desired capital stock to output it appears reasonable that an expected rise in demand will induce new investment. This suggests that expected demand and therefore usually a change in the volume of employment or/and real incomes in the recent past determine investment (and not saving and the rate of interest as the classics assumed). As entrepreneurs can be trusted to know how many machines or real capital they require to produce a given volume of output, they can also be trusted to calculate how many additional machines they will require to meet any expected greater volume of demand. In other words, if they expect demand to grow, entrepreneurs, knowing their Capital/Output ratio, will adjust their investment to suit the expected additionally required output. It follows that expected increases in output induce new investment, which sets in motion a *multiplier* which raises demand so that the process becomes a self-fulfilling prophecy. This process will continue until either the supply of one of the factors of production can no longer be increased or until the share of savings out of the newly generated incomes has leaked out of the circulation leaving too little additional demand to suffice to convince entrepreneurs that it is safe to carry on increasing their stock of real capital profitably.

The process can be summarized as follows: if investment is designated (I) and national income (which is the money value of the goods and services becoming available to a nation from economic activity) (Y), and (t) stands for a unit of time (say, one year) associated with that national income, then an expected rise in (Y) in the year (t + 1) would induce new investment equal to the expected change multiplied by the known Capital/Output ratio (v). Given that investment sets in motion a multiplier effect, the result will be that actual demand in period (t + 1) will increase more or less in the measure which the entrepreneurs expected. But what is it that in the first place led entrepreneurs to *expect* that demand would expand? The answer to this question is that it is usually past experience. If in the period (t–1) demand had grown beyond the volume they could supply with their existing stock of capital, then knowing their capital/output ratio and the volume of output which they could not readily supply with their existing stock of real capital, they have a reasonable indication of how much more capital they should acquire.

The logic of this is simple. If past experience has shown that the increase in demand for final goods is rising $(Y_{t-1}-Y_{t-2})$ and the capital/output ratio of the firm is (v), and the proportion of income saved is s, then to meet this increase in demand the entrepreneur will have to add new capital equal to $v(Y_{t-1}-Y_{t-2})$, which is I. In short, experienced changes in demand induce changes in investment. In other words, the *Multiplier* sets out to show how the level of national income reacts to changes in investment, and the *Acceleration Principle* sets out to explain what determines investment.

$$I_t = v(Y_t - Y_{t-1})$$

$$Y_t = \frac{I_t}{s}$$

$$Y_t = \frac{v}{s}(Y_t - Y_{t-1}) = \frac{v}{v-s} Y_{t-1}$$

or, as after some algebraic manipulations, the above is conventionally written:

$$I_t = \alpha \Delta Y_{t-1} + b$$

where α is the accelerator coefficient, Δ the change, and Y_{t-1}, the proxy for the expected change in output. This is called the *"naive"* acceleration principle, but giving a dog a bad name does not make it bad. "Naive" or not, it represents the essentials of how Keynes visualized the determination of investment.

The idea is of course more complex than this representation suggests. Time lags and negative savings at low incomes, as well as conditions in which the marginal propensity to save is not equal to the average propensity to save, must also be considered. If this is done the interaction equation becomes something like this:

$$Y_t = \frac{v}{s}(Y_{t-1}-Y_{t-2}) + \frac{Z}{s}$$

where Y_t designates national income in period t; v the normal capital-output ratio; s the proportion of income saved; Y_{t-1} national income in the previous period; Y_{t-2} national income in the period before that; and Z the amount of negative saving that would take place at zero income.

The interesting thing about the last equation is that the interaction of the multiplier and the acceleration principle does not lead to a cumulative up or down movement but subjects these tendencies to fluctuations. In fact fluctuations will occur because of the inability of income to rise (or fall) beyond a certain limit, or the intervention of external factors. Moreover, the amount of capital that may be used to produce a given output is somewhat flexible and firms do not regard their output as given even if they consider the demand schedule for their products as remaining constant. Similarly long-term expectations play a role in decisions so that even if last year's demand was falling, long-term expectation may still induce investment, while increasing demand may not convince entrepreneurs that the trend can continue long into the future. Some economists would even invoke, out of context, Keynes' remark about entrepreneurs' "animal spirits" to suggest that investment defies any mathematical model. But in fact all this leads only to one certain conclusion, namely that it would be rash to declare that investment is an easily calculable function of the rate of change of national income. In short, even if it were legitimate to combine stocks and flows as done with the capital/output ratio, the capital stock adjustment principle would still not really sufficiently account for all the forces which affect investment.

The example cited is taken from trade cycle analysis. It is typical of the way in which in the 1950s the economics profession dealt with the Keynesian heritage. It did not abandon the belief in equilibrium and incorporated Keynes' essentially causal system as a special case into the old theory. It continued to regard disequilibria as short-term deviations which, though inherent in the system, can be or even must be counteracted. Almost everyone seemed to be in agreement that governments have the power to prevent the level of economic activity from fluctuating and that they must eliminate the social losses caused by fluctuations, but not that these could be structural rather than short-term aberrations. In the words of Matthews: "the government can and should regulate the flow of aggregate spending in such a way as to keep demand and employment at the desired level, it must stimulate spending if there is a tendency to unemployment and... restrain spending if there is a tendency to inflation." The instruments by which governments were thought to be able to accomplish this task seemed to be obvious, namely the regulation of consumers' expenditure and investment. They believed they were able to regulate consumer expenditure by varying the level of taxation, by subsidies, and by augmenting or reducing state pensions and changing the rules governing consumer credit. Private investment they thought to regulate by varying the taxation of profits, subsidizing investment when necessary, and licencing; investment, by monetary measures, varying government expenditure and by administrative decisions. In short, economists believed that governments were able to stabilize the economic system by *fiscal* means aided by their *monetary powers* to influence the rates of interest.

Before long Hicks in his celebrated ISLM model, by incorporating the effect of national income on the rate of interest, transformed the Keynesian *dynamic model* back into an interdependent system of simultaneous equations. In fact this converted Keynes' general theory into a special case in the neoclassical tradition. Others introduced market imperfections, particularly sticky wages, to explain long-term massive unemployment, and improved the *Accelerator Principle* by more sophisticated versions in which the ratio of capital to output is taken to be affected by "user cost of capital" and more sophisticated time-lags so that its impact on the system became less powerful and immediate. Harrod and Domar restored some of the dynamics to the Keynesian model using the interaction between the *Multiplier* and the *Acceleration Principle* to find a relationship between investment and savings which would suit stable economic growth with full employment, and Pasinetti added a capital stock adjustment coefficient which takes account of investors' expectations. It turned out that stable economic growth with full employment requires equality between the quotient of the aggregate propensity to save and the capital/output ratio. The conclusion was that when such a warranted rate of growth exceeds actual growth, savings surpass investment, and when it falls short of it, they are deficient. At first sight this meant that by carefully assessing that rate of growth which would be dynamically consistent with full employment it should indeed be possible to sustain economic stability by fiscal and monetary means. But how does one assess the long-term rate of growth? In his paper on "perspectivistic distortion" J. Reijnders showed that all such trends depend on the dates on which the time series begins and ends, and this makes any such extrapolation into the future unreliable.

Eventually Harrod's idea was also supplemented by Solow's variable capital/output ratio and by Kaldor's aggregate variable-propensity to save. In effect, Solow's addition to the Harrodian model was again a return to the neoclassical tradition. A flexible capital/labour ratio would equalize the aggregate propensity to save, to the product of the capital/output ratio and the natural growth rate. On the other hand Kaldor's addition to the model takes a technologically restricted constant capital/output ratio as a given, and adopts a flexible propensity to save. Pasinetti claimed that Kaldor ignored the fact that workers also save and therefore share in profits. He distinguished between

wages and profits, and workers and capitalists. But he too postulated that profits are proportional to the supply of savings and equal to the rate of interest,
which makes the propensity to save out of workers' income insignificant for
determining the share or rate of profit. On the basis of the same distinction
between workers' and capitalists' saving Samuelson and Modigliani divided
the system into two saving regions, in one of which capitalists' income is essential for the rate of profit from capital, and in the other, workers' propensity
to save affects the capital/output ratio.

The result of all these modifications was that the long-term message inherent in the acceleration principle was lost, namely that investment is induced
by changes in consumption and that consumption depends on the level of
investment. In simple words, it was forgotten that the level of net investment is
a proportion of the difference between the desired capital stock and the actual
capital stock, or that the level of aggregate net investment depends on the
expected change in output. This so-called *naive accelerator*, which assigns no
role to interest rates, was what Keynes regarded as the prime determinant of
investment. Taking account of "user cost of capital" and "time lags" and making the accelerator coefficient more flexible may well be very useful for the
explanation of conventional business cycles, but unless one assumes that most
businessmen are fools the long-term message stands, namely that effective
consumer demand induces investment and that investment generates demand,
and that if for a lengthy period effective consumer demand is not allowed to
rise in line with productivity, investment will turn from product innovation to
process innovation and unemployment will be lasting.

It was Kalecki who saw this. In his equation national income is determined
by the propensity to save out of capitalists' income and by the distribution of
the national income between wages and profits and the volume of investment.
In what is an almost Marxist conception, he distinguished between capitalists
(savers and consumers) and workers (consumers) and showed how profits and
consumption are related to each other. Unfortunately his dictum: "workers
spend what they earn and capitalists earn what they spend," though appropriate, caused a good deal of misunderstanding and diverted attention from his
important argument. Had he formulated the distinction in terms of "income
from work and income from profit," rather than in the sociological terms "workers" and "capitalists" the picture would have been much clearer. It would at
least have silenced the critics who pointed to the fact that many workers earn
both an income from work and from their savings. Kalecki divided the system
into an income side and an expenditure side. As no one can have an income
without it being someone else's expenditure the totals of both must be equal.
He designated profits as the sum of capitalists' incomes and wages the sum of
workers' incomes. On the expenditure side he added up investment with capitalists' and workers' consumption, and assuming that workers spend all their
earnings on consumption made workers' expenditure equal to wages. In this

way capitalists' expenditure on consumption and investment is equal to profits. This leads to the conclusion that capitalists' share in national income rises by the amount they invest, while the multiplier is increasing aggregate output. But even if they consume part of their profit rather than invest it, their income will not diminish. Capitalists' income is maintained without regard to how they spend it, which means that the volume of investment at any given level of technology determines the division of labour between the production of consumer goods and investment, and that the level of technology and the volume of production capacity determine the output of the various types of goods. It follows that for growth with full employment there is a determinate volume of consumer goods to meet the flow of wages, and a determinate volume of capital goods produced in line with capitalists' profit expectations.

In 1993 R.Ph.G. Walsteijn demonstrated that an extension of the Kaldor-Pasinetti approach could bring the argument back to its Keynesian origins. Investment and consumption are both positively related to growth, while changes in the path of economic growth are confined by full employment equilibrium. In his opinion a detailed study of the Kaldor/Pasinetti extension of the Keynesian original model, and of the relationship between income distribution and economic growth, should yield new insight especially when the role of the government sector and international trade are also taken into account.

All these improvements to the interpretation of the interaction of the multiplier with the acceleration principle are very illuminating and relevant for the explanation of the conventional business cycle, but they have little to contribute to the better understanding of the *long-term* processes to which the economy and society have been subjected since the late 1970s. They do not take account of the consequences of the separation of ownership from control of investment; the shift of emphasis from product to process innovation; the growing globalization of production and distribution; the scramble for funds under the influence of "tight money" policies; monopoly and power; the psychological effects of long-run depression and unemployment; the division between market and stock exchange activity. In short, they do not take account of all the slow-moving forces transforming traditional capitalism into a different type of quasi-capitalism for which the old behavioral assumptions can no longer be taken to be valid. The offshoot of this is that while business cycles are inherent in the market system their analysis cannot explain the tendencies which are the causes of our present ills.

In conclusion: economic growth with full employment requires that effective demand increases in line with productivity. As the diminution of market competition and of Trade Union power can no longer assure this course, the state remains the "independent actor" who can fill the gaps. The state must regulate demand as well as investment in a manner which matches productivity. In other words, it must regard the *naive* accelerator as a long-term macroeconomic guide to intervention, and the *multiplier-accelerator interaction* analysis as a guide to reduce the impact of short-term fluctuations. The former the state must do by supporting effective demand through creating employment in the public sphere and reducing interest rates for investment in the private sphere when unemployment grows, and the latter by the conventional instruments of fiscal and monetary policy. It simply must take employment rather than GNP as the guide to economic policy. It must abandon the static conception of the role of money and the assumption that inflation can only be the product of increases in the money supply, and consider the possibility of alternative causes for a rise in prices and seek ways to neutralize them. But without strong public pressure such a course of action can hardly be expected to be taken by the people entrusted with the conduct of the affairs of state in most industrial countries. Too many of them come from the same milieu as the management of industry and therefore share their interests, prejudices and limitations. The problem is therefore political and requires an *educated* democracy. Given the current state of affairs this places an enormous responsibility upon trade unions and on intellectuals. The former must organize responsible resistance to the policies designed to reduce social security and wages; the latter must examine and explain the true causes of the current economic ills. That these are neither easy nor personally very rewarding tasks is obvious, but if "capitalism with a human face" is worth pursuing there seems to be no alternative.

8

Distribution: Some Methodological Observations

Perhaps the most interesting descendant of the eighteenth century French theoretical economic tradition was Léon Walras (1834–1910). His work went almost unnoticed during his lifetime, not only because he presented his findings in mathematical terms (which was not in fashion with the economics profession of the time), but also because of his political ambiguous position. He claimed that Free Market economics presents as working well a system which works badly, and that Marxism presents a system which will not work at all. "Certainly economists have not demonstrated scientifically the principle of free competition. Fortunately for them free competition organizes production more or less well. In going into ecstasies over the admirable manner in which it does this they regard their task as accomplished. But socialism must proceed differently. It must distinguish itself from *economism* [the Free Market paradigm] above all in its knowledge of political economy, and it must explain why and how this or that principle will lead to and maintain equilibrium of the demand and supply for services and products. In doing this it will advance from the literary to the scientific stage. This is what the collectivism of Marx fails to do."

Taking *general equilibrium* as his point of departure, Walras examined the simultaneous determination of all prices and all quantities of goods in the economic system. Assuming that people act rationally to maximize utility, and employing a *numéraire* by which all prices can be equally expressed, he concluded that the system can be represented by two sets of equations for each of the (m) commodities present in the market. One set of market equations represents price and the other set represents quantity. As each commodity exchanges for all others less one (m—1), that is that every commodity exchanges for all commodities except for itself, the number of equations for each commodity in the entire system must be two. One set may then be regarded as demand equations and the other set as supply equations.

$$(m—1)m \text{ Demand equations}$$
$$(m—1)m \text{ Supply equations}$$
$$\text{ie, } 2m(m-1)$$

59

As the number of unknowns is also 2(m—1), because half of the unknowns are the *value* of each commodity in terms of every other commodity and the rest the *quantities* of all commodities in terms of all others, the number of equations is equal to the number of unknowns, and the equations can (at least in theory) be solved. A similar approach was later also adopted and adapted in Wassily Leontief-type input-output tables to assist politicians in making economic policy decisions.

The problem with this method is that the demand for one good can only increase at the expense of another and because the price of one has either risen or fallen. In other words, the model recognizes only *substitution effects* and ignores *income effects*. For example, capital goods can only be used more intensively in the production process at the expense of another type of input, such as labour, and only because the relative price of the former has fallen. In short, economic growth and a general rise or fall in incomes is disregarded. In later models of this type some income effects have been included as exogenous factors. For example, in long-term *indicative plans* the results of technological innovations which affect production coefficients (which are taken as constant in the short and medium term input-output models used by planning offices) have been allowed some latitude for correction. But the basic conception remained that the substitution effects of changes in relative prices provide the mechanism which moves the system from one equilibrium to another.

However, if we can believe W. Jaffe, then, unlike modern neoclassical economists, Walras never thought that what he was describing or analyzing was the workings of the economic system as it existed. What he intended to do was to demonstrate the possibility of formulating axiomatically a rationally consistent economic system in order to find out whether an economic system based upon conditions that to his mind constituted economic justice in exchange and distribution could exist. In the words of R. X. Chase, "his aim was prescriptive or normative and not positive or descriptive. His object was to formulate (invent?) an economic system in conformity with the idea of social justice." Whether this was his aim or not, and the idea that this was actually his purpose has been challenged, the fact remains that his method was evidently static and based on the untenable proposition of perfect competition and on the belief that prices and wages are determined by and within the system.

Pareto, who in 1892 succeeded Walras in the Chair of Economics at Lausanne, extended the mathematical conditions for the general equilibrium of Walras. Excluding all ethical elements, in order to stress the formal character of positive economics he justified inequality of incomes on the grounds of what he believed to be a constancy of income distribution across countries and through time, a kind of natural law.

Classical economists had been concerned with the causes of the wealth of nations and with its distribution among the factors of production within the framework of population growth, finite resources and free competition in a private enterprise system. They recognized labour as the source of *value* but ignored the worker's property rights in the fruit of his labour while they meticulously observed all other property rights. They found poverty in the midst of riches deplorable but not a legitimate cause for intervention because they regarded it inevitable. They saw the social order as part of the natural order by which in spite of their natural selfishness and rapacity the rich are led by an invisible hand to make nearly the same distribution of the necessaries of life as that which would have been made had the earth been divided into equal portions among all its inhabitants. They looked upon the poor as dependents of a kind, with a good right to protection and with a duty of subservience to their betters, but denied that they had a *right* to food and employment. In the words of Malthus, "as the rich do not in reality possess the power of finding employment and maintenance for the poor, the poor cannot .... possess the right to demand them." Society "will always consist of a class of proprietors and a class of laborers; but the condition of each, and the proportion which they bear to each other, may be so altered as greatly to improve the harmony and beauty of the whole."

Having attained social and economic power by the middle of the nineteenth century, the bourgeoisie was entering its first period of consolidation. Its "laws of motion" became laws of dynamic stability and the study of growth became the study of the laws of equilibrium. The classical economists' implicit theory of growth yielded place to theories which explained the economy in "close analogy to statical mechanics" and treated the Laws of Exchange as the Laws of Equilibrium of the lever. Mobility continued to be accepted but only as running in place. In its entirety the system had to remain immutable, but individuals were allowed to find their places in the social structure on the basis of their competitive ability. Progress, in the economists' terminology, became the accumulation of capital, the advancement of cost-reducing technology and the spreading of trade and enterprise. Human beings became "labour power," and nature became a "factor of production." The main concern of economic theory became measurement of utility and its maximization.

Claiming that judgments involving basic issues of fairness, justice or morality are beyond its special competence, the new economics restricted itself to the study of "the relation between ends and scarce means which have alternative uses." In other words, it confined economic thought to the study of what is (or will happen) under specified conditions, without concern for what should or ought to be. The paradox of a society technologically capable of producing affluence for all, and the dire reality of the persisting widespread poverty, was none of its concern. The legitimate business of economic science was the theory of the firm, the pricing of goods, services and factors of production, that is microeconomics, in the competitive markets of a static system. In place of the cost of production theory of value it introduced the subjective value theory of price determination; in place of a socially determined theory of income distribution it produced a marginal productivity theory of income distribution; in place of class struggle it conjured up the vision of an harmonious system in which the reward of each factor of production is related to the marginal productivity of its employment.

This conception of economics eliminated the inconsistency between the strict observance of property rights in general, and their non-observance with regard to workers' property rights in the fruit of their labour. If *utility*, and not as the classics believed *work*, was the true source of value then profit ceased to be "theft" of inadequately remunerated work. All this does not imply that economists were deprived of humanity, but it does indicate how the choice of an economic approach or methodology determines which strata of society are and which are not served by its practitioners. The new economics simply accepted the oligarchy's point of view that the poor differ from the rich, and that this was the cause of their poverty. Moreover, they believed, as Pigou actually said, that the equal distribution of the national product between all people would be "seriously doubtful."

It was in this climate in which in 1916 Vilfredo Pareto published his *Traité de sociologie générale*. His intention was "to seek experimental reality by the application to the social sciences of the methods which have proved themselves in physics, chemistry, astronomy, biology and other such sciences." Taking for granted that human nature is immutable—a datum—which is driven by some primeval, hedonistic passion (*residues*, in his terminology) which are kept in line by an imposed order, he presented society as a collection of independent variables held together by the gravitational attraction of self-interest and restricted by the system. He saw society as an aggregate of individual components characterized by the fact that change in one part of the system leads to adjustive changes in all other parts. Individuals may advance socially and economically or fall behind; but society in its entirety remains unchanging. Human nature is the same at all times and everywhere; there is no room for improvement and learning from experience and no growth of social consciousness and foresight.

His famous discussion of élites begins with the simple proposition that people are intellectually and physically *unequal* and remain so. The more capable form the élite. If there is social mobility then this is due to the circumstance that at any time some people do not really deserve to be in the positions they find themselves. They are merely assigned there, mostly by the accident of birth, without having the necessary qualifications. The genuine members of the élite hold on to their position because they belong there, those assigned to it without the required qualities may hang on for a while but eventually yield their positions to others who are more capable but initially less favorably placed than themselves.

In fact Pareto did not wed the social sciences to the natural sciences, as later students of his work sometimes suggest, but regardless of the question whether this methodology is suitable or not, forced the social sciences into the Procrustean bed of a mechanistic approach which is acceptable in the natural sciences. He ignored the dynamic and holistic character of society and imposed upon it a conception borrowed from the principles of equilibrium in solid bodies. His hedonistic conception of human nature and static perception of society also explains why, in spite of his many forays into the study of history, he never really understood the complex relationship between economic, social and cultural phenomena. For him all human actions are divisible into two categories: those relating to economic matters, in the pursuit of which man acts rationally, and all others, which he considered irrational—the expressions of sentiments. Social values and culture in general are no more than confusing attempts to "rationalize" the irrational. The possibility that his *residues* may also be little else than the reactions communicated by emotional and verbal contamination to successive generations until, overladen with habitual rules, they appeared to be intuitive and inevitable, entirely eluded him. It never occurred to him that his *residues* are simply what at any given time social consensus makes to appear "natural" or "inevitable"

Unlike Walras who was probing into the feasibility of economic justice, Pareto's approach purged political economy of its social context and turned it into a set of purely systemic deductions which depend upon assumptions which at best cannot be directly checked and at worst are plainly wrong. To make economics more "exact," more like the natural sciences, and capable of providing quantitative predictions, it excludes all disequilibrating forces, such as technological innovation, population growth, changing attitudes and tastes. It disregards the whole organic nature of society by tacitly assuming that it is dealing with short-term processes alone. The fact that the entire system depends upon the equilibrating tendencies of the *price mechanism*, which is a manifest long-term process, is overlooked or considered to be irrelevant. Economic growth is made exogenous and relegated to the sphere of technology, and new attitudes to the sphere of sociology and psychology. All change becomes exogenous; its impact on the economic system can be studied but the likelihood that it may itself be the product of the system or that it may alter the structure of the system is disregarded.

In other words, by ignoring the dynamic and organic character of society, Pareto and his latter-day disciples made mathematical predictions easier but hardly realistic in macroeconomics. There simply is no way by which the Walrasian model can be used without resort to the deceptive assumption that the world is progressing toward free competition or that the exogenous variables are independent of the model. Even the ingenuity of Solow and Samuelson cannot change this and release the purely indigenous self-adjusting economic system from its static moorings. To circumvent the issue by claiming, as Milton Friedman does, that there is little difference between economics and the natural sciences because "in both there is no *certain* substantive knowledge," is definitely not the way to inspire confidence in the practical powers of prediction of this type of economics.

In fact, however, there is a difference: nature is "given" and though its laws may be differently interpreted in various times it is independent of man's wishes and desires. A man may construct a rocket to overcome the gravitation of the earth but this will not abolish gravitation. An economic system however is a social construct whose laws change once the system changes. *Natural Laws* are the product of observations and so are the laws governing the conduct of societies, but the laws by which societies abide are man-made, the historical product of societies and therefore open to change. The laws of gravity cannot be abolished, but the laws governing the conduct of people living in an economic Free Enterprise system would simply not exist in another type of social organization. A return to Feudalism, or the imposition of a planned command economy, would wipe out the profit motive and with it the whole body of economic laws based upon the notion of an equilibrium-seeking price mechanism.

Individuals and entire societies can learn, and sometimes do learn, from their experiences and adjust their behavior accordingly, and molecules cannot. The neoclassical notion of the *optimum* rests upon a timeless conception of society which leaves people no room for learning from experience but at the same time grants them perfect foresight. To say that resources are distributed optimally when it is impossible by transferring them to make one person better without making another worse, implies that what people hold to be desirable at one time must remain so at another and that while choosing between alternatives they are always conscious of the consequences of their choice. But in reality positive choices need neither be rational from an individual's point of view nor leading to socially optimal results. For this reason the neoclassical approach gives only an illusion of scientific objectivity: it achieves precision by quantification at the price of divorcing itself from empirical reality.

Neoclassical economics cannot claim to be a value-free scientific approach. To fit the Walrasian model it is laden with assumptions about how society ought to be instead of how an observer sees it or it really is. The model does not provide the "positive scientific knowledge that enables us to predict the consequences of a possible course of action," which Friedman rightly expects from a scientific method, but a methodology imposed upon questionable and even erroneous assumptions. For the model to be valid society must be static and it is not; utility must be narrowly materialistic and it is not; competition must be universally free and it is not; each factor of production must be equally rewarded in relation to its marginal contribution to output, and it is not; profit must be constantly maximized, and it is not—in fact all *ceteris* must remain *paribus* which seldom is the case. In short, the entire system of assumptions upon which the validity of the model depends is shaky, but its discussion was declared heresy and since the 1970s punishable with excommunication from the economics profession's establishment.

All this does of course not deny the existence of a mechanism of allocation by prices, but is does refute the hypothesis that the system is gravitating toward harmony and optimum. Economic laws are the specific product of social arrangements and relations which are with the passage of time constantly transforming. Notions about equilibrating tendencies need to be seen in their social context and in the light of the ends they serve. Pareto and his disciples' notion of an equilibrium-seeking system reflected, and continues to reflect in its modern guises, the urge of the ruling oligarchy to protect its position by freezing the existing social and economic structure of society. In contrast to this, the notions of equilibrium in the works of Tinbergen, Leontieff, Harrod, Domar, and Kalecki are of a different order. Their notions of equilibrium which gained prominence after World War II, do not treat quantification as a purpose in itself, as a kind of surrogate scientific reality, but as a tool to help solving "real world" problems. It was this approach which, when the power structure of the old élite was in disarray, dominated the historical interlude of "regulated capitalism" and for a quarter of a century gave Capitalism an almost "human face." It accepted that reality does not conform with perfect competition and attempted to discover ways and means to deal with problems on the basis of reality. Its protagonists did not plan to change social reality in the vain hope of attaining perfect competition; they did not attempt to curb the influence of Trade Unions or abolish free enterprise or the power of capital; but they accepted reality as it is. Like the scientists in other modern sciences they set themselves a more modest task, namely to devise the necessary instruments for sustaining economic growth with full-employment within the given perceived reality.

Adam Smith, like Newton, believed in a separation of *a fact* from its *observer*, but modern science insists on linking them. The old approach left mankind at the mercy of forces beyond himself and outside of his control, the new approach makes man part of these forces. The old science described nature for the purpose of understanding it and to take this description at all times as a guide to human action. Modern science describes nature with an eye to imitate, reproduce, or control it. The order it imposes on nature is governed by the wish to predict. Consequently experience becomes the basis of scientific laws, and as experience can never yield absolute certainty, all it can show is that *ceteris paribus* an action taken several times in the past yielded similar results. Sometimes, as in the case of Mendel's experiment, the probability of the recurrence of the results can be defined in a precise value, the belief in the *absolute* is replaced by exact *probabilities*. With this the future becomes no longer determined by the old principle of "cause and effect" but is allowed a defined measure of uncertainty. Man's future becomes neither teleologically nor strictly causally determined but is allowed a calculable measure of uncertainty.

J. Bronowsky likened the calculable limits of this freedom to atoms in a stream of gas under pressure. On the average they obey the pressure, but at any instant any individual atom may be moving across or against the stream. In other words, given a degree of uncertainty, large events may be predicted but not small ones. However the last mentioned are precisely those which receive most attention in the neoclassical approach. They are the quintessence of microeconomics; the substance of a system which allows individuals to find their places in society on the basis of competitive ability without worrying about the general direction the system in its entirety is taking. In this way economics maintains that true knowledge is founded exclusively on sense experience, here and now, and has no use for a global and historical perspective. The "large events" which might provide a clue to the future are relegated to the world of mystics and utopians, and it is simply assumed that life imposes greater order while in fact the system is drifting into disorder. Worse, the study of how this drift is affecting us is actually discouraged in spite of the biological evidence that organisms and species have perished because they could not read the symptoms of change in the past and present, and synthesize them to foretell the future. Life implies action, human living thoughtful action, and thoughtful action involves choices. Therefore whether choice is free or determined, the action it elicits is in fact always directed toward the future. But mankind can either try to control this future or else accept whatever comes. This is a point entirely ignored in neoclassic economics.

Since Copernicus and Galileo the platonic search for the underlying plan for all natural phenomena has been gradually supplemented by pragmatism, by the wish to make use of scientific knowledge for practical purposes. So the practical applications of science played an ever-increasing role in historical development. The steam engine was invented before the laws of heat had been stated, and electrical engineering was earlier than Maxwell's equations. The practical applications offered a solid basis for a thorough knowledge of the phenomena, and eventually helped to find mathematical forms adapted to the observations and to concepts which led to formal transmissible understanding. The two tendencies did not conflict, but the emphasis changed. Science became important because it was *useful*; not because it enabled us to read God's second book—the Book of Nature.

For most scientists brought up on Newton's mechanics, which had ruled successfully for two centuries, it was difficult to accept the new "non-Newtonian" reading of the universe. The existence of absolute time, independent of space, had been no less an essential feature of their comprehension than Say's Law is with present-day economists. Like Newton's physics, the theory of relativity connected many complicated phenomena in a surprisingly simple way. Many physicists co-operated in testing the predictions and in analyzing various observations on the basis of the new ideas so that the theory was shown to be a useful approximation to one of motion in which the velocity of light could be ignored. But the real conceptual change came only in the 1920s with quantum theory. Only then the combined effort of many physicists resulted in further undermining the familiar conceptions and the validity of Newtonian mechanics was further limited. All this does not suggest that behind the variety of phenomena there may not be a simple unifying principle, but it is a principle that has not yet been discovered. In fact a problem facing physics today is that relativity and quantum theory are difficult to unite. The point is that it was the expansion of the known reality that drove physicists to change their theories.

Little of the sort has happened in economic theory. In spite of the fact that in all industrialized countries oligopolistic tendencies are profusely documented and that a major share of the national income is government-controlled, which means that its distribution is not determined by the *price mechanism* but by ideological or socially acceptable criteria, the philosophical background of economists has remained unaltered. One important reason for this is that determining how far the *real life* economy is removed from *perfect competition* is an empirical question which cannot be easily examined and accommodated in the ruling paradigm. Nonetheless the problem needs to be faced, and for this the traditional mechanistic approach in economic theory must be supplemented by a methodology which affected also *modern* science, by a methodology based on observations free from trust in a single universal mechanism and free from the exclusion of variables which, because of our present state of knowledge, make quantification difficult.

9

Distribution of National Income between Strata of Society

The economists of the era of *Regulated Capitalism* recognized that a person's income depends on a great variety of factors of which many have little if anything to do with market forces. Nobody denied that the entire income structure might rise or fall with the varying fortunes of the economic system, but this does not mean that personal or household income differentials will remain the same. They depend on initial wealth, on sex, profession, education, personal ability and status, in short on the customs and traditions of society. Sometimes they are influenced by market forces and other times market forces are influenced by them. But they have a direct effect on aggregate expenditure and through this on the overall volumes of saving and investment and on the rate of economic growth.

A general rise in household incomes in very poor societies, or in rich societies by the end of a recession, may well increase consumption. The share of the *new* income consumed will rise in comparison with the share of *new* income saved. Average savings will increase but relative to average consumption they will lessen. Thanks to the greater effective demand for consumer goods investment may be encouraged, and because of the higher interest rates resulting from the relatively diminished savings may be discouraged. In rich societies, or in periods of prosperity, given that consumption is on the whole already on a satisfactory level, the consequences will be different. The share of the *new* income consumed will lag behind the share saved. Relative to average consumption average savings will rise. The diminished rate of increase in demand for consumer goods may reduce incentives to invest, or the lower interest rates encourage investment. It follows that changes in the general level of earnings affect a redistribution of the national income between savings and consumption. A redistribution of income in favor of the lower income groups in a poor society, or in favor of those groups in richer societies which are below the poverty line, will have a strong negative effect on total savings and a positive effect on consumer demand. In rich societies it will have little or no effect on total savings (because it does not matter if the saving is done by corporations or by households) and it will only have a moderate effect on consumer demand. This means that the proposition that high wages in a rich society will cause a deficiency of savings can only be substantiated if it can empirically be shown that the total volume of savings from profits and from wages taken together is less than from profits when wages are reduced. It also means that if investment is *not* induced by low interest rates alone, or by a sudden spurt of new inventions which do not replace old processes and products but increase the overall volume of employment, or by some "animal spirits," it is evident that income distribution has a major influence on the volume of investment. A rise or a fall in the income of each strata of society has a different impact on effective consumer demand and saving. In short, a rise in social security transfers are therefore the most likely to raise the demand for consumer goods at the cost of savings, while wage increases at the middle level of earnings, or above it, will have the least effect on the demand for consumer goods and the overall volume of savings. The point is simple: the poor cannot save, and the rich cannot consume, much more than they habitually do.

The conclusion to be drawn from the foregoing proposition is that for the economic system as a whole high wages cannot diminish savings but low wages can reduce investment and employment. As wages cannot exceed productivity, since no Trade Union wants the enterprise in which its members are employed to be driven into bankruptcy, assuming its leaders are not fools, excessive wage claims can only result from misinformation or distrust in management. Inflation is therefore more likely to be the outcome of imperfect market competition than of wage increases. If productivity is rising, given that a certain share distribution between investment and consumption is necessary to maintain effective demand in equilibrium with investment and that wage increases cannot exceed the rise in productivity, the passing on of higher wages to consumers in price hikes can only be affected under imperfect competition. It must therefore be concluded that the true source of inflation is imperfect price competition and not wage increments. In this sense Friedman's advice to relate the volume of the money supply to the rate of economic growth is perfectly correct, but if and only if, competition is reasonably lively.

However, while wages cannot for any length of time exceed productivity they can be far below it; and this is the real crux of the matter. When this happens consumer demand cannot suffice to clear the markets and incentives to invest become divorced from savings. At this point the emphasis shifts from investment in *product innovation* to *process innovation*, and in spite of the initially greater supply of savings the scramble for funds to finance the development and application of the new production-cost-reducing equipment will cause interest rates and unemployment to soar. This means that under imperfect competition the provision of correct information to employees' representatives about the profits and development plans of the firms in which they work, and powerful labour unions, as well as a careful regulation of minimum wages and social transfer payments by the state, are necessary conditions for the adjustment of consumption and savings in the proportions required to sustain growth with full-employment. It also means that government policies designed to restrain inflation by wage restriction or by allowing a certain rise in unemployment to the same effect are ill-advised. The former can seldom be sustained in periods of full employment and the latter have a tendency to become cumulative and uncontrollable.

Unfortunately this is not all there is to it. In the past, when *process innovation* went together with a commensurate fall in market prices and therefore with a rise in *real incomes* and effective demand, the loss of jobs in the sectors in which the innovations were applied gave rise to other jobs to meet previously unsatisfied or even unknown demands. This happened in the era of *mechanization*, in the age of the conveyer-belt so splendidly depicted in Charlie Chaplin's "Modern Times." In the last decades *mechanization* has been superseded by *automatization* and this makes a great difference. *Mechanization*, particularly the conveyer-belt, separated production into fairly simple and routine tasks which could be learned on the job in a few days. Even farm workers who had never worked in industry before could almost immediately be absorbed into the industrial labour force. With the progress of *automation* many of these jobs have become superfluous. Chip-controlled robots can go through the same motions previously performed by the people serving the conveyer-belts and can do so with greater precision, for a longer time each day and with less risk of interruption. Moreover, in most production processes the initial price of chip-controlled robots and their depreciation cost is low in comparison with wages. In addition, the application of the silicon chip to control the robots' operations often makes the use of robots more flexible than human labour. As a result the progress of automation segregates the demand for employees into at least two separate labour markets, one of highly skilled and another of unskilled workers. Entrance to the former labour market requires certain personal qualities and years of "unpaid work," in obtaining a higher education. Entrance to the unskilled labour market requires little or none of this. As automatization also increases task specialization, frictional unemployment among skilled labour is often intense, but due to the particular qualification required for various tasks, the wage rates for this type of work remain high. This is not true for the unskilled segment of the labour market. Here, when reduced production cost is not passed on to consumers, the overall demand for labour will diminish, and competition for vacant jobs, sometimes temporarily made worse by a massive immigration of unskilled workers from other countries, keeps wages low or even falling. Before long society divides into people with a high income and reasonable job security and people with a very low income which is equal to or just above social security disbursements and with little if any job security. The former are able to provide their children with the education required to enter the upper income labour market, and the latter not. As job competition among the unskilled drives their income close to social security they also have little economic incentive to find work. After having been out of work for long and finding it increasingly difficult to locate employers willing to engage them, many give up the struggle and arrange their lives accordingly.

There is of course nothing unusual in a separation of society into upper and lower classes. Ancient Rome had slaves ("speaking instruments") and Roman citizens. Feudalism had legally-institutionalized hierarchies. Nascent Capitalism, Mercantilism, believed that there were even psychological differences between the rich and the poor and that high profits stimulated economic activity in one class and high wages stifled economic activity in the other. Moreover, seeing the differences between their own way of life and the behavior of those upon whom the wretched conditions of their existence imposed another mode of conduct, the rich saw their ideas about the inherent difference between the classes confirmed and put the blame for privation on the poor themselves. But neither the empires of antiquity nor any type of feudalism produced an industrial revolution. Even mercantilism did not turn manufacturing into industrialization as long as foreign markets were its driving force. It was only when domestic effective demand became a considerable source of profit that Capitalism turned to mass production and that spectacular technological innovation began raising peoples' living standard. But this was happening at a time when reality was closer to perfect competition than it has become in the later decades. Therefore, if trust in perfect competition is abandoned, the problem of income distribution is not only normative, a question of the kind of society people *wish* to live in, but a matter of survival because without a growing effective demand industry can only innovate in cost reduction, that is in cutting back expenditure on labour and materials. In other words, when the economy becomes too far removed from perfect competition, then without state intervention to redistribute the national income in favor of the lower income groups, unemployment will rise continually. Eventually the entire fabric of society will be undermined and Latin American conditions will appear. Children with no real chance to afford more than the compulsory education will shirk classes and take to a life of crime or drugs; and adults will either resign themselves to poverty or enter the "black" economy and work for employers who avoid making their contribution to social security and taxes.

Once such a situation is allowed to last for any length of time the system becomes beyond redemption. The cost of social security will rise above what even well-inclined governments can collect in revenues, and public services will be abrogated. The better-off will concentrate in well-separated ghettos protected by privatized security arrangements and will provide for themselves the services they require. The blessed meek among the poor will resign themselves to the situation and escape reality by religious fundamentalism, and wait patiently for the time when they will inherit the earth. The more assertive will either try to extricate themselves from their condition individually, by ingenuity or sharp practices and crime, or they will organize themselves to take collective action to overthrow the system.

After the war Joseph Schumpeter recognized that the size of the units of production was becoming much larger and that their ownership was separating increasingly from their management. What he failed to recognize was the tendency of the managerial bureaucracy to develop into a "class" or "estate" with values and desires of its own. He was under the impression, at that time correct, that society was moving toward greater democracy and greater state control over the management of private industry. The possibility that business management would control government simply eluded him, as did the possibility of increasing unemployment coinciding with, and even becoming the cause of rising prices. The inverse relationship between unemployment and prices, or as Phillips later showed, between the rate of change of money wage rates and the rate of unemployment, seemed so self-evident that neither Schumpeter nor other economists found it necessary to consider the possibility that what was true for the period 1861 to 1957 need not necessarily be also true for other periods. This, however, is what has been happening since the late 1970s.

Similarly, Schumpeter's famous theory of economic revival through the cumulative process following upon the invention of a new product or technique, or as the result of the evolution of a new market, did not take into account the distinction between *process innovation* and *product innovation* under private oligopoly or monopoly when state control is inadequate, and it discounted the distinction between *product-expanding* and *product-replacing* innovation. In the past, when the invention of the internal combustion engine added a totally new range of previously unknown needs, its exploitation required extra labour. The new inventions in the realm of micro-electronics and robotica mainly *replace* the equipment previously required to satisfy old well-established needs by new equipment requiring less labour than had earlier been necessary. Some spin-offs of the "electronic revolution" were indeed new products, for example television and video equipment and the personal computer. The two former did not replace the radio, and the market for the latter was greater than the market for typewriters had been, but coming together with other labour-input reducing innovations they contributed little to the demand for labour. In other words, while Schumpeter's elaboration of the process by which a fundamentally new invention can, and on several occasions in the past did, bring about a self-sustaining process of economic recovery and growth, his model is of only limited predictive value. Its validity depends on specific characteristics of competitive markets. In predominantly competitive economies, or under a system in which the state is able and willing to skim off excessive oligopolistic profits in order to regulate the volume of demand and employment, at the cost of reducing the *rate* of economic growth, the Schumpeterian model would probably be true. But under powerful oligopoly without forceful state regulation its validity is doubtful. Schumpeter was impressed by the democratic climate and by the drift toward economic state regulation in the immediate post-war era. Had he written in the 1980s, conceivably his views might well have been modified and less optimistic.

A truth too often forgotten by economists is that the social framework is constantly in a process of transformation and that in the long run almost nothing remains *ceteris paribus*. This makes extremely precarious any prediction on the basis of extrapolation from data reflecting patterns in the past. There is a great volume of very sophisticated statistical analysis of historical data relating to the idea of long cycles in economic development. As historians know, and economists ignore, most of the series of data upon which these ideas are based are notoriously unreliable. Moreover, two consecutive harvest failures, a war-scare, an actual war or an epidemic, or any other important economically-exogenous events, influences the series and distorts the general trend. In other words, without a careful *historical* interpretation of the statistical data and without a good examination of their particular institutional background, the trends cannot be usefully extrapolated to predict the future. This means that the most ingenious mathematical treatment of this type of time-series can be no more than an *imposition* of patterns borrowed from other sciences on data of dubious validity with little predictive value. They may or may not tell something about the past, but they can say little about the things to come. It is, however, precisely this type of mathematization, divorced from the study of history and sociology, which has become the focus of attention of economic science since the 1970s.

The point is that the past and the present are not like the future, but the future is not entirely unlike the past and the present. Both the past and present provide signals holding a meaning for the future, which can with the passing of time be interpreted in an ongoing process of correction. If this process of reading the signals is guided not by expediency but by truth, science undergoes two tendencies. One stresses the unity of nature and the other its diversity. The one stresses the abstract thought which goes beyond the fluctuating impressions obtained by our senses, and the other emphasizes the results of reality that must be judged by these impressions as they present themselves. From this point of view the search for abstract truth in economics is a valid exercise. But then it must not depend on presuppositions which can neither be empirically verified nor falsified in an ongoing process of correction in the light of the social and institutional changes which are constantly affecting the conduct of individuals and entire societies. In other words, the search for abstract truth in economics must be holistic and take into account the dynamic character of society, and not mechanistic and scholastic. It must use mathematics, but it must not allow mathematical patterns to take the place of the study of reality.

A case in point is the internationalization of modern economies. Walras as well as Keynes focused attention on what may be considered national economies. Their models assumed closed systems with foreign trade as a kind of added factor which is either self-regulating or can be regulated by currency manipulations. International trade was seen as a matter of *comparative advantage*—the different price ratios between countries. The question of employment and of income distribution between countries, and between various strata of society in the diverse countries, was simply thought of no consequence. But today, particularly for small open economies, the question of income distribution and how at each level of income people divide their expenditure between domestic and imported goods is highly relevant. Perhaps this can be illustrated by the following example. In the Netherlands in 1993 a cheap foreign-made bicycle was priced somewhere in the range of 600 to 800 guilders and a low-price domestically-produced bicycle in the range of 1200 to 1700 guilders. The quality of the imported bicycle was certainly inferior to the Dutch product. For a long time the bicycle trade was selling about two million bicycles a year, approximately one million imported and one million home-produced. Since the onset of the depression overall sales have not fallen much, but the share distribution of sales moved sharply in favor of the cheaper foreign bicycles. This example illustrates how a reduction in the lower ranges of income can affect the demand for labour in an open economy. It also indicates how changes in social security disbursements can have a positive as well as a negative affect on domestic employment. The difficulty is that it is very hard to determine the precise level of income at which such shifts in demand are taking place. But even when the watershed is ascertained, the impact of such shifts will differ from one country to another depending on the precise composition of the country's range and structure of production. It is not inconceivable that a rise in the incomes of the lower stratum of society may increase the demand for labour in firms producing mainly for the domestic market and at the same time decrease the demand for labour in firms producing for the export market. The higher incomes may increase the demand for Dutch bicycles and at the same time price Dutch cheeses out of foreign markets. All this seems logical enough and may be worthy of precise statistical examination but it is only part of a much wider problem.

Since the days of Ricardo the problem of international trade had been studied in the shadow of the theory of *comparative advantage* and *reciprocal demand*. In the 1960s a new phenomenon emerged, namely the tendency of large enterprises to transfer labour-intensive tasks which do not require much schooling to low-wage countries. In this sense the economy has really become "global." But this implied a loss of unskilled jobs in the rich countries and the dooming of workers in poor countries to persistent poverty. In other words, the internationalization of production opened up a previously unmatched supply of unskilled labour. By the logic of the market system this means that to sustain unskilled employment in the rich countries the wages of unskilled workers in these countries must fall as low as those acceptable in the poor countries. It also means that social security benefits must become even lower than third world wages to encourage the unemployed to look for work. This places the advanced open economies in a dilemma. They cannot prevent the unskilled jobs from being exported to low-wage regions, because international competition forces producers to take labour where it is cheapest, and they cannot maintain adequate living standards for a considerable part of their populations, because they would fall if free competition were allowed to take its course.

This problem is exacerbated by the internationalization of the flows of capital. The transfer of investment to a number of countries, like Hong Kong or Taiwan, where even skilled labour is relatively cheap, or to countries with low taxation and little state regulation, and just as little protection of the natural environment, cannot for long leave the social structure in the advanced economies unaffected. The rich will become richer, the poor and a good share of the skilled labour force will be reduced to third-world living standards. It is difficult to see how anything else can happen unless economic growth in the developing countries accelerates at an unlikely pace, its fruits are equitably distributed, which is equally unlikely, and taxation and regulation in the poor countries is practically overnight adjusted to match that of the highly advanced nations.

The conclusion is that *laissez-faire* cannot sustain the humane characteristics of our cultural heritage, and that macroeconomic theory as it is taught today is not only founded on outdated and therefore misleading postulates, but is also methodologically unsuitable for offering advice on how to encounter future social hazards. Too often it is forgotten that the objective of modern science is not only to observe but to predict so that man can choose a *desired* course of action. To be sure, the methodology of modern economic science needs to be positive but its objectives normative. Most of the economics establishment macroeconomic theories fail on both counts: its postulates are no longer based on fact but on preconceived ideas and its objectives miss a historical perspective. It assumes that rising productivity equally benefits all strata of society in proportion to their levels of income and ignores the growing discrepancy between the earnings of unskilled and skilled labour. It assumes that income is distributed by some mechanism which relates wages to marginal productivity and ignores the fact that women usually receive less pay than men for similar work. It assumes that the maximization of utility is reflected in material rewards, and ignores the craving for status and power which attends the separation of the ownership from the control of economic resources. It assumes competition works and ignores when it falters. It assumes a society in which the acquisition of wealth is pursued by legitimate means, and ignores the great riches obtained by drug-barons, gangsters, fraudulent bankers and all other kinds of malefactors engaging in great variety of shady economic activities. It assumes democracy, and ignores the privileged access to the media of information insured by high social, business and academic position making the voice of economic advantage louder than the voice of truth; without informed choice between alternatives democracy becomes a sham.

The point is that once the veil of false objectivity is lifted from economic science, the erroneous preconceptions are corrected, and the state is allowed to play an active normative role, there appear many ways by which these social and cultural consequences of the recent drift of the economy can probably be averted. A crucial advantage the developed countries still have over the poorer is their extensive economic infrastructure. This includes not only the physical assets, such as good communication networks and a great variety of ancillary trades, but also advanced education and training, work-discipline, faith in the legal system, reasonable protection by and against the state, and, though it is fast eroding, confidence in general. All this is essential for the proper functioning of a highly specialized and integrated economic system. In fact the affluence of the industrialized nations depends on it, because unless all the component parts fall into place with clockwork precision their economies fall into disarray. Though threatened by recent developments, these prerequisite conditions for sustaining a high level of productivity are still present in the economically advanced countries and missing in the rest of the world. It is this economic and intangible infrastructure which provides the *comparative advantages* of the industrialized nations. It is therefore in this sphere that the solution to the economic problem arising out of the transfer of labour and of capital to the low wage countries must be sought.

To stop the flow of work and capital to the third world is neither practicable nor morally desirable, but the improvement of the industrialized countries' physical and social infrastructure will be to everyone's advantage. Rather than adjusting unskilled labour's wages downward to compete with those in low wage countries, the acquisition of skills should be encouraged in the high wage countries. Free higher education and the extension of the teaching curricula to provide extra time for the subjects which tend to foster independent thought and good responsible citizenship would be a good beginning. Next to this investment in *human capital,* the communication network must further be improved and extended to accommodate the increasing trend toward industrial specialization. Social security and public health must be sustained at a high level to create the necessary sense of confidence and communal consensus. But all this is beyond what private enterprise can do. It is here that the conflict comes to light between the immediate pressures on individual firms as they compete to survive and their collective long-term need to maintain prosperity. For this reason only a power which is free from the dictates of the competitive short-term profit-seeking market can perform this task. In other words, there is no inherent mechanism, no "invisible hand" in the free market system to sustain the material and intangible infrastructure assuring the adequate performance of the modern economic system. Only the state, and sometimes local government, have the power to recruit the necessary funds for this infrastructure, and only they can legislate and enforce the rules to restrain abuse.

10

Distribution between the Private and the Public Sector

Given that the Free Market does not provide a mechanism which adjusts the short term needs of individual enterprises to their long term collective requirements, and assuming that the state can perform this coordinating task, the question arises in what proportions the national product must be divided between the private sector and the state. The simple answer is in such manner that, with full employment, increasing productivity is precisely matched by increasing effective demand for goods and services. Under conditions of perfect competition this would be more or less the outcome of the income effect of falling prices. Increasing productivity would reduce production cost and competition would decrease prices and thus raise overall demand. In the real world of imperfect competition this is the exception rather than the rule.

One way to solve this problem is to counter the negative effects of imperfect competition by legislation. Many governments have tried to restrain monopoly, but with only moderate success. Another way to solve the problem is by progressive taxation. This is supposed to make the pursuit of monopoly profits uneconomical; inordinate profits would simply be taxed away. This kind of taxation would face the monopolist with the options of having his profits go to the tax collector or himself returning them to consumers by moderate pricing, or in donations and grants to support museum, concert-halls, football-clubs, public gardens etc. Alternatively, if the monopolist does not behave in the expected manner, the state would return the extra profit to the public by funding similar objects out of heightened tax-revenue and by spending more on the country's infrastructure and social security. Leaving aside the question whether companies' donations should or should not be taxed, and whether it is better that the government rather than the monopolist decide on what the "extra money" should best be spent, it is clear that where it has been tried progressive taxation had has also only limited success in regulating the economy. The point is that legislation as well as taxation are notoriously prone to circumvention.

In Britain the *Fair Trading Act* of 1973 defined a monopoly supplier as one who controls "a quarter of the market" for its produce. The *Monopolies and*

79

Mergers Commission is supposed to prevent such situations. In the USA the *Federal Trade Commission* is expected to achieve the same end with the help of the antitrust laws. Since the *Sherman Antitrust Act* of 1890, and the *Clayton Antitrust Act* of 1914, various legislators have tried to prevent corporations acquiring the whole or part of another corporation where the effect of such an acquisition may lessen competition substantially or tend to create a monopoly. In both Britain and the USA the results of these efforts have been meager.

The bid to return a large share of monopolistic profits to the public by way of taxation has fared little better. The revenue from corporation taxes is usually less than one third of the revenue collected by the state in personal income tax; personal income tax of someone earning $100.000 will be about 35% of his income while someone earning $10.000.000 will pay just under 50%. The point is that neither *legislation* nor *taxation* has been able to sustain the income distribution which would be necessary to maintain the market-clearing balance between investment and consumption. In the 1960s and 1970s, when wages and profits sometimes exceeded the rise in productivity, most economies have been plagued by inflation; and since the 1980s, when wages began lagging behind rising productivity, most economies are plagued by massive unemployment.

In the era of Keynesian regulated Capitalism many attempts were made to regulate the economic system by both fiscal and monetary controls. The measures taken were usually *corrective* and not *prospective*. Taking for granted that in spite of distortions the system is after all tending toward equilibrium, governments helped it along after events showed that consumer demand exceeded productivity or that a shortfall of demand reduced incentives to invest. In other words, governments took inflation as a sign of excessive consumer spending and unemployment as a sign of underconsumption. In the first event they tended to raise taxes to skim off the excessive purchasing power and in the second event they reduced interest rates or created extra employment in the public sector.

Several governments, for example the French and the Dutch, went even further than this. They turned to medium term planning in the sense of using Leontief or Tinbergen type input-output tables to estimate the probable outcome of different economic policy decisions. For a time, particularly in the 1960s, this system worked reasonably well. There was a good measure of economic growth, full employment, and a constant rise in the public material welfare. The negative aspect was a constant rise in prices. After the oil crises this rise accelerated so that by the end of the 1970s several governments decided that the reduction of inflation must be their prime economic policy objective. Conforming to the idea that wages are the main cause of rising prices, and ignoring the possibility that there might be other more important causes, they were ready to allow a measure of unemployment to restrain consumer demand and hence prices. In other words they transformed the Keynesian system of regulation from a system designed to assure the full employment of labour into a system designed to reduce the rate of inflation.

The result of this transformation was that full employment ceased to be a political objective. Stated otherwise, the protection of the share of savings was given priority over employment. The wishes of the rich flouted the needs of the poor. Naturally, there was a lot of lip service to create the impression that once the "war on inflation" was won all would come well, and that there were no "real" implications for the unemployed because the social security arrangements made sure that nobody would actually go hungry. What the champions of this policy were either unable or unwilling to see was the rise in the cost of the social security this policy engendered. Before long government deficits soared and either taxes needed to be raised or expenditure to be cut. Given the circumstances, as raising taxes was politically out of the question, social security was gradually reduced. In the place of "nobody actually goes hungry" came "there is too much abuse of social security, it deters people from seeking work and it can no longer be financed; it is the fault of the unemployed themselves that they cannot or do not find work."

In summary, instead of fighting inflation at its true roots and the abuse of social security where it needs to be tackled, a policy was introduced to restore the pre-war social and economic relations—"what's good for General Motors is good for the American people." None of this could have happened without the transformation of democracy from its post-war content into the advertizer-manipulated system of the 1980s, where people may vote but are deprived of the information they require to decide what they are really voting for. This relationship between democracy and economic policy will be discussed later, but here the salient point is that the restoration of full employment as the paramount objective of economic policy is not alone a social or humanitarian requirement but an economic necessity if society is not to revert to pre-war conditions or move on to the South American crime-infested model of excessive riches among dire poverty.

Leaving aside the social and political difficulties involved in obtaining and sustaining the full employment level of consumption, the share distribution of the national income between investment and consumption involves technical problems which are hard to work out. For example, in real terms any investment in capital comes at the cost of a reduced volume of goods available for consumption relative to consumer earnings. The labour engaged in the production of capital does not immediately contribute to the supply of consumer goods but earns the means for obtaining them. Consequently a rise in the share of labour engaged in the construction of new capital would cause consumer good prices to rise at least until the new capital is yielding its productivity-increasing and cost-reducing results and is passed on to consumers in lower prices. Under conditions of *perfect competition* price stability is therefore necessarily impaired in the short run but not a real problem in the long run. This is not true when competition is imperfect and producer prices are not forced to fall in line with increasing productivity. Then, the rise in consumer prices will be matched by either higher wage claims or by falling living standards. Attempts to forestall this by the imposition of price controls have almost always proved to be ineffective. The alternative to price controls mentioned earlier, namely the taxing of such profits as reflect the lack of competition, would raise not only the legal problems of restraining tax avoidance and evasion but also the question of how much of the mark-up is justified by Research and Development expenditure and future investment plans, and how much must be regarded as monopoly profit. An added difficulty is the assessment of depreciation. If a certain piece of equipment can adequately perform for five years it may in fact be outdated and due for substitution within two years or may continue in use for ten. This means that tax allowances for R&D, innovation and depreciation are in practice almost unassessable by an outsider. The managers of a company alone may have an insight, but no reason to divulge such information correctly to the tax authorities. There is of course the possibility of estimating the mark-up by adding up stockholders' earnings and the remuneration and perks various managers receive in excess of what could be called a normal compensation for their work. In a measure this is done by the progressive nature of personal taxation but it hardly touches the real core of the problem.

Moreover, the trade-off between skimming off excessive profit and the need for savings to promote R&D and economic-growth advancing innovations raises another difficult problem, which becomes increasingly acute with the progress of globalization. Firms, especially large firms, supplying an international market can often simply not survive without a large outlay in R&D and innovation, not because of price competition but because they cannot hold pace with the advancing and changing requirements of their customers.

All this leads to the conclusion that the conventional correctives which may be employed and have been used to adjust supply and demand to attain or sustain relatively stable economic growth with full employment and rising living standards may well be founded on a misconception of the working of the economic system and the role of the economics profession. We misconceive the working of the system; arthritis increasingly torments the invisible hand which can no longer manipulate the factors of production toward equilibrium, and the economics profession fails to see that its task must not be to adjust the life of human beings to the needs of an assumedly equilibrium-seeking system but to adjust the system to the needs of human beings. To put the last in Biblical terms, the Good Lord did not create Man to serve the economy, but modern economics was created to serve the needs of mankind.

When we take this perception as the point of departure, *unemployment* moves back into the center of the economic science. Labor ceases to be dehumanized, "*a factor of production*", and becomes human and the focus of attention.

Unemployment and poverty become a source of social isolation, corruption, racism, political instability, proliferation of crime and drug abuse, ill health, unhappiness, and a general deterioration of civilized modes of conduct. It follows that the prime objective of economic research and policy must be neither economic growth nor the restraint of inflation by means of reducing living standards or allowing unemployment to reduce wages, but the restitution of full employment and adequate living standards for all, and, given the attainment of this aim, finding the means and ways to sustain economic growth with as little inflation as may be possible. In practice this means that the first objective of government must be to provide full employment and the opportunity for all to receive education, and then to attend to any negative by-products of success. The question must cease to be how much the government can afford to pay for the unemployed to be given work and the inadequately educated to receive good schooling, and become how the economy can be adjusted to pay for these requirements. The first questions economists must seek to answer is how much it costs to create full employment (in the collective sectors) and to improve education, after the cost of unemployment and an ill-educated youth is deducted. Then the multiplier effect of the newly created jobs on the generation of employment and incomes in the private sector must be estimated. Next the prospective demand in the various economic sectors needs to be analyzed to adjust government employment and education to future needs, and taxation needs to be adjusted to produce the necessary funds to implement the changes. With the statistical data we can now command, all this can be calculated. The point is that there is nothing amiss with economists' logical deduction, but there is much wrong with the choice of the questions they attempt to answer. As said before, scientists' philosophical background seldom influences their answers, but it does determine their questions, and the final outcome can depend on this.

If we take the new approach suggested here, the first step must be to make a careful listing of the unemployed by age and professional qualifications. The next step is to make an inventory of vacant jobs and jobs which can serve the public good but remain unfilled because of funding problems. The former should show how much must be spent on education and training to reduce frictional unemployment, and the latter to determine the cost of taking young people off the streets by extending education, the cost of investing in the physical infrastructure to serve the future growth of industry, and the cost of providing better housing, health care, police and care for the old and infirm. The third step must be to estimate the savings which will result from reduced unemployment pay and from lower public expenditure resulting from savings on public health, private policing and damage to property by the jobless. The increased disposable income generated from new employment must be calculated with an eye to the tax revenue accruing to the state from new direct and indirect taxes and from the multiplier effect of new employment. Finally, in order to assess the real cost of the realization of all these measures, the new revenue must be compared to the cost of implementation and taxation must be adjusted to it.

Keynes was of the opinion that the volume of employment determines *real wages*. His point was that workers can perhaps influence the general level of money wages, or the distribution of the wage bill between the various producers, but not the level of real wages. A rise in money wages will raise prices because consumers will *think* that their earnings have risen but in fact the higher wage cost and the increased readiness to pay more because of the illusion of higher incomes will cause prices to rise as well. The same, he believed, would happen when wages were reduced. When wages are reduced the purchasing power and hence the propensity to spend will diminish, prices will fall and incentives to invest decrease. Consequently the volume of employment will diminish. Moreover, assuming that firms produce the level of output at which marginal costs are equal to marginal revenue and that this usually is at a point where average cost is rising, higher wages will tend to raise productivity and falling wages to reduce it.

The following diagram should illustrate the point.

The curve *marginal output* designates the marginal productivity of labour, i.e. the contribution each additional unit of labour adds to output. The X axis measures the number of workers employed; and the Y axis the value of each worker's output, the wage rate per worker which is the same for everyone employed, and the market price of the firm's unit of output.

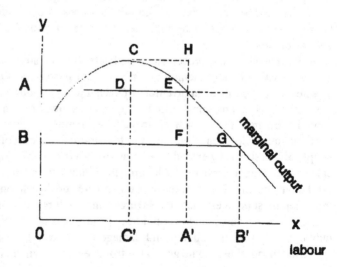

At output C with the volume of employment C' the firm produces at minimum cost per unit of output—it makes optimal use of its capacity. But as the market demand for its produce at a given price may be larger than what it produces at this point, say equal to the product provided by OA' workers, the profit-maximizing firm will produce a larger output, namely the one for which it requires OA' workers. If it produces less (for example at optimum utilization of its capacity) it will miss the profit indicated by the area CDE. If it produces more it will do so at a loss because the value produced by each worker after A' are employed will be less than what consumers are prepared to pay for the additional produce. It follows, according to this (Neoclassical) reasoning that a reduction of wages from A to B would increase employment from A' to B' because at this cost (assuming that prices are stable) the firm would increase profit by the area EFG. Supposing that firms really behave in this manner and do not or cannot adjust their capacity to demand so that point C would shift to point H, and that they really operate under conditions of diminishing returns and not, as is often likely in periods of recession and depression, at a level of output and employment which is to the left of point C, all this seems to make sense. But from a macroeconomic point of view things look different. Here *income effects* may well thwart this apparent logic. From this point of view all depends on whether the increased income generated by the employment due to the reduced wages is larger or smaller than the loss of income engendered by the fall in the wages of those previously employed. In other words, the outcome depends on whether the area ABEF is greater or smaller than the area FGA'B' less the social security disbursed to the unemployed and the fall in market prices which may accompany the fall in wages. In the one event effective demand will diminish and unemployment will increase; in the other event effective demand will increase and employment will be stimulated. Where classical and neoclassical logic goes astray is its assumption of the universality of the inverse relationship between the volume of demand and the height of prices, namely that as prices fall the demand for a good or factor of production increases. While on the whole this may be true, it need not be applicable to the demand for labour, because for the economy as a whole labour is not only a factor of production but also a source of consumer demand whose earnings determine the level of consumer prices from the demand side. As wages fall, demand decreases and the decreased demand may well reduce firms' volume of employment and increase their productivity.

This, however, is only one part of the doubts Keynes cast upon the logic of the classics (neoclassics). Another point he raised in this connection concerns savings. Classical theory assumes that savings and hence the rate of interest determine investment. Keynes believed that investment determines the rate of savings. At almost every level of income above subsistence people save (and are forced to save) part of their earnings. Everyone's expenditure is someone's income because it cannot be otherwise. But if everyone saves part of his or her income and every subsequent income is also divided between spending and saving, the flow of income and saving can go on until all the initial earnings have leaked out of circulation back into savings and there is nothing left to circulate. But this, as has already been explained (see pages 48–50), will happen when the initial stock of money is equal to the total of the savings generated by the flow of incomes. By that time the total of incomes will have increased by some multiple of the initial investment, depending on the manner in which earners decide to divide their new incomes between saving and spending. But the total of savings will be equal to the stock of money which set the process in motion. It turns out that savings are determined by investment and not investment by the volume of savings. This is the lesson of Kahn's *Multiplier*, which was taken over by Keynes. In short, according to Keynes, investment determines the volume of savings, and the propensity to consume determines the volume of employment and of income. In this way the original source of the entire process is investment which depends on potential investors' *expectations*. But, with some exceptions such as the discovery of a new invention, expectations are based on experience: a growing demand raises and a declining demand dampens them. This means that if lower wages reduce the volume of effective consumer demand by a greater figure than increased employment raises it, entrepreneurs' expectations and incentives to invest will falter and employment will continue to decline.

Keynes exaggerated the new income-generating power of the multiplier. The textbooks upon which many later followers of Keynes were brought up did worse. In fact the value of the multiplier in a country like the Netherlands is nowadays little more that 1.7 over two years, but the principle is correct. Expectations and investment are the kingpin of the market system because they are the source of both savings and employment. However, Keynes assumed a fairly competitive economy in which prices are eventually determined in the market-place and influence the volume of employment. He underrated the pace of technological progress and the speed at which the share of capital, material and energy cost were to overtake the share of labour cost in many important industries, and he did not take account of the drift toward monopoly and globalization. In other words he recognized that production determined prices and demand but he could not foresee that prices and the volume of output would be determined by producers in accordance with investment plans rather than by the pull of market forces. He was therefore convinced that fiscal measures could influence effective demand and investment, whereas present reality suggests that effective demand is determined by manipulated prices. In summary, Keynes disagreed with his predecessors about the way the price mechanism influences production and employment, but he did not question the working of the mechanism as such. It is at this point that his conception falls short of present-day reality and needs to be amended.

Fiscal and monetary instruments of economic regulation continue to be important instruments but only supplementary to direct government investment. However the latter raises psychological obstacles which are difficult to overcome. For generations few questioned the need for a state budget to finance military expenditure. During the Cold War these budgets increased with little objection from the public. Most people were simply accustomed to this type of expenditure and regarded it as an unavoidable requirement for preserving peace and security. To be sure, this has not always been the case. In earlier ages the English Kings often met with strong objections when they required Lords and Commons to pay for wars or to increase their military might. But in time military expenditure became a permanent item in state budgets and except when it was perceived to be greatly increased it usually went unopposed though often challenged. Several decades ago the proposed to levy taxes or rates for the protection of the environment also initially raised protests; today few people even remember that such an item was not always a constant part of local or central government expenditure. The same may well be true of a tax to pay for full employment. Naturally, politicians will be reluctant to introduce a "new" tax particularly in the climate of opinion they themselves have created against state intervention. But once both industry and labour are made to realize that this is no less essential for maintaining their customary way of life and security than military expenditure and the protection of the environment, more likely than not the objections will soon soften. Once the recognition that without full employment and reasonable provision for the old and infirm public life will fall into disarray, that without widespread education industrial progress will grind to a halt, and that without the state providing for employment and education the middle class will steadily sag into poverty, the objections to state intervention will also wane. There is a world of difference between solidarity and charity; the one is firmly rooted in self-interest and the other in compassion. To allow the state to spend on the provision of employment and the better education of the young is certainly no charity; it is the cost of self-preservation.

Once the premise is adopted that unemployment is as much a national calamity as war or an environmental catastrophe, and that employment is the source of savings and incentives to invest, the economic profession will be able to concentrate on solving the problems arising out of the need to finance full employment and the further problems arising out of the efforts to do so. It will no longer calculate how much the state can afford to sustain the unemployed but will be able to study where the new employment is best utilized. It will abandon its long-standing underestimation of the contribution of services and human capital to economic growth and be able to combat inflation at its real sources. Naturally, the money initially required to finance the deliverance from unemployment must come out of *income tax* and not from corporate taxes. But corporation taxes must be cleansed of hidden untaxed personal incomes so that the higher earnings will be appropriately taxed without reducing the funds required for the substitution of depreciated capital and without lessening the resources available for R&D and innovation. Income tax and property tax may well have to be raised initially but this will hardly have a negative influence on effective demand. This is because income and property tax initially increased and spent on new employment will raise consumer expenditure by the amount taken out in taxes. By virtue of the multiplier, demand will even increase. As ultimately investment always turns out to be equal to savings the entire problem of the distribution of the national income between the share of savings and the share of investment disappears and full employment itself produces the optimal solution. The only real difficulty that remains is that the proposed approach cannot be successfully adopted in isolation by one or two small countries. It can only be embraced by a large federation or association like the USA or the European Community. This is because the composition of demand tends to differ from one strata of society to another. It is therefore not impossible that the loss of income of one strata to pay for the rising income of another may not only influence the marginal propensity to save but also the structure of demand. For example, a move from poverty to a higher income may increase the demand for quality goods which may not all be produced in a small country. The loss of jobs in the low quality producing factories will then not be made good by the new jobs generated in the same country. Obviously, such difficulties need to be taken into account, but their presence cannot deter the efforts to extricate economics from the theoretical morass into which the transformation of human beings into a factor of production has led it. In short the misguided philosophical background has to be abandoned and replaced by a conception which places persons, not capital, in the focus of attention.

11

The Problem of the "Social Welfare Function"

One of the problems with the mechanistic approach which has dominated mainstream economic thought since the late 19th century is its neglect of the social and socio-psychological context in which the economic system functions. It simply assumes that people behave in the same way at all times and everywhere. This assumption is not restricted to economics. John Rawls developed an entire theory of justice on the basis of the idea that if choices are made without the chooser being aware of the eventual consequences of his choice for himself personally his choice would be "fair." What Rawls is taking for granted is Aristotle's assumption that it is "a peculiarity of men that they possess a sense of the just and the unjust." Willy-nilly this implies that what he or the current American middle class assumes to be fair *is* fair. Aristotle believed that this "common understanding of justice as fairness makes a constitutional democracy," and that "the basic liberties of a democratic regime are most firmly secured by this conception of justice." Aristotle lived in a society which accepted slavery as a normal condition. Had Rawls lived in another era, or even today in a tribal West African environment, he would hardly have adopted this kind of assumption. To believe that behind the "veil of ignorance" (that is, ignorance about their own position in society) people would elect to live in a society in which each individual enjoys equal rights, and inequalities would only be justified on the basis of competition and in so far as they operate to everyone's advantage, presupposes an egalitarian competitive culture in which changes in inequality can be justified only if they do not reduce the welfare of the worst-off. But this was the specific historical product of post-war Capitalism. Take out this presupposition and Rawlsian justice becomes a travesty. As said before, an egalitarian society is not inscribed into any historical plan, and people consider "just" what they have been accustomed to regard as such. The same is true for competition. Members of Guilds did not and were not allowed to compete with each other. They did not find their places in society on the basis of economic competitive proficiency. Kings were born into their status and their privileges were considered fair. Tribal chiefs are selected from particular families and their elevated social position is taken to be self-evident.

Classical Capitalism regarded *justice* as equality before the Law; Socialism dreamt of "from each according to his abilities, to each according to his needs"; post-war liberal Capitalism tried to create a society in which each person finds his place on the basis of competitive ability and in which the less able will still be assured of a share in the steadily increasing affluence. The last mentioned is the conception upon which Rawlsian justice is founded. It is the democratic conception based on majority voting, but it is a conception shared only by a particular and relatively small part of world population. But even in its idealized form it has its flaws. It is based on the assumption that a society's objectives can be represented as a function of the manner in which resources are allocated—the *Social Welfare Function*. As Kenneth Arrow has indicated, a social welfare function can only be a valid concept if social objectives can be derived from the preferences of individuals. In this sense it is equivalent to a "decision rule." This raises the question if a system of voting can be devised that is both rational, decisive and egalitarian. The answer must be negative; there is simply no way to reconcile the conflict between collective rationality, decisiveness and equality of power. This is in effect the message of Arrow's *"Impossibility Theorem."* He showed this by presenting five reasonable axiomatic prerequisites defining the conditions any procedure of social decision-making should fulfil in order to satisfy all three requirements. The first is the technical requirement that the choice be uniquely determined. The second axiom postulates a positive association of collective and individual values. This is a Pareto optimum: if each and every member of a society prefers A to B, then A should be ranked higher than B in the social welfare function. And if one of the alternative social priorities rises in the individuals' perception without there being other changes in the order of priorities, it can be taken that it rises in the social ordering. The third axiom postulates that the choice depends only on given alternatives. This means that if there are three contenders for the presidency of the European Community then the dropping out of one candidate will not influence the order of preference of the other candidates. The fourth axiom postulates that cultural or religious interdictions must not determine the social choice, irrespective of individual preferences. The fifth axiom postulates that the chosen method of decision-making should never result in one individual imposing his will and overruling everyone else's preferences.

Given these reasonable propositions Arrow proved that if there is any variety in the ordering of preferences by individuals there is no method of social decision-making which can satisfy his axioms. An oft-quoted example is Condorcet's paradox of voting. D.H. Blair and R.A. Pollak in their article on rational collective choice present the paradox as follows: "Suppose a committee consisting of Tom, Dick and Harry must rank three candidates, x, y and z. Tom's preference ranking of the candidates is x, y, z. Dick's is y, z, x and Harry's is z, x, y. Majority voting between pairs of candidates yields a cycle: x defeats y, y defeats z and z defeats x, all by two votes to one." In this situation of pairwise ranking the way out would be to specify an agenda, that is to list the order of voting. "For example, the agenda might call for an individual vote on x against y, followed by a second stage in which the winner is matched against z. Under this agenda our three-member committee would first vote for x over y and at the second stage z would defeat x. It is easy to verify that under each of the three possible agendas in this situation the alternative taken up last emerges as the victor: the agenda determines the result." If the agenda is selected randomly the choice of the winner is arbitrary, if the agenda is determined by the machinations of its setter the result is determined by him.

This is not the place to discuss the entire investigation of the "impossibility theorem" but the conclusions set out by Blair and Pollak are simple. "Three widely shared objectives—collective rationality, decisiveness and equality of power—stand in irreconcilable conflict. If society forgoes collective rationality, thereby accepting the necessary arbitrariness and manipulability of irrational procedures, majority rule is likely to be the choice because it attains the remaining goals. If society insists on retaining a degree of collective rationality, it can achieve equality by adopting the rule of consensus, but only at the price of extreme indecisiveness. Society can increase decisiveness by concentrating veto power in progressively fewer hands; the most decisive rule, dictatorship, is also the least egalitarian." So in the end, as Winston Churchill said, "democracy is the worst form of Government except all those other forms that have been tried from time to time."

Subsequent work questioning the "reasonableness" of Arrow's axioms or on relaxing their degree of stringency has divided economists. Some believe that the concept of a *social welfare function* is best abandoned altogether and others adopt the point of view that economists may accept any given such function without concerning themselves with how it is obtained. But the essential point remains that attainable social welfare, whatever people take it to be, remains a matter of culture, namely what people have been accustomed to regard as fair.

This is not all there is to it. By ignoring the constantly changing cultural environment economists and others take on board erroneous behavioral assumptions. Classical Capitalism was founded on *confidence*. Hugo Grotius (1583–1645), who believed in the rationality of man and man's ability to create a better society in accordance with the needs of man, proclaimed as the binding principle of behavior *"pacta sunt servanda"*—"bargains must be kept." Adam Smith thought that people are confined to legal means in their pursuit of riches and must not resort to the obviously simplest means for obtaining their wealth (such as highway robbery), because of "a divinely ordained harmony of egoistic and altruistic impulses in man." In his *Theory of Moral Sentiments* he declared that man's actions are determined by the values of society—by the approval of his fellow men. As already quoted, "the rich man glories in his riches, because he feels that they naturally draw upon him the attention of the world." But if the riches he acquired came to him by illegitimate means this "real" objective of his efforts is flouted. In other words, the legacy of the belief in divine retribution, the fear and acceptance as just of social opprobrium, and the dread and acceptance as fair of the penalties imposed by positive law, provided Capitalism with a measure of *confidence* without which it could not have developed. Similarly, the Age of Reason made *truth* amenable to human understanding and transformed truth into something good in itself. Without this the marvelous advancement of science would not have been possible. The romanticism of the 19th century emphasized individualism and stimulated creativity, originality and a sense of *noblesse oblige* or paternalism in employers' attitude toward their employees. Together with the teachings of the Church and the fear of riots, all this helped to mitigate the harsh logic of the competitive society and for the poor often smoothed the roughest edges of the system. Nonetheless the living conditions of the industrial working class were appalling in the nineteenth century and it was beset by a fear of destitution and starvation which imposed the work discipline without which the complex clockwork of industrial production would have soon ground to a halt.

All this bequeathed to modern capitalism a climate in which competition was circumscribed by legality; economic success dependent on efficiency; work discipline on fear of unemployment; and science on the quest for truth. Moreover, it also bequeathed to modern society respect for individuals' courage, originality and honesty. In short, a particular concatenation of historical circumstances provided industrial society with a culture which suited a widely shared type of economic progress. Lately, however, this culture has begun to wane. Technological advancement still produces economic growth but the mechanism by which its fruit used to be distributed is faltering.

Until the seventies living conditions in the industrialized countries improved and almost all classes shared in the fruits of the rising productivity. A social security system seemed firmly established in the western world and served as a safety-net against poverty and destitution. But almost imperceptibly the culture which had supported this social and economic miracle and had found its political expression in early post-war democracy was losing its emancipating powers. In the eighties this type of democracy, which had sustained the equilibrium distribution of national incomes between consumption and production even when the price mechanism was inadequate to meet this need, began to wane. The mesh of the safety-net became less tight and its slackening precipitated new conditions no longer compatible with the old patterns of economic growth and distribution. Step by step the meaningful early post-war democracy was transformed into a more or less merely ceremonial affair.

There were many reasons for this erosion: the failure of education to keep up critical and normative traditions; the drift of the mass media of information from informing toward persuading the public; the tenacity of the materialistic individualistic patterns of culture which post-war society inherited from the era before social security had reduced the fear of destitution; the perseverance of the urge to compete, itself also a legacy of the ages of dire scarcity, and its reinforcement until it seems part of "human nature."

In the social sciences this process went together with a confusion between *objectivity* and *non-involvement* and between *desirability* and *profitability*. Many modern social scientists confused objectivity with non-involvement and simply did not understand that the very doctrine which postulates the exclusion of normative judgments from scientific inquiry is itself a normative judgment; and many other scientists confused profitability with desirability and did not see that economic rewards are not always a good indicator for social benefits. The former simply confined their work to efforts to make "the system" work without bothering about its ethics; and the latter allowed market forces to determine the direction of their research with little concern for its social consequences. In this way the success of positivism in the natural sciences confounded methodology with objectives in many other fields of study. In literature, for example, the teaching of linguistics gradually replaced literary, ethical and aesthetic criticism. In sociology the study of methods and techniques for statistical analysis at the micro level reduced interest in dynamic macro processes. In economics the refinement of mathematical instruments replaced the integrated study of social and economic phenomena and focused attention on prices to near-exclusion of income effects. Economists plainly failed to recognize that a concept like *economic efficiency* is meaningless unless the meaning of the *best* allocation of resources is established, which is of course a normative issue. They overlooked the fact that unless one adopts a very deterministic view and altogether repudiates free choice, it is obvious that all human action involves a normative choice, namely a decision to prefer one course of action to all others.

And so, in its effort to make economics as much as possible like the natural sciences, most of the economics profession engaged itself in the perfection of the ruling theory without questioning its logic or ethical values, and abandoned the study of the dynamics of historical developments. Shedding tears about the impossibility of finding *absolute* criteria for deciding what is *good*, it declared itself impotent to make value judgments and adopted a position of moral relativism. In this way economists left the determination of values to the people who assert that there is no absolute universal ethics and that materialistic self-interest, though it may be sometimes mitigated by some "irrational" impulses, is all there is, and that everything else is nonsense. In this way economics lost visions of a more humane social reality and adopted a belief in universal egoism as its theoretical foundation. We have wonderful new technologies capable of providing plenty yet which cause poverty and destitution; we can produce mountains of surplus butter and pork and lakes of milk and wine, but the greater part of humanity ekes out a living on the borderline of starvation; we have marvelous media with the facility of spreading knowledge to all corners of the earth and used instead for escapism; but all this did not awaken the economics profession to the need to re-examine the real life distributive effects of the "invisible hand" and of its other fundamental premises.

In fact it was not only economics which became increasingly estranged from social reality. Democracy as a whole lost the social conception upon which the Welfare State had rested and drifted toward becoming an institution for assessing the relative power of pressure groups vying to obtain material advantages at the expense of others.

12

The Disintegration of
Western Civilized Society

In summary, what distinguished liberal or democratic capitalism from other systems was its ability to internalize most opposition. Treating labour as a factor of production whose price is determined by demand and supply in the market place, and regarding trade unions as monopolists, it transformed class struggle into wage negotiations. It allowed labour to oppose inequity but only on the system's own terms, that is as long as the system itself remained unchallenged. Similarly, liberal capitalism did not crush symbols of discontent. It internalized them by making them into a part of the system. Long hair, protest songs, even "subversive" literature, were not prohibited, but turned into fashions. In economics the discussion of real issues was sidestepped by focusing attention on technicalities. Keynes was not rejected but incorporated into a "neoclassical synthesis" which reduced his ideas into a "special case" within the old paradigm. Opposition which could not be internalized, for example questions about the rationality of the system itself, was placed beyond the pale. It was subjected to the establishment's powers of "repressive toleration." No mass arrests or executions; smear campaigns against Churchmen and *Berufsverbote* against socially committed active people (teachers in particular) were equally effective. Just like its communist counterpart in the eastern bloc, the capitalist oligarchy discovered that *compliant and unimaginative people* can serve it best. Democracy remained intact, but the mechanisms which make it meaningful gradually wore out.

During the post-war prosperity people felt little need to complain about their welfare and became accustomed to the system. They seldom questioned the equity of the institutionalized pay structure and the status differences within their own organization but compared their incomes and perks with those received by similarly-ranked employees in other businesses. This was a reversal of the process which had characterized the transformation of the feudal system of the Middle Ages into Capitalism. Medieval social and economic coherence was *vertical*. It was based upon a personal congruity of interests. A powerful master or landlord was better able to protect his serfs and tenants than a weaker one; and an affluent serf was better able to contribute to his master's strength than a poor serf. When a lord refused to contribute to some military adventure of the King he did so for himself, but in effect he also did so for his vassals and serfs. After all, in the end it was they who had to foot the bill. In other words, the feudal system rested upon a common interest which united each economic and social hierarchy against all others. The farmer relied on the aristocrat's protection and assistance, and the aristocrat relied on the farmers' surplus product for his income, his power and prestige.

Capitalist society created another type of social and economic alignment which was *horizontal*. People became aligned by belonging to similar income groups or by the nature of their occupations. The new alignment was a *class* system. At least subjectively the interests of the upper strata were no longer congruent with those of the lower. On the microeconomic level they were in fact antagonistic. Each individual capitalist's economic interest were directly opposed to his workers' because in the short run every wage claim affects profits. Therefore, in spite of competition among themselves, capitalists acted in unison against labour, and workers, though usually less successfully, against employers.

In the post-war era a new system gradually superimposed upon this antagonistic relationship a revived *feudal nexus*. As working conditions in large oligopolistic enterprises tended to be more favorable than in small firms (which have a much harder struggle for survival in their competitive environment) employees in the more powerful corporations felt that they were working for a "good master." They developed an *esprit de corps* which not only protected the firms from outside criticism but also undermined labour's class cohesion. This newfangled *industrial feudalism* was not confined to the private sector but spilled over into public administration. As a result of this the common interest of workers in an equitable share in the fruits of their labour was increasingly overshadowed by particular group interests which have no bearing on the wider issues affecting workers as a class. Slowly these common economic issues ceased to determine workers' voting on election days.

The process was accentuated by the new media of information. In theory radio and television are excellent media for the promotion of democracy; they can disseminate the necessary information to improve everyone's rational choices. In practice they degenerated into instruments of mass diversion and offered neither a reflection of reality nor true alternatives for democratic choice. The point is that television viewers receive programmes chosen according to viewing statistics. This not only gives a particular slant to the selection of programmes but also determines the manner in which they are presented. Discussions become popularity contests; points of view are "sold" without adequate background information, and difficult intricate problems are avoided. Consequently people watching television or listening to the radio are constantly subjected to the intellectual climate of public relations experts. The make-believe world of the soap operas becomes so familiar that viewers can no longer distinguish reality from fiction. They are socialized into the world invented by public relations agents who have less concern for *what* they sell than *that* it sells. Children are shown so many scenes of violence in which the "good" only win because they are even more violent than the "bad" that they take violence to be a normal way to settle a dispute. Adults are shown so many products by which materialistically successful people become "beautiful people" that they forget that it is not the products but the image created by the advertising agencies that makes them what they seem to be. The constant subjection to these make-belief images invented by the public relations experts creates a mental climate in which people cease to measure themselves against reality and enter a world in which the old values simply fade away. But a materialistic society without these values is bound to disintegrate and fall into a Hobbesian war of everyone against everyone else and so become unable to sustain the intricate networks of modern industrial production.

There are of course also excellent and informative programmes but they are few and hardly popular. On most channels discussions on *fundamental* economic questions are not offered. The establishment's point of view is just taken for granted. Viewers are simply told that high profits reduce unemployment as if this was some long-established truth. The possibility that the causal sequence of profits and employment could be the other way around, namely that for many firms greater employment raises profits, is simply left unmentioned. In this way the freedom of choice of viewers and listeners is restricted to the alternatives of either wage cuts (and reductions in social security expenditure) or greater unemployment. The other alternative, that the impact on the volume of employment of the *income effect* may perhaps outweigh the gains from wage-cuts, is proclaimed a matter settled by the "experts," too difficult to be understood by the general public, and of too little public interest to be offered for discussion. In this way listeners and viewers become passive consumers of ideas offered by a certain type of people. This tendency to rely for good judgement on the "experts," as if such matters were akin to repairing a broken machine where no personal interest on the part of the mechanic is involved but only his professional competence, and to deny people's common sense goes even further than the media. Work and working conditions are left to be decided by trade union officials, and workers' solidarity is transformed into union discipline—into the collective pursuit of narrowly defined materialistic self-interest.

In this climate of competitive individualistic utilitarianism the political cohesion of the working class is lost and democracy is divested of its progressive emancipating powers. By the 1980s, democracy had indeed been so enfeebled that it lost the ability to sustain the state's distributive mechanism which for three decades had assured the distribution of the national product, between capital, labour and receivers of transfer earnings, in the proportions necessary for maintaining full employment. However, at the same time that democracy was losing its socially emancipating powers, the Free Market system was also losing its economically essential mechanism. By the end of the seventies even the establishment's professional economic literature acknowledged the drift toward business concentration and monopoly. To be sure, in some branches of wholesale trade and certainly in retail trades, price competition continued to play a role, but its influence on the large-scale manufacturers who set the floor below which prices cannot fall became slight. For a time the re-emergence of Japan as a major trading nation and the rising economic role of the "Asian Tigers" seemed to enliven competition but it did so insufficiently to become a real substitute for the waning domestic market mechanism. The growth of *multinationals* and *globalization*, the concentration on core activities, soon put an end to this illusion.

Entrepreneurs have continued to be interested in innovation but mainly to reduce production costs—costs not prices. Where producers kept on vying for their respective market shares they did so more often by advertising and tied services than by price competition. In effect huge business conglomerates were increasingly not only determining prices but the structure of demand. The enormous cost of establishing new production plants made entrepreneurs wary of setting up competing ventures. The rapidly spreading amalgamation of firms into market-controlling conglomerates allowed consumers a choice only among the goods offered to them by conglomerates with combined sales monopolies. In other words, it restricted consumers' freedom of choice to the assortment of goods which suits their technological convenience. Increasingly enterprises became concerned with changes in revenue resulting more from advertising than from price modifications. In short, many conglomerates became able to determine both the supply and the demand side of their markets. People remained free to choose, but their choice was limited within the bounds of what the mighty offered them to choose from. As Henry Ford is supposed to have said, the customer is free to prefer a car of any color as long as it is black.

In former times, competition obliged producers to pass on cost reductions in lower prices to consumers, but in the 1980s this distributive mechanism lost its power. Competition of this kind diminished, and effective demand ceased to increase sufficiently to keep employment and consumption on a long-run upward path. In the past such a deficiency of price-reducing competition was sometimes made good by higher wage claims, but by the end of the seventies this type of "competition" between capital and labour also weakened. Wage claims and social security payments still sustained consumer demand in line with the rising productivity, but, unlike market competition, could not keep prices down. As a result the wage hikes, and the taxes to pay for the increasing social security cost, were passed on to consumers by continuously rising prices. And so, in spite of mounting productivity the familiar inflationary spiral kept accelerating.

Mistaking the symptoms of the problem for its causes, governments tried to curb inflation by monetary measures. The results were disastrous. Prices, wages and interest-rates continued to rise and unemployment and the cost of social security soared. Producers adjusted their output targets downward in line with the lower rate of growth in consumer demand, and placed even greater emphasis than before on cost-reducing innovation. In the most powerful oligopolies rising productivity kept profits high enough to use internal resources for investment. The weaker firms, which had to borrow funds, were faced with increasingly severe liquidity problems. Many production plans were postponed and new ventures with long gestation periods were abandoned. Employment in the production of consumer goods diminished and work in the capital goods industry became more and more specialized and added frictional to structural unemployment. Finally, increasing unemployment and high interest rates made traders careful when replenishing their stocks.

Confronted with a combination of unemployment and inflation or stagflation, many governments abandoned efforts to regulate the economy by the Keynesian instruments. They declared fiscal policies ineffective and sought refuge in a mixture of monetary measures with supply-side economics. Taking for granted the neoclassical postulate that saving equals investment, and reviving Say's Law which asserts that supply creates its own demand, they adopted policies designed to redistribute the national income with the intention of raising the share of profit. They believed that reduced consumer spending would contain inflation, and that increased savings would bring down interest rates and restore employment. In fact inflation became moderate but interest rates and unemployment remained high and the unemployed became socially marginalized. Illiteracy, drug-abuse and crime proliferated. In many towns entire districts became unsafe, and the humane achievements of the earlier post-war era were steadily eroded.

Unfortunately Keynesian economics and the coming of the Welfare State had hardly touched most peoples' individualistic profit-seeking mentality and perhaps it even further encouraged it. This was particularly unfortunate because this version of individualism could not cope with the new situation. Despondency and dissolution spread and undermined confidence and labour-discipline. Many young people gave up the hope of finding adequately-remunerated work and turned to alternative ways to satisfy their urge for action and advancement. Others, who worked for low wages, simply resigned themselves to living in relative poverty but ceased to feel responsible for the work they did. Those who earned better wages saw their real income dwindle and put the blame on taxation to sustain the "undeserving" poor and the inflated state bureaucracy. In short, the mechanisms which kept the capitalist system's clockwork moving began to be erratic. The improvements in social security had reduced the fear of destitution without providing a new mechanism to take its place and deprived the system of its major instrument for the enforcement of

work discipline; the rise of oligopolies and of multinational business conglomerates had reduced competition and deprived the system of the mechanism by
which income was distributed in line with rising productivity, and progressive
taxation had reduced entrepreneurs' opportunities to become rich in the manner they had learned to expect and deprived the system of its genuine entre-
preneurial élan. But no new mechanism had as yet materialized to keep the
modern industrial system properly functioning.

Classical capitalism had always differentiated between legitimate and illegitimate means of acquiring wealth; but in the era of regulated capitalism (and
not necessarily for the reasons given for it by Lady Thatcher) the threshold of
public disapprobation became lower. The transgressions became less distinguishable from tolerated practices and they became more difficult to prosecute. Workers' fear of unemployment continued, but it was less compelling
than it used to be. Absenteeism increased, tea-breaks lengthened, and a large
number of workers defrauded the community by claiming unemployment benefits though they were working secretly. Many employers made use of the
most clever stratagems to evade taxes and to deceive their customers and workers. At one time or another, almost everybody came face to face with these
malpractices, so that many people came to regard them as "natural." Consequently more and more people began to resent working responsibly and
honestly for normal wages and to paying taxes and national insurance contributions. Dishonesty is of course no new phenomenon, but the blurring of the
boundaries between what is and what is not acceptable was new. Coming at
the time when the old efficiency-promoting mechanisms of capitalism were
waning and the economy becoming so complex that one part could not adequately function in separation from all others, the blurring of these boundaries took on an ominous significance. It threatened the entire fabric of society
and reduced the prospect for replacing the individualistic economic mechanisms of capitalism by a system based on social responsibility. In fact it nurtured the social climate which ushered in and made widely acceptable the
conservative reaction of the 1970s and 1980s.

The old sense of decorum was waning and with it the hope that the Free
Enterprise system could function without fear of destitution as its driving force.
This led many people to take it as self-evident that without reasonable prospects for personal material advancement, without the fears associated with
unemployment, and without the sense of decorum to make working-men feel
responsible for and take pride in their work, the efficiency required to maintain high living standards could not be sustained. They recognized that *individualism* and *competition*, the foundations of the capitalist system, by their
internal logic were approaching a paradoxical conclusion. *Individualism*, having
been released from the fetters of an older culture, was rapidly becoming short-
sighted pure self-interest; and *competition*, having "competed" out of business many competitors, was becoming an illusion. But they did not consider

new alternatives and fell prey to the Thatcherite delusions that some kind of idealized pre-Keynesian capitalism could be revived, and that the old capitalist mechanisms could somehow be restored. As a result unemployment was ignored, made the responsibility of the unemployed themselves, and destitution was presented as the result of the destitute individuals' mismanagement of their affairs.

Disregarding these developments the economics profession kept itself occupied refining methods for achieving the *best* allocation of scarce resources, never asking the question: best for whom and best for what? The point is that the acquisition of wealth by ingenuity instead of force was an essential feature of capitalism. But the profit motive and fear of starvation which were present in earlier generations, and continue to be present in many poor countries today, did not promote industrial progress. To raise living standards a specific social and cultural environment is required, because it is the reigning social values which determine how these desires and fears direct the conduct of society. However the economics establishment all but excluded this verity from its science.

Values are the product of current economic forces, but they are also inherited from an earlier period. They are imparted to the young by their parents and teachers and thus reflect the real needs and values as well as the aspired reality of a preceding era. This gives society a degree of stability and continuity, but holds back its more rapid adaptation to current changes in its material environment. The spiritual legacy of the Middle Ages in western Europe left the would-be rich of later generations with a feeling of discomfort in the pursuit of their wealth. It tempered their profit-seeking so that the new individualism which accompanied the new material opportunities was prevented from killing the goose that was to lay the golden egg. It imposed legality, rationality, even a degree of humanity, upon the quest for riches, and confined rapacity and exploitation within legal boundaries in which, on the whole, ingenuity rather than brute force became the source of wealth. Self-love was circumscribed by social and religious conventions. Without these cultural constraints capitalism would never have achieved its great economic success. Lately, however, the constraints are being swept away by a new unbridled utilitarian culture. For this reason, it is not only ethically undesirable, but outright nonsensical to attempt to restore to capitalism to its old mechanism of fear to keep the poor in line and of the prospects of high profits to encourage the rich.

The socialization process which in the past had imposed on capitalism the necessary remedial modes of social conduct now tends to impose new practices which are the product of capitalism itself and have a different effect. Values and mores are communicated to successive generations by elders who impart their wishes in a moralizing setting of rules variously rationalized. As these emotions become overladen with habitual rules, the rules themselves appear to be intuitive and inevitable. In this way the real need to compete in order to survive, which was practically unavoidable in pre-war capitalism, gradually invested egoism with moral quality. At home and in school competition was taken for granted. Success was rewarded by approval and failure treated with contempt. During the post-war era of prosperity the urge to compete lost its earlier rational context in the Welfare States, but having become habitual continued to appear intuitive, as "human nature." The *means* by which competitive success is attained faded into the background and success itself became moral quality. A pharmaceutical enterprise facing the choice between investing resources in a medicine for treating river blindness, or in the promotion of a new perfume, will choose the perfume because the Africans and Asians afflicted with river blindness are too poor to be considered an attractive market.

In the same way as after the end of the Middle Ages faith continued for a very long time to be an area of life with boundaries which it was extravagant to overstep, so did the pursuit of narrow materialistic self-interest continue to govern people's life in the period of post-war regulated capitalism. Just as in the era of the Enlightenment, reason only gradually took the place of revelation and religion ceased to be the force governing mankind, so does the spirit of relentless competition linger on in our time. That the objective causes which first gave rise to this spirit may no longer appertain has little immediate influence; that our technology has attained a level of such efficiency that if its fruits were equitably shared it could provide a standard of living in Europe for all people which even the upper middle class would consider adequate does not matter. The heritage of the darkest ages of capitalism persists. The urge to compete and the narrow pursuit of materialistic self-interest have become "human nature."

But is it? In wars soldiers have been known to lay down their lives to protect comrades; families help each other without expecting direct material rewards; parents care for their children, brothers for their sisters, and countless hospital nurses care for their patients beyond the call of duty, and, in spite of Gary Becker, rich men have been known to fall in love with poor women and rich women with poor men and many of them lived very happily ever after. All this is ignored or relegated to the sphere of irrational or exceptional behavior. Even collective forms of self-interest, like anti-pollution and anti-atomic energy movements, are rarely acknowledged as indications of the possibility that individuals' self-centered materialism may be transient and subject to alteration by changing circumstances and by education. The fact is that "human nature" is more involved than a calculating machine and the human brain is more complex than a computer.

Education does therefore play an essential role in the socialization of the young. Its contribution to the formation of the necessary frame of mind to maintain the efficiency assuring high living standards is no less essential than technological instruction. To teach people how to use sophisticated technological equipment is not enough. To obtain good results they must also have a reason to employ it diligently. The belief that in education money is better spent on providing competent technicians than on improving general knowledge and critical thought is therefore deceptive, and at a time when fear of destitution and expectation of plenty are waning it may be downright wrong. It is not that technology is unimportant in maintaining efficiency, nothing could be further from the truth, but the imparting of social values to the young and encouraging them to think critically is of no less importance for industrial efficiency. And it is in this sphere that modern education fails and industrial feudalism wields a paralysing influence.

In the 1950s and 1960s the young were still taught at school the traditional literature which exalts the humanistic and liberal values of the past, but at home and in the world around them they were confronted with a materialistic and utilitarian reality. It was not that in school they were not encouraged to compete and admonished to aim at material success in later life, but their studies also imparted other values. As a result they were bewildered by the hedonism and bureaucratic insensitivity of the world of their elders. By the end of the 1960s they attacked capitalism because they saw it abandoning democracy, freedom of expression, individualism and human rights. Paradoxically the student movement employed Marxist terminology in the pursuit of a much older creed, namely original Christianity. Believing that they were following a new Marxist revolutionary path they did in effect cling to the traditional values when they revolted against the rising wave of the new-fangled type of self-centered materialism and industrial feudalism. They resented the world of Stalin and McCarthy, of the Official Secrets Act in Britain and of the Algerian lobby in France, of the re-emergence of the old guard in public service in Germany, and, eventually, of the trauma of Vietnam. But they had no clear conception of a *positive* alternative. They lived in an era of hitherto unknown social and economic security which had bred in their elders, who had suffered for long a life of deprivation, a climate of brute materialism, of unrestrained consumerism. Deprived of a clear perception of the way they want to form the future, the revolt was no more than an explosion of frustrations and in the end degenerated into "We want it all and we want it now."

Moreover, the primitive Marxism adopted by the young totally ignored the fact that in the 1960s the European working class was not living on the verge of starvation and in fear of unemployment. The industrial working class had much more to lose than its proverbial chains. Parliamentary democracy and trade unions had served it well. They had provided social and economic security, paid holidays, and a multitude of consumer durables. And so, while unable to win wide support from the industrial working class, the students' crude Marxian rhetoric did not enthuse the workers but alienated them and most of all they alienated the poorest deeply religious foreign workers, the hard-pressed self-employed, and the sections of the liberal intelligentsia, though the latter was no less frustrated than the students by the ethical void into which the affluent society was sinking.

Finally the failure of the student movement, and the subsequent sprouting of several politically naive terrorist groups, also accelerated the repressive tendencies without which industrial feudalism cannot flourish. Instead of alienating the working class from the new oligarchy, the student movement effectively scared it into its arms, and led it to accept the various measures apparently necessary to "protect" democracy which actually denuded it of its emancipating content. All that remained as opposition to the new order were single-issue groups such as the movements for the protection of the environment, against nuclear rearmament, and women's lib. However, these groups have neither the design nor the power to save the economic and social achievements of the Keynesian era, though they are well within the Jewish and Christian tradition of the liberal bourgeoisie, namely respect for human rights and justice mitigated by compassion. The only real countervailing power to the establishment's crude materialism was the slowly developing understanding between Socialists, progressive sections of the bourgeoisie and of the Church. Particularly in the Third World, where poverty, inequity and repression are worst, the slogans of socially-engaged priests became hardly distinguishable from those of the Marxists, which is hardly surprising if it borne in mind that, in spite of their long history of animosity and mutual vilification, Marxists, Christians and the bourgeoisie basically share one and the same cultural background and value system.

Special attention in this context needs to be accorded to what happened to science. Ever since Adam and Eve were expelled from the *Garden of Eden* poverty has afflicted and continues to afflict humanity. Thanks to the advances made in science during the era of capitalism society obtained powerful means to reduce this curse. This gave to science and technology a special position in the public's imagination and bestowed a particular social standing upon the people who engaged in scientific research. As economic progress became more and more the fruit of technological advancement which resulted from scientific investigation, scientific research met with growing universal approval, except of course where it came into conflict with religious taboos. Workers learned to appreciate its role in raising living standards, though from time to time its technological application caused fleeting bouts of unemployment, and capitalists regarded it as a key to competitive advancement. Almost everybody, with very few exceptions, believed that science was promoting economic growth and that such growth was to everyone's advantage.

This gave to scientists a special position in society. Believed to be the champions of man's ascendancy over "the niggardliness of nature" scientists received a social status far above the one which capitalist society normally reserved for people of their income and wealth. The masses romanticized scientists' work and regarded the scientist as a selfless servant of truth and human progress, and entrepreneurs saw in him or her a useful tool for the advancement of their own interests. As a result of this scientists escaped class conflict and developed for themselves a sub-culture which placed ingenuity in pushing back the frontiers of ignorance above personal material rewards.

Well into the 1950s many young people who chose a scientific career were motivated by a social commitment to assail poverty, injustice and diseases. Young architects dreamt of building bridges to unite the world, young biologists of raising the yield of crops, young lawyers of improving the administration of justice, young physicians of eliminating illnesses and epidemics. There were those who hoped only to obtain well-remunerated jobs, or who simply studied because their parents wished them to do so, but they hardly set the tone for the scientific community or marred its public image. Not that there were no greedy scientists, but these were not the people who determined the cultural climate in the scientific community, nor did they sully the image of the scientific community as a whole in the perception of the general public.

In the 1960s all this began to change. The reasons were many, but the most notable were the emergence of previously unknown hazards which looked as if they were imposed by science on mankind and its natural environment, and the increasing subjection of scientific research to crude capitalist profitability. Scientists continued to push back the frontiers of ignorance, but they no longer determined the *direction* in which their work was leading. Publicly-funded research was increasingly determined by the Cold War, and privately-financed research by business *profitability* rather than the public good. Gradually the public image of the scientist as the champion of human progress was superseded by the vision of a Dr. Strangelove who releases immense destructive forces which he cannot control, or of a scholar who places his services at the command of irresponsible profit-seeking industry, often conducting socially irrelevant research such as finding a new flavour or color for a toothpaste.

Young people came to study economics and sociology not because they wished to improve the world but because these could provide them with a well-paid job in government or industry. They discontinued thinking about how things *ought* to be and confined themselves to the question how things were and how they could be done efficiently in the best interest of their employers. Capitalism simply internalized the scientific community into the system and rewarded researchers according to their contribution to its functioning in the way it is. Many sociologists and social psychologists became advertising agents using their sciences not to enlighten people about true requirements but to convince that one brand of washing powder was superior to another although they were perfectly aware that there was no difference. Economists ceased asking awkward questions about the social and macroeconomic consequences of certain types of investment and restricted themselves to the study of ranges of profitability. All this did not go unnoticed and step by step the position scientists held in the general public's perception waned. Like the Church the scientific community became emasculated in the struggle against poverty and destitution.

Worse than this, the application to the social sciences of the positivistic methodology which bases its findings on facts that can be experienced rather than on ideas formed in the mind, and which had been tremendously successful in the natural sciences, introduced into economics a fateful confusion between methodology and objectives, between the *is* and the *ought to be*. It misconstrued the entire purpose of the social sciences and of macroeconomics and deprived them of a social vision and purpose by presenting sham non-involvement as scientific objectivity. The poor are poor because they are "losers," an observable fact and hence a truth. Had a researcher at the end of a decade of Nazi education asked 100 young Germans whether Jews were an inferior race, a cancer which unless exterminated would afflict and destroy the healthy Aryan nations, he would certainly have received a statistically over-whelmingly significant affirmative reply, another statistically confirmed truth. Statistics was transformed from an instrument into the sole source of evidence for *truth* and mathematical rigor into the hallmark of scientific perfection.

Again, it would be rash to conclude that there were not also some socially redeeming forces at work in the 1980s but none of them actually threatened the core elements of the economic system. Such is its power to internalize that any social opposition is simply integrated and subjected to its mechanisms. Blacks cease to be discriminated against because of the color of their skin, but with few exceptions they continue to be discriminated against because of poverty and lack of education. Women cease to be discriminated against because of their gender, but find themselves discriminated against because of uncertainty of tenure and the extra cost to businesses when they have children. The environmentalists are no longer laughed out of court, but the cost of environmental protection is passed on to consumers without any really serious efforts being made to desist from environmentally hazardous activities. In other words, profit and competition rule supreme. Only the short run functioning of the economic and social system, the *is* here and now, is relevant and worthy of scientific analysis and action; its dynamics in the long run, the direction it is taking, even if it may be leading to disaster, is of no concern. It permits opposition, but only when it can subject it to its rules. All criticism which cannot be integrated is shrouded in a cloak of silence, declared irrelevant, or proclaimed unscientific.

This reinterpretation of the role of science and its search for truth, and of the role and power of the media in the advancement of this process, are well reflected in the recent rise of *post-modernism* and the novel aspects of *neo-pragmatism*.

13

Truth and Expediency: Some Introductory Philosophical Observations

Economists and other social scientists have recently been heard to say that they are not interested in truth; that what matters is that their papers are interesting, persuasive, or suggesting new ideas. The purpose of this chapter is to outline some of the developments in the philosophical assumptions of the sciences which led to this devaluation of the concept *truth* and to throw light on the consequences of abandoning it. It is needless to say that the limited purpose of this chapter imposes on the discussion some inevitable simplifications which would be unacceptable in a more complete historical survey. The intention here is to draw attention to the connection between the scientific approach in different disciplines which may have affected the historical observations in the preceding chapters.

The first thing to notice is that the lack of interest in the concept of truth is justified in two ways. The first is the assumed impossibility of attaining true knowledge, and the second a political, or moral, claim concerning the misuse of knowledge. These are not new claims. Plato, for example, accused the sophists of being the enemies of truth, but their main objection might have been to the authority which Plato and his followers claimed for themselves on the basis of their superior knowledge. In the middle ages, nobody doubted that God had created the world according to a design and a purpose. Heretics argued that the church failed to understand God's purpose. And humanists understood, so Stephen Toulmin tells us in his Cosmopolis, that as nobody can ever discover the design, they had better be tolerant and allow all interpretations to coexist. Toulmin proposes to adopt the same policy with regard to science. Since we cannot know how the world *really* is, we would do well to act on moral rather than on scientific grounds.

Similarly, Richard Rorty in his *Consequences of Pragmatism* identifies this humanist approach with pragmatism. Realists, he says, claim that truth is a relation between representations, namely ideas and theories etc., and a represented reality. But pragmatists disregard reality. Pragmatism means that science is about coping with current practical concerns without imposing on them an ontological status. Hence, knowledge is not about truth, but about (socially) acceptable reasons for action or warranted assertibility. If we get rid of traditional notions of objectivity, on which scientific method is based, he claims, we shall be able to see the social sciences as a cultural construct continuous with literature. Historians and anthropologists will help us turn a member of another culture into "one of us"; sociologists will do the same for all sorts of "outsiders" in our own culture, and psychologists for the eccentric and the insane. All of them will enlarge and deepen our sense of community. If this is the task we expect of them, we need not worry about how their style is related to the quantificational style required by the Galilean tradition, because we do not expect them to discover a hidden nature of man.

There are therefore two distinct questions: of what sort of knowledge, if any, we can assert that it is true and objective, and whether we need to rely on truth in order to achieve a social goal. Starting with the first question we must note that both the meaning of truth and the way it is pursued, which had dominated natural philosophy since Plato's time, have drastically changed in modern science. Plato's aim, and one which lasted well into the seventeenth century, was to discover the *Grand Design* behind the distorted phenomenal experience. Rationalists like Descartes and Leibniz, also identified laws of nature with objective reality. They believed that since this reality was best grasped by the rational mind, logical thinking was a more reliable source of knowledge than the human senses. Galileo believed that the language in which this universal design was written into "the book of nature" was mathematics, and Newton's laws confirmed this belief.

From the beginnings of the new science the aim to discover the "grand design" met with philosophical objections. Among the rationalists, only Spinoza faced the problem we call *today* the completeness of knowledge: if the world was completely determined by natural laws, then true knowledge must include knowledge of "the machine" to its last detail. Only God, or Nature's self knowledge, in Spinoza's opinion, has access to this absolute truth. Bishop Berkeley had no doubt that Truth (with a capital T) was in God's grand design of nature, but he was equally convinced that the human mind could not possibly perceive it: we have no access to knowledge of things that are independent of our minds. For empiricists, Hume's well-argued rejection of induction did the rest: his proof that there was no valid method for inferring general laws, let alone the grand design, from perceived evidence, terminated the belief that the human intellect could lead to certainty about scientific descriptions which go beyond the empirically observed phenomenal world. Moreover, Hume argued that what seems to be pure rational thought is no more than well-entrenched habits of thought, and therefore not more but less objective than perceptions. It follows from this that since perceived phenomena are by definition subjectively experienced, all attempts to remain within the limits of the phenomenal must in the end lead to antirealism.

Although this conclusion still preoccupied the scientists and philosophers who took part in the Vienna Circle at the beginning of the present century, it never attained a *dominant* position in modern science. Modern scientists have always presupposed that sense perceptions, the phenomena, are caused by the real world and that the real world is governed by laws which, on the whole, can be discovered. A central theme in the modern philosophy of science may therefore be regarded as an attempt to refute Hume's skepticism. It is acknowledged that no certainty can be claimed for causal laws inferred from habitually-observed regularities, but the degree of certainty can be increased by satisfying two requirements. The first is to check the effect of what Hume called "habits of thought" by the experimental method, and the second is to treat every inductive generalization as a hypothetical law which is only probably true. Although the second requirement was not put in this form until well into the 20th century, it reflects a much older belief that induction is always speculative and that only deduction leads to certainty, but also that deduction does not lead to *new* knowledge. It only makes consequences of knowledge explicit. Curiosity about the unknown always leads to speculation, and induction is its simplest form. The question is how much speculation we should tolerate.

Until close to the end of the nineteenth century these two requirements were considered sufficient. The idea was that causal laws, the basic general statements in any theory, can be tested for truth separately, one by one, by confronting them with facts. This is *the correspondence theory of truth*. According to this conception of truth, a hypothetical generalization is a provisional step in research: truth is always in the observed details, in the examined facts.

Since the beginning of the present century, and particularly by the time these ideas were examined in the Vienna Circle, a shift of emphasis has taken place. From the dominant effect of examined *facts* on the acceptance of a theory the emphasis shifted to the effect of an accepted theory on the *examination* of facts. It was conceded that with the experimental testing of a basic scientific law, other laws of the theory within which it appears are always taken for granted. For example, if such a test involves measuring temperature, it requires the use of a thermometer which is constructed on the basis of theoretical generalizations in the same or a related theory. This realization led to the conclusion that the only way a theory can be proven true is to show that all statements involved in it support each other. This is called *the coherence theory of truth*.

The obvious flaw which the members of the Vienna Circle saw in this theory of truth was that, although it is reasonable to require that the system of causal laws and their consequences which constitute a scientific theory must be logically consistent, it is *not* reasonable to assume that every consistent system must necessarily be true. However, they claimed not to have *replaced* observed truth by logical consistency, but to have combined them. They thought that together with the experimental requirement, and with the presupposed causal relation between the real world and human perception (the observed phenomena), this new conception of truth could be accepted. They realized that it meant giving up the idea that one can ever be certain about the truth of any particular statement independently of the rest, but they thought that the more extensive a theory becomes the more likely it is that a fault will eventually be exposed by an inconsistency. Nevertheless, although not always explicitly recognized, this change in the conception of truth introduced an additional constraint on scientific theories: only in domains where it was justified not to expect internal contradictions could scientific methods be applied. In other words, whether or not the real world was logically ordered, logical consistency turned into a necessary strategy of scientific inquiry. And the obvious question arising (but not yet raised) from this presupposed methodological condition is whether, for example, psychology or economics can be a science.

The realization that ascertaining the truth of particular statements depends on the truth of the theory in which they appear was one of the sources of two currently popular post-modern ideas. One is contextualism—that facts *are* facts only within a particular framework of discussion, and the other is that facts are constructed rather than discovered: what we call a fact is a true statement, and if there is no way to distinguish between ascertaining the truth of an observed fact from ascertaining the truth of the entire theory; and if an entire theory is a logical construct of the human mind, then so must be each fact. However, the full impact of these ideas evolved later. Another consequence of the coherence theory of truth, or rather of the constraint imposed on science by the requirement of logical consistency, which evolved later within the realist approach, is that absolute truth, in the sense of having a complete knowledge of reality, is most probably unattainable. However, in the present discussion of changes that occurred in the modern realist approach, the important point is that the presupposed general belief in a causal relation between the real world and phenomenal experience, remained intact, and so did the aim of science to describe the real (ordered) world as it is. But the belief in the way to reach this aim (the epistemological assumptions and requirements underlying this aim) changed, and with it the meaning of realism and of objectivity.

An objective description, a description independent of the human mind, came to mean that the way the phenomena are subjectively experienced needs to be removed from the description of the world. Feeling heat, seeing red, seeing a flash of lightening, are all explicable as caused by external events, or by their interactions with our sense organs. Their scientific description as molecular motion, as light waves of a specific length, or as an electric discharge to the earth, are obtained when these experienced interactions are removed. In spite of its complexity, Einstein's argument for his theory of relativity is worth mentioning because it does not only highlight the significance and generality of this principle in modern realism, but it also served as a metaphor for the post-modern idea of the relativity of observations.

That the position and velocity of a moving target measured by two observers moving relative to each other (for example by one person on a ship and another on shore) yields different results was well known to Galileo. Descartes' invention of coordinate systems (his analytic geometry) was the mathematical tool designed for "calculating away" these subjective effects on measurements. The meaning of this is that by using the Galilean transformation laws it could be shown that results obtained by one observer could always be transformed into those of another, showing that the laws of mechanics were the same irrespective of the coordinate system relative to which the values of the variable inputs to the equations were measured. Moreover, knowing that the laws were the same, the relative positions of the observers could be ascertained in the same way. The problem which Newton expressed as a relativity principle was that when two coordinate systems move relative to each other with *constant* velocity, there is no way by which we can discover this fact: the objective relative movement cannot be discovered by calculating away observed differences because the observations are the same. Einstein's revolution occurred when a way was believed to have been found to overcome this relativity principle: the constant velocity of light derived from Maxwell's equations was believed to be constant relative to the absolute coordinate system attached to the universe as a whole. Hence, by observing the velocity of light relative to any other coordinate system one could discover whether or not it was moving relative to the universe. The astonishing result was that the measurements of the velocity of light were found to be always the same, independently of whether they were taken by people in coordinate systems moving or stationary relative to each other.

Apart from leaving Newton's relativity principle as it has been, this apparently incredible fact undermined some well established ideas about objectivity. Prior to this discovery a collision of objects in space and in time, namely their simultaneously reaching the point of collision, were believed to be always an objectively ascertained event—the assertion being absolutely true—in the sense of not being dependent on the coordinate system relative to which it is observed. After the discovery the objectivity of simultaneous events was undermined: in a thought experiment Einstein has shown that two rays of light emitted from a source in the center of a moving coordinate system (for example in a room moving so fast that its velocity would make a difference to observed calculations) would be observed to reach two fixed points (for example the walls of the room) simultaneously by an observer within this coordinate system (within the room) and not simultaneously by an observer outside it (who will see one wall running away from and the other approaching the rays of light). Einstein's conclusion was that, since the observed fact that the velocity of light remains constant cannot be ignored, and the laws of mechanics must be the same in all coordinate systems, the Galilean transformation laws had to be discarded in favor of new transformation laws which were to ensure this validity by calculating away the difference in observations. He argued further, that no matter how counter-intuitive the idea is that simultaneity of events turns out to be a subjective feature—which seems objective only to observers within the same coordinate system—this idea must be accepted, because only in this way could it remain true that a scientific description is true and objective.

If science is to be empirically tested, then, objectivity came to be identified with intersubjectivity. Intersubjectivity does not mean universally accepted but universally *acceptable* once the effect of the particular position—the subjective point of view of the observer—can be calculated away. In this way objective truth remains tied to the phenomena as a methodological constraint on the scope of scientific description.

This constraint was accepted by modern science as a measure of protection against metaphysical speculations which attempted the impossible—originally against religious dogmas, and later against any all-encompassing explanations that purport to go beyond the evidence. To this day most *empirical* scientists are convinced that such speculative attempts are not only futile but present a major obstacle to obtaining the best possible objective descriptions.

This notion of objectivity refers to the resulting description. But the concept of objectivity refers also to an attitude of "neutrality" towards research. Scientists must not only be prepared to disregard their particular interests, convictions and intuitions (their habits of thought), but also learn to create the means for calculating away that evidence of their own senses which must be considered subjective. All measuring devices have always been designed with this purpose in mind. The simplest examples are measuring-rods for length or distance, instead of relying on visual evidence, or a thermometer instead of relying on the feeling of warmth.

Although the two meanings of objectivity retain the emphasis on empirical evidence, and involve a departure from the rationalists' belief in the power of the mind to grasp the presupposed logical order of the universe, something has remained of the latters' belief in this power, in the form of the required logical structure of scientific knowledge.

In the seventeenth century, when the universe and everything in it were supposed to have a fixed structure, rationalists not only believed that this structure was necessarily logically consistent, and therefore accessible to a logical mind, but they also believed that the power of the human mind to grasp this structure was more reliable than the power of the human senses to perceive it. This was the belief which was undermined by Hume's pure empiricism. Kant claimed to have shown the way by which Hume's skepticism could be overcome without speculating about the structure of the universe behind the phenomenal evidence. He argued that such abstract notions as space and time constituted a precondition for perceiving positional and temporal relations between objects, and therefore, they characterized the perceiving mind, not the world. He proposed that the logical structure given by science to phenomena, including the idea of causality, equally characterized the human mind. In other words, all these structural features of the universe were imposed on the world by the mind.

Like the modern version of realism, Kant identified the scientifically understandable reality with phenomenal reality. Moreover, to say that realism *presupposes* the causal relation between the real world and sense perception, implicitly embraces Kant's view that causality is imposed by the mind. Similarly, the identification of objectivity to intersubjectivity admits the same to a certain extent, only that to the assumption of sense experience being common to all human minds, Kant added the common human logical thinking. Neither Kant nor the rationalists before him regarded logical thinking as a description of a psychological phenomenon. It was described as a power of the mind because it *could* impose, or according to rationalists, could discover, an ordered view of the world. And the realists' conception of intersubjectivity as universally *acceptable*, rather than as universally accepted, is not very different. What is common to rationalists, Kant's idealism and modern realism is the conviction that the possibility to think logically is common to all human beings and that to be a rational scientist means to think logically, independently of any transitory effects of social or psychological factors.

However, just as from its early days of triumph the new Galilean science had been challenged by empiricists, so its new version, reaching its peak of popularity in the nineteenth century, has been challenged by a new view of knowledge which emerged in the wake of Darwin's theory of evolution. To a large extent the problems which preoccupied the Vienna Circle arose out of the contradictions between the view of modern realism described above and this emerging new view which they inherited from Ernest Mach. While Kant thought of an eternal human mental power that could impose structural laws on observed phenomena, logical positivists thought of evolving minds, and adopted Wittgenstein's thesis (proposed in the *Tractatus*) that the truths of logic rested on the nature of the language of logic, and not in the nature of the human mind. This may be interpreted as saying that logical thinking is not a *natural* cognitive "tool", but a cultural one, resulting from the obviously invented logical language—a tool without inverted comas. It *may* be, rather than must be, so interpreted because no alternative interpretation of the world (usually described as a narrative mode of thinking) is devoid of any logical principles. In other words, we do not know whether logical thinking is natural, and if it is natural, to what extent it shapes what we consider knowledge. What we can say, according to the evolutionary view, is that whether or not logical thinking is an invention, it nevertheless characterizes the function of reasoning today just as the practices used in agriculture characterize this human activity in a nearly universal human reality in spite of being a cultural invention.

Whether a cognitive or invented tool, then, scientists retained the belief that logical thinking is at least as reliable for bringing us closer to those real structural aspects of the world that can be understood, as observation can bring us closer to the world that can be seen. Logical thinking is opposed to having unexamined beliefs, just as observing is opposed to casual seeing, whether observing means natural looking or looking with the aid of invented instruments. This is why logical positivists, like realists, still thought a neutral attitude to be possible and the discoveries of science to be acceptable as universal and unique.

The real challenge to this belief, posed by the new evolutionary view, came from the converts to American pragmatism, initiated by C.S. Peirce, W. James and J. Dewey. Both Mach and the pragmatists thought that the scientific endeavour must be seen as an improvement on natural cognition, as an improvement on the natural creation of knowledge we call common sense, whose function is to cope with, or adapt to, one's reality. The problem is that the reality people have to cope with is mainly the reality of a socially organized world. Hence, if this reality is so different for different people, how can one speak of neutral observers? How can one remove what Hume had called the habits of thought?

The progress of technology in the western world did not allow the pragmatist view to affect the conviction that the natural sciences were objectively true: how else could these sciences have led to the successful coping with the natural environment? But in the social sciences there is nothing to match this evidence. However, in the social sciences the question is not confined to evidence alone.

If the pragmatist conception of science is correct, an explanation of behavior can ignore neither the motives of people attempting to resolve (cope with) particular problems, nor their reasons for choosing one way for solving them rather than another. It follows that in psychology an adequate explanation of a person's behavior must always be given in terms of motives and reasons, or as often stated, in terms of desires and beliefs. And in any social science an explanation must be given in terms of a community's common desires and beliefs.

The first difficulty arising from this conclusion is that pragmatist psychologists, anthropologists or other social scientists, are pragmatists when they think about the explained people, societies, or cultures, but remain modern realists when they bother to think about their own approach to research. They seldom approach their fieldwork with the aim of solving anything for either the observed people or for themselves. They usually consider themselves neutral observers.

The second difficulty arises when social scientists study some aspect of their own society, where they are part of the observed people. In this case, consistent pragmatism requires that they think of their social science as a means of improving their own natural cognition in the attempt to cope with their social environment. Hence, the very purpose of neutral observation, or of reaching maximum objectivity, becomes controversial. The same problem has been raised by social philosophers like Habermas who claims that even if a distinction between observer and observed *could* be made, it should not be made within one's own society. In his opinion, when social scientists in the modern scientific tradition adopt a neutral point of view, they necessarily focus attention on existing social structures which incorporate the common desires and beliefs that are most influential or most powerful at that moment. It therefore tends to perpetuate the status quo rather than offer solutions to real social problems.

To relate this arguments to the conception of truth we may put it as follows: realists identify truth with a description of the world as it is, where the description may change but the world stays the same. The replacement of "the world as it is" by "the phenomenal world as it is" admits that the information we absorb from the real world as it is is "filtered" through our sense organs: we do not see the full range of light-waves, nor do we hear all sound waves. Phenomenal reality is different for human beings, bats or lions. However, these filters are common to all humanity, and hence we can obtain intersubjective science based on the evidence of our senses, and with the help of instruments, we can to some extent reach beyond them to the world as it is. In contrast to the senses, linguistic categorization—the mental filters of thought—are not as intersubjective as perception, and in the pragmatist view, this is because this categorization—the basic organization of knowledge—is determined by its success in coping with phenomenal experience in various aspects of life, and this success is not uniquely determined. Even when we believe to be pursuing pure understanding, to say that scientific knowledge is an extension of common-sense knowledge implies that scientific categories are at best corrections of common-sense categories, and hence, like the latter, they are imposed on experience according to the success in their application. This means that categories, and the knowledge based on them, are considered true, when their application makes prediction possible, thus providing the ability to control that aspect of life which they describe. It is only because the natural sciences often deal with intersubjective experience, that their categories too can be intersubjective, and their discoveries can be thought of as universally true. But even this consideration depends on the special value attached to the distinction between facts and values.

Logical positivism shared with realists the distinction between facts and values. Neither denied that a society can make use of knowledge to attain its aims according to its values, but while realists justified the distinction by their conception of objectivity, logical positivists justified it by their theory of meaning: the meaning of a concept is (or should be determined by) the method of its verification. Truth can be verified only where empirical knowledge is concerned. Hence, the concept is meaningless when it is applied to aims or values. The distinction between fact and values is simply the distinction between cases where the concept of truth can be and cannot be applied. Pragmatists and hermeneutics, however, rejected the distinction between fact and value as arbitrary. According to pragmatists, the distinction rests on the assumption that theories are like tools which one can use at will according to needs; that one can separate the use of knowledge from its purpose and history of acquisition. Pragmatists deny this possibility: if, as they maintain, the truth of a sentence is determined by its value for prediction and control then the wish to predict and control is not less factual than the observed results. In the social sciences in particular, they see no reason to consider those aspirations and values which are the common desires and beliefs of a community as less important in determining the truth of a description than those chosen by empiricists to be the sole features qualified to be called facts. And the hermeneutics see no reason to ignore the aims of scientific descriptions in all cases. In their opinion, the social sciences ought to be the tool for the emancipation of every human being from existing social ills, in the same way as the natural sciences ought to be, and initially have in fact been, a tool for liberating mankind from material scarcity. The conception of truth ought to be related to this aim.

In order to understand how these objections to the realist and logical positivist view of truth developed so as to undermine, or even threaten, the entire scientific endeavour, we must consider several aspects in the development which combined to produce this effect. Since the central theme in this discussion is the effect of changes in science itself which contributed to this threat, and these changes (like the already discussed change in the conception of reality) involve practically the whole history of modern science, we can discuss here no more than a few central issues which influenced the conception of truth in the social sciences more directly than others. It should be borne in mind that only for convenience, only to make their exposition easier, the issues are treated here one by one as if they had evolved separately from each other.

The most conspicuous feature in the post-modern philosophy is the central role given to a language both in the theory of mind and as a factor in shaping social relations. The former arose out of the *naturalization* of language, the idea that a natural language is a cognitive "faculty of mind" representing the most elementary way people can understand the world. The idea is related to the conception of the mind as an information processing device—part of a wider change in the conception of reality in which information takes a central position—but also to a controversial disagreement about reductionism, arising from the evolutionary approach.

Reductionism can be understood as either a metaphysical doctrine or as a methodological principle. The first means that the universe is organized in a hierarchy of complexity from the bottom up: properties of the elements on any level of organization (for example the molecular level) are the result of, and cannot have an effect on, properties of elements on a lower level (on the atomic level, in this example). A paradigmatic example for this reductionist view is the explanation of pressure in the theory of gases: the behaviour of a gas contained in an enclosed volume is described in terms of the pressure and temperature within this volume. Both are completely determined by molecular motion. Nothing is added to the gas, in spite of the fact that molecules need not be mentioned when pressure and temperature are measured. And the latter have no effect on the properties of the molecules, as found when studied on the molecular level.

There is a difference between the realist and the logical positivist interpretation of this hierarchy. Logical positivists are nominalists: the concept "pressure", in their opinion, is merely a name we give to the observed (the phenomenal) effect of molecular motion on their container. To say that this concept adds nothing to the description means that, on principle, it could have been given in terms of molecular motion alone. The use of the added concept is necessary because by introducing a compact mathematical formula it makes understanding possible. The methodological principle of reduction, then, by which the branches of science are hierarchically organized, is accepted purely on grounds of convenience. From which follows that if it will be found convenient to organize knowledge differently, it can be done. According to realists, the universe is in fact organized hierarchically, and barring possible mistakes, this organization of science correctly reflects the organization of the real universe. Although pressure is a property of a gas which emerges only from the condition of the molecules described by the theory of gases, the property is perfectly real. Moreover, according to them, far from being a mere matter of convenience, the methodological principle, is due to the logical constraint imposed on the organization of knowledge discussed in connection with the coherence theory of truth. It is the necessity to organize knowledge in logical systems that does not allow to mix levels of organization, if contradictions are to be avoided in the descriptions. This is because terms must retain their meanings, namely the way they are defined, throughout their use in a logical system. But pressure is not a property which can be assigned to a molecule, just as the properties of a water molecule cannot be assigned to hydrogen or oxygen.

This metaphysical difference between realism and logical positivism has no practical scientific consequences because both agree that there is no top-to-bottom influence in the hierarchy of the sciences. A more substantial controversy is introduced when this bottom-up principle is challenged. As we shall soon see, the challenge occurred on a lower level than the mental, but for the moment it is sufficient to note that with the acceptance of evolution—with the rejection of the Cartesian distinction between soul and body—speech and thought are seen as natural phenomena which, by the reductionist principle, ought to be explicable as arising from properties of, or processes in, the brain. Just as in the case of gases, the terms used in a theory of mind may be different from those used in the description of the brain, but nothing that can be understood as a higher mental level, a more complex brain function, ought to have any effect on functions of the brain described on a lower level. In fact, the meaning given to the presupposed causal relation between the world and the *perceived* phenomena (discussed at the beginning of this chapter, in connection with the interpretation of the coherence theory of truth by the Vienna Circle) adhered to this principle: psychologists in the empiricist tradition interpreted the principle as applying to sense perception alone. Concepts arise on the basis of these perceptions; they represent a higher level of brain activity, and they do not affect perception. But with the consideration of a language as a natural cognitive system, this interpretation of the principle has been challenged by some psychologists, who claim that the presupposed relation holds between one's environment and beliefs. While psychologists in the empiricist tradition take for granted that the perception of objects is a purely visual event, these psychologists claim that already on this level there is no way by which knowledge based on sense perception and knowledge based on higher levels of interpretation of the world can be distinguished from each other. For example Gibson argued that for a visual identification of a table there is no way by which one can distinguish between the perception of the features that can be explained in purely physiological terms and the perception of what the table "affords us", such as a surface to put things on. In other words, the perception of a table is determined by the conceived belief, expressible in an observation-statement like "this is a table", which distinguishes it from an object differing from it only in size, which affords us a place to sit on. In general, according to this view, more often than not one sees what the conceptual structure of one's world dictates.

The reductionist principle is challenged even more strongly when the relation between psychology and sociology, or any other social science, is considered in the light of the central role given to a language. The early pragmatist behaviorist approach stressed the effect of customary behavior on a conceptual structure. For example, since measuring is an important element in western activities, the assessment of distance, lengths and other measurements have had an effect on the modern person's cognitive system, and the related concepts entered the language. This is why William James focused his attention on psychology. For him, however, a particular language was a result rather than a cause of different patterns of behavior. Neo-pragmatists shift their attention to anthropology because in their opinion individuals acquire their *conceptual schemes* (roughly the set of concepts associated with what they take to be true or false) from the community into which they were born, and the medium by which their conceptual scheme is acquired is that community's language. Hence, if a society is a system of organized individuals, then there is a clear top-to-bottom influence: common actions depend on a common cognitive scheme, but the latter passes from person to person within a community.

What looks like a pure observation-statement is in fact a well established belief in a community which we call a common-sense belief.

It follows from this, that when neo-pragmatists assign to a language a central role in coping with reality there is no bottom-up construction in the description of how a language functions: a natural language represents a system of beliefs well established in a community, which determines what an individual take to be common sense. Beliefs are expressed by sentences. The meaning of each word in the language is determined by its role in expressing the meaning of a sentence, which is the same as saying that the meaning of a word is determined by its role in determining the truth of the belief. A new belief is always formed as a response to existing beliefs that for some reason raise doubt, and this is also how the meanings of words change. Two points are important. The first is that the sentence held true comes first, and its meaning is established by use and communication in a population, and thus is imposed on a person's mind from top-to-bottom. And the second point is that in order to understand what is meant by thinking of a language as a cognitive faculty of the mind it is necessary to understand what is meant by saying that a sentence *expresses* a belief. The term "express" may suggest a possibility of distinguishing between a belief and its expression. This is indeed what is implied when one says that a particular change in the language was a result of changes in cognition, which in turn is determined by changes in some pattern of behavior. The implication means that a distinction can be made between, for example, what J. Fodor calls *the language of thought* and its expression by a spoken language. But the central idea in the neo-pragmatist version of the naturalization of a language is that this is not possible: it makes no sense, in their opinion, to distinguish between *saying* that the senstence "snow is white" is true and *thinking*, believing, or knowing, that snow is white. All of them simply mean that the sentence is taken to be true.

This naturalization of a language implies a change in the conception of phenomenalism. As we have seen, modern realism changed the conception of phenomenalism from being a distorting obstacle to the possibility of perceiving the real world as it is, into a limiting factor of science, limiting the scope of what we can know or should consider true knowledge. But if perception from its earliest formation comes structured by a natural language, as neo-pragmatists claim, then the existence of different languages means that there are as many *perceived* worlds as there are different languages. The neo-pragmatist conclusion from this version of phenomenalism is that it is legitimate to say that a language as a whole represents an intersubjective view of reality common to the speakers of that language, but it is not legitimate to say that people speaking a particular language may claim that their representation of reality is better, or more universally intersubjective, than the representation in the language of other people, let alone the possibility to represent the world as it is.

Although this is the central idea in support of relativism, other changes in the approach to science had their effect on the concept of truth. As noted earlier, a major factor in changing the conception of knowledge has been Darwin's theory of evolution, where the central concept is natural selection. Darwin's idea was borrowed from Thomas Malthus: organisms reproduce themselves beyond the capacity of their environment to sustain their offspring. Hence, the latter compete for survival. Darwin observed that although similar to their parents in their main properties, offsprings were not exactly the same, and Nature somehow favored those who were best adapted to environmental pressures. The idea that Nature favored them, rather than that their own success leads to survival, was due to his firm belief in Newtonian science, and its mechanistic view of the world. According to him evolution was directed by a force external to the organism, which he called natural selection. Although he did not describe *how* natural selection worked, he and his followers were convinced that its description as a *mechanism* was appropriate, and that it must eventually be discovered, because without it, natural selection appeared to be directed by the organisms' purposeful attempt to adapt to new circumstances. This was, in fact, Lamarck's theory, which preceded Darwin's. Lamarck maintained that evolution occurred as a result of an inherent tendency of a living creature to adapt to its environment. He thought that this tendency explained the constant increase in the complexity of organisms. Darwin rejected the idea. Like all events in nature, natural selection must have a causal explanation. The mechanistic view of the world did not allow adaptation to be purposeful, hence natural selection must find its place in the ever increasing hierarchy of complexity without introducing purpose.

The strange point in this disagreement is that Lamarck retained the reductionist idea that properties emerging in a population are based on properties of individuals. But the retainment of this bottom-up process has been achieved by introducing purposeful behavior to living creatures. The rejection of the latter retains the mechanistic view of nature but at the expense of "pure" reductionism.

It took more than fifty years for the modern view of evolution to come up with a mechanism of natural selection. Its description introduced two more basic concepts: the gene, which as a molecule in a gas remains on the whole as unaltered in the higher level description of an organism, and mutations—occasional mistakes either in the reproduction or in the recombination of genes in the process of fertilization—are responsible for the dissimilarities between parents and offspring which Darwin observed. Mutations occur in individuals, but natural selection, as a force which alters species, acts on populations, and its description requires the use of statistics.

Statistical methods have been used earlier. In the nineteenth century Gauss introduced the normal curve (the so called bell curve) to deal with the distribution of errors, as a response to the fact that in astronomy measurements often yielded different results. The distance of a star from the earth was obviously taken to have an exact constant value. Hence the variability of measurements had to be attributed to errors. In his theory of gases, Boltzmann used the same curve to describe the real variation of molecular motion. The molecules remained unchanged but the important point is that, although their real movements are not errors of the observer, they have no effect on the properties of the gas as a whole. In spite of being real their total motion is precisely determined by mechanics, and the variation can be seen as fluctuations about an average, so that this average, called the expected value of every molecule's speed, is sufficient for determining the pressure and temperature of the gas. The fluctuations, then, can be ignored.

Statisticians call a gas, or a species, or any system of components to which their method applies, a *population*. The important innovation in the description of natural selection is that the variability *within* a population cannot be ignored as it is in the theory of gases: mutations are chance events, the occurrence of which cannot be exactly determined, and these small changes in individual organisms can accumulate and eventually cause a change in, or a splitting of, the species.

The mechanism explains both variation within species and natural selection. Real variation is due to the fact that many mutations lead to neutral changes, changes which afford neither advantage nor disadvantage with respect to the survival of the species. A significant disadvantage is a change which leads to the death of the organism before the age of reproduction, and a significant advantage is a change which increases its chances of survival beyond that age, thus increasing the proportion of those individuals in the population that carry the genes which determine the advantageous property.

Concerning the conception of truth, we should note that when the distribution of errors was introduced by Gauss, its purpose was to remove subjective error. In other words, to calculate away subjective differences in order to obtain an objective measurement. When statistics was first accepted as a respectable method for obtaining objective measurements, psychologists, social scientists and even statisticians, tended to see all variation as akin to error. With the impact of Boltzmann's theory of gases, and particularly when the existence of indeterminate chance occurrences was accepted in particle physics (the ground flour of the hierarchically constructed universe), the use of statistics spread to all branches of science as representing real variation. But even then, psychologists and social scientists thought of variation as unimportant deviations from, or fluctuations around, a fixed structural pattern.

An important theoretical support for this assumption has been that the mathematical equation of both distributions, namely of the distribution of errors and of the distribution of random variation, is the same. And the support seems to be strengthened by the fact that evolutionary theory can explain the similarity: the fact that the distribution of errors forms a bell curve can be explained as representing a distribution of real differences in people's ability to measure exactly, arising for example from differences in their acuity of vision. The curve of the distribution of errors represents the random variation of this visual property which, being neutral with respect to survival, remains stable in the population. The problem with this support is that the stability of such variation cannot be the same for the whole human species at all times. A hunter with poor vision in the Stone Age had a smaller chance of survival than an astronomer in the nineteenth century who could use spectacles and a telescope.

The point of this example is that, at least where the human species is concerned, it introduces a cultural factor in the determination of what can and what cannot be considered random variation. In other words, what came to represent a given fact has depended on the cultural environment within which modern people lived, on the ways they could survive and on the knowledge that enabled them to produce spectacles to increase their chances for survival.

The dependency of survival on a level of cultural development, and in particular on science and technology, is not surprising in itself, but in the context of the contribution of the use of statistics to the recent devaluation of the concept of truth, the point is that it revived doubts about phenomenalism and objectivity, or the possibility to attain universal intersubjectivity. This is because in a mathematically-described theory, every calculated measurement is expected to fall on the particular mathematical curve which corresponds to the relevant causal law, and the methodological requirement is that only if the law covers all observed cases can it be considered true or real. Where statistical laws prevail, hardly any observed case falls on the calculated curve, and hence most cases seem to violate the law. The assumption behind the conviction that in spite of this fact, a curve drawn according to statistical calculations describes a real causal relation between the variables, is that actual measurements are fluctuations about this real causal relation that can be ignored. As a result, truth seems again to be hidden behind the phenomena. Consequently the method threatened to turn phenomenalism again into a screen between observers and reality, unless there is a very convincing reason to believe that such a causal relation in fact holds. But what kind of good reasons can we have except the reliance on measurements?

When Logical-positivism and pragmatism became influential, statistical methods were a-priori supposed to represent either errors or such fluctuations that could be ignored. Hence, in their opinion there was a reasonable escape from this unwelcome threat to phenomenalism in the form of their own definition of truth, which did not require such unobtainable good reasons, independently of observations. Since, according to them, the function of all knowledge is to cope with environmental pressures, a law can be considered true when its application makes prediction possible, providing the possibility to control that aspect of life which it describes. Prediction and control warrants the assertibility of the law, and not any realist assumption. But once it is accepted that a statistically described curve represents real variability, which as shown in evolution, may affect the future behavior of the correlated variables, this identification of causality with predictability looses its validity.

The dissociation of causality and predictability is accentuated with the solution of the question how mutations can accumulate so as to cause a splitting of a species or the emergence of a new one. Mutations are chance events and thus not predictable. But the solution in question is based on the observed fact that the properties of species do not appear to change one by one. If an organism is seen as a system of interacting processes, then as long as the system works well—as long as each process responds to external stimuli as expected—the interacting processes do not interfere with each other. This is described as saying that the expected output to a given input in each described process is not affected either by the fluctuations around its own expected value, or by those around the expected values of other processes. This is the situation when internal variation can be ignored. But when an external stimulus, like a sudden appearance of a new predator, or any physical or chemical change in the environment (described as a new input to such a system) requires a drastic change in response (described as an output of the system as a whole) the adequate response cannot anymore be the expected one. Instead, an unusual combination of particular fluctuations causes a drastic change in the organism's internal state, and then, if it does not die, its system of processes is reorganized to meet the challenge. Such situations are points of bifurcation in the description of the population: up to that point the component organisms can be considered similar and their behavior is predictable. But after it, more than one reorganization is possible, and the form which a particular system will take after its own reorganization is unpredictable.

The idea of non-predictability does more than undermining the idea that absolute truth can ever be obtained. Knowledge of an absolute truth, as noted in connection to Spinoza's mechanistic view, is knowledge of a world that is copletely determined by natural laws to its last detail. As we have seen when discussing the consequences of the coherence theory of truth, the constraint imposed on science by the requirement of logical consistency introduced the idea that such complete knowledge of reality is most probably unattainable, because not all areas of research can be arranged in logical order. But as long as "the world as it is" is supposed to be so ordered, this impossibility reflects a human limitation, rather than reality. However, if the world itself is supposed to be contingent, to include chance events which *on principle* may evolve in different ways, then non-predictability is due to the real world, and not to our limitations. For example, in spite of Darwin's and Lamarcke's disagreement about the attribution of purpose to an organism, both interpreted evolution as inevitable progress, as a necessary result of a cumulative effect of adaptations of species to their environments; as an ever increasing complexity of organisms better equipped to deal with their environment, culminating in the appearance of mankind. But if an organism is described as a system that may be reorganized in different ways, then (as for example S.J. Gould maintains) neither increased complexity nor progress, in any sense of the word, are guaranteed. It is then non-predictability that becomes inevitable: absolute truth, in the above mentioned sense, is not merely unattainable: it does not exist. The question is whether this is the only possible interpretation of knowing the world as it is.

The dissociation of predictability from causality is accepted by statistitians as a fundamental cautionary principle, that no extrapolation from a curve is legitimate unless we have very good reasons to assume that the validity of the law can be extended in time. Only in this case can predictions be made, because only then the supposed trend can be expected to continue and deviations can be ignored. In other words, while the nature of evidence shifted from the realist notion of verification (or falsification) to the pragmatist notion of satisfaction of a need to predict and control, has had no serious effect on most branches of natural science, this is not the case in the social sciences: when social scientists take prediction and control to be the only purpose of science, and use statistics for attaining this purpose, they implicitly presuppose that no change in the trend is possible. But this is the assumption that pragmatists ought to reject if their approach is based on the theory of evolution. And this is indeed the rejection implied by the dependency of statistical assumptions on cultural (as opposed to natural) developments as the example of the hunter and the astronomer suggests.

The result concerning objectivity as a scientist's neutral attitude is similar. Logical positivists in the Vienna Circle assigned the greatest value to evidence given by individual scientists. They could do so because, in their opinion, when these observations differed from each other they could be regarded as random deviations from a correct expected value and therefore could be ignored. Only the statistically obtained expected value counted as an objective, or true, observation. When social scientists use statistics they do not ask themselves whether they are justified in considering the variation in their own observations to be insignificant, or random. They implicitly presuppose it.

In conclusion, the presupposition that differences in observations can be ignored introduces an unacceptable bias into some types of research. Alternatively stated, the use of statistics in science has introduced a new constraint on the validity of a scientific theory—on the type of research that can justifiably be considered scientific. If the coherence theory of truth restricted the possibility of creating an objective science, by allowing this possibility only in domains where logical contradictions were not expected, the use of statistical methods restricts their extension in time: claims of objectivity for such created science is allowed only when variation between particulars is supposed not to affect predictions, and only to the period that predictability is likely to hold. Moreover, it confines the validity of equating objectivity to intersubjectivity to those descriptions where, at least on principle, it can be legitimately assumed that variations between subjective observers can be ignored.

These two constraints reflect the pragmatists' and hermeneticts' worries in different terms: they raise the question whether a true description according to the approach of the natural sciences is at all possible in human affairs. Whether it can ever be assumed that no contradictions are to be expected in a system of desires and beliefs, and whether it can ever be ascertained, or reasonably argued, that internal differences between individuals concerning their interests and beliefs can be described as mere fluctuations that can be ignored.

Assuming that at least some aspects of social affairs can be studied scientifically, the question arises whether the method of studying them is nevertheless essentially different from that used in natural science. Whether a Lamarckian approach is not introduced when we consider cultural evolution. If knowledge is assumed to be experienced as useful for survival, we can ask how does a society choose which knowledge to transmit and which to reject? Both modern and post-modern intellectuals may agree that, for example, the assumption of universal rationality is not a thesis about a natural human mind but is the cultural legacy of the Enlightenment. But even if they agree on this assumption, and hence agree also that the aim of modern science similarly evolved in the same tradition, they may still differ about whether they can or ought to transmit this legacy. Modern scientists and philosophers have always assumed that the assumption of universality was to enhance human freedom and welfare, but post-modern thinkers fear that hidden assumptions of universality behind factual diversity lead to the undemocratic suppression of subjective wills and rationalities. This difference leads us to the second of the two questions we posed on p.108: whether we need to rely on truth in order to achieve a social goal.

Only if the possibility of choice is acknowledged does the moral question arise. But the attempt to insert humanity into the general process of evolution brought with it another possibility. In fact, the shift of emphasis from individuals to populations, and from isolated causal relations to systems of such relations, brought with it a new mechanistic view of the world, of the mind, of societies, and also of knowledge.

Metaphorically we may say that the model of a system ceased to be the industrial machine (which in the nineteenth century replaced the original Newtonian clockwork as the metaphor) and became an information-processing machine. In an industrial machine the structure and the behavior of the machine remain the same throughout the entire process of production. In an information processing machine like a computer the hardware structure also remains the same but its internal processes and behavior do not. Its behavior depends on the impact of information on its internal processes, the software. An input is described as information when it changes that internal state of the system which regulates its behavior. For example, when a new input changes the stored information in the nervous system of an organism and thus affects its behavior.

This view of an organism as an information-processing machine is quite general. In fact, what has been described as hardware in the previous paragraph can be described as the output of the genetic information stored in DNA. Although the process is still not known, the non-reductionist aspect of this view is in the fact that genes are the same in all cells, but different genes are activated in them presumably by input-information being transmitted to them in various locations, thus bringing about their different structures and functions. An organism whose behavior is guided by such internal interaction of its stored information is a self-sustaining system in the sense that it reorganizes itself according to the impact of incoming information. The consideration of genetics and physiology in this way does not concern us here. For our discussion the point is that this view suggests that both a human being and a social system can also be seen in this way. According to this view, changes occurring in both can be explained by analogy with the approach to natural systems, because any input (whether sense data or interpreted sentences) constitutes information in the sense described above.

A difference between this and the old mechanistic view is in the fact that the future of all systems in a state of transition or of self reorganization is not predictable. This non-predictability, in the sense of being in fact indeterminate is, however, restricted to states of transition even in the case of changing social systems. This restriction is obscured by the fact that even in stable states of complex organisms and societies the very complexity of interacting causal relations makes predictability, in the epistemological sense, very difficult if not impossible. But on principle, complexity in itself does not imply non-predictability although it is less precise than predictions based on isolated causal laws.

Seen in this way, the idea that the behavior of people in a society must be explained in terms of interests and beliefs is interpreted as saying that interests and beliefs are the products of information; they are the software stored in the brains of people, and the carrier of this type of information is a language. In a homogeneous and stable social system, variable interests and beliefs are regarded as no more significant than random fluctuations in a natural stable system. When a society is not stable it may look for a time to be on the point of disintegration, but in fact, barring the actual death of all its members the system reorganizes itself to meet the challenging destabilising effect. In this case, the resulting form of reorganization is unpredictable.

A language too is considered to be a system, and like mathematics in the realist view, it has an objective existence, in the sense of being independent of *particular* minds, and as in modern realism, objectivity is taken to mean universal intersubjectivity. When the categories of a language are believed to be the most basic carriers of information, as neo-pragmatists claim (as well as those psychologists, like Gibson, who claim that these categories affect perception), then different languages are metaphorically compared to different coordinate systems in mathematics: Just as Einstein's argument has shown that what seemed to be universally intersubjective to earlier physicists, for example the simultaneity of events, is in fact intersubjective only for those who observe the events relative to the same coordinate system, so what seems to scientists in our society to be intersubjectively acceptable facts are in fact intersubjective only to the speakers of the same language.

If a set of beliefs in a society is seen in this way, then Kuhn's idea of normal science means that normally scientists believe in the set of sentences which most members of a scientific community take to be true and objective (real information). And this intersubjective assertion is the only meaning of truth. When the system of beliefs is stable, personal deviations from common beliefs are ignored as having no effect, and eventually disappear. But occasionally there is a point of bifurcation: two ideas compete for recognition, and when one of them wins the contest the system of beliefs reorganizes itself to accommodate this result, and with this reorganization, basic categories in the language may also change.

To say that the system of beliefs reorganizes itself, is the essence of the new mechanistic view. Just as an organism has no effect on the process of natural selection so, according to this view, people have no say in the way systems of belief change. Obviously people decide which ideas to accept and which to reject, but these decisions simply represent outputs of lower level systems of desires and beliefs, which are as mechanistically explicable as any other form of behavior. By another interpretation, the one which restores a Lamarckian factor to cultural history, people may control, if not always do control, the reorganization of the system, so that purpose and reasons find their place.

Both interpretations are possible within the pragmatist tradition, where a particular linguistic expression is created within a specific context of coping with a particular aspect of real life. Within such a context the meaning of the linguistic expression is determined by its function. The idea that a language and a way of life are related in this manner is not new. In the 1920s the linguist Edward Sapir concluded from this assumption that languages vary without limit because ways of life do; and starting from the same assumption, the anthropologist Whorf who studied the culture of the Hopi argued that without our understanding their language we cannot understand their culture, but without understanding their culture we cannot understand their language. Hence he concluded that cultures are closed systems.

Two points stressed by the neo-pragmatist version of the same assumption are important. The first is that since the meaning of every word is determined by its use in a particular context, the meaning of the word "true" is no exception. And the second is that the truths of logic are also no exception. The second point was introduced by Quine. In the introduction to his *Methods of Logic,* Quine explains why the principles of logic (and mathematics) seem to be necessarily true or accepted a-priori independently of any experience. It has been a decision of empiricists, he says, (a decision associated with the correspondence conception of truth), to allocate priority to statements with empirical content when claiming objectivity for a system as a whole. There is however another priority (associated with the coherence conception of truth, or with the idea that beliefs form an inter-related system) which arises from the fact that there is never a unique system of statements that is compatible with experience. Faced with unexpected experience we are never forced to reject a particular statement. Therefore the more fundamental a component of a theory is to our conceptual scheme, the less likely we are to choose it for revision. This is the central pragmatist principle, in Quine's opinion. It is "a conservative preference for revisions which disturb the system least". An all-pervasive fact, concept, or theoretical principle which in the past has served us well is psychologically simply too "expensive" to be discarded. The principles of logic (and mathematics) are so central to our conceptual scheme that in practice they enjoy immunity from revision. Therefore they seem to be inherent in the mind.

However, a neo-pragmatist observes that experience is organized as logical systems only in western societies, and that the priority given to logical thinking in these societies is not universal—it is not shared by all other societies. Hence, the presupposition of modern realism, that for a scientist (or for one who attempts to understand the world as it is), to be rational is equivalent to thinking logically, is also not universal. Consequently the *possibility* of obtaining an intersubjective description even of the natural world becomes questionable.

Concerning the first point, that the meaning of truth, as the meaning of any other word, is determined by its use in a particular context, neo-pragmatists suggest that the logical positivist idea, that the meaning of a word is the method of its verification, may be retained as the meaning of truth in the empirical sciences because there it is used in this sense. But we should neither transfer this use elsewhere, where it cannot have this meaning, nor interpret its assertion in the realist sense.

As we have seen, both realists and logical positivists accept the distinction between facts, those empirical statements ascertained as true, and values, to which the term does not apply. The idea, however, does not fit in a theory that explains all behavior as being guided by desires and beliefs, and that attributes a central role to a language in shaping these beliefs. In such a theory of mind the concept of truth must be as central as the perception of objects has been for empiricists. When an object is seen, no question arises about its being there, but the very nature of a belief is that taking it to be true implies that it can be false. In other words, if one replaces the empiricists' presupposed causal relation between one's environment and one's sense perception by a relation between one's environment and one's beliefs, and the latter is equated to a sentence being taken true, then it is not *possible* to do away with the concept of truth in any domain of action, let alone a domain of inquiry.

Donald Davidson, for example, explains that if a response to environmental stimuli is supposed to be guided by beliefs, then sentences rather than words must be considered to be the basic carriers of meaningful information, and this means that the meaning of a word is derived from its function in understanding the sentence. If this is supposed to hold down to the level of perception, then this must be equivalent to deriving the meaning of every word by observing the conditions under which the sentence is held true. In his opinion, this dependency of meaning on the conditions of truth presupposes that a user of a language must have a primitive notion of truth which characterizes human thought.

A primitive concept is a concept that cannot be defined in terms of other concepts, and that the explanation within which it appears cannot do without it. In other words, in Davidson's opinion, if the language gets the central cognitive position which it holds in the neo-pragmatist view, then no matter how basic or common it is, no pattern of behavior can exist that is not based on a guiding belief, whether the belief is about the physical reality, about other people or about morality.

In short, when pragmatists equate a belief to a tendency to behave in a way which proved successful in the past, from which they conclude that a statement is true when one can act upon it with confidence, they forget their own assumption that tendencies to behave are determined within a context of a particular interpretation of reality, and that any belief which enters an interpretation, whether scientific or moral, must be taken to be true if one is to act upon it at all. It follows that the idea that knowing is coping successfully with one's external reality *presupposes* the concept of truth rather than defines it.

All that a pragmatist can claim is that the scientific way of ascertaining truth is not the only way we use, or ought to use, the term. But this claim is obvious. Even if we accept the pragmatist-behaviorist assumption that the belief that "$2 + 1 = 3$" is a universal truth evolved together with the invention of numbers and learning to count, it is still reasonable to maintain that because practicing the skill of mathematics has been divorced from its application in various domains, this truth is understood to be different from that of saying that one has two brothers and one sister, or from considering whether numbers are mere names or are the real alphabet of God's language. In each of these cases the reason for holding the statement to be true is different.

The same example shows how the primitive, undefined, concept of truth gets a particular meaning which has to do with the way truth is ascertained. This is not very different from the fact that in ascertaining that economic efficiency is good or that equity is good we may use different criteria of goodness, but in order to make the distinction one has to have a primitive conception of good and evil.

Realist social scientists may accept this differentiation of the concept of truth, but if they do, neo-pragmatists still hold that a difference between them remains. Davidson, for example, explains that if realists agree with him that a primitive concept of truth must be attributed to the human mind, they take his argument to mean that we in fact must have such a primitive concept. But in his opinion, we do not know whether we do or do not have it. All he has shown is that if one holds that all knowledge depends on having a language, and this implies the differentiation of a primitive concept of truth, then the existence of a primitive concept of truth must be presupposed by those who hold this theory. It is a *theory*, a description of phenomena which requires presuppositions, but this does not *prove* the existence of the presupposed. The existence of my father, he explains, does not prove my existence. But if he is to be described as my father, then my existence must be presupposed. In the same sense, the neo-pragmatist theory of mind must presuppose the existence of a conception of truth, but another theory need not do so. In order to conclude from this theory that we in fact must have a primitive concept of truth, we must prove, or at least assume, that this theory is the only possible description of mental phenomena. But this is exactly what pragmatists learned not to assume.

A modern realist approach admits the possibility of drastic changes in theories and concepts as a response to new information. As we have seen, the well established transformation laws lost their universal validity and the concept of simultaneity lost its invariability when Einstein's theory of relativity replaced Newton's. But in the neo-pragmatist theory of knowledge a system of beliefs seems to have acquired a life of its own. Beliefs compete for survival in their "environment of ideas". They take hold or change in the minds of people but, like natural selection, a cultural selection works on the system as a whole. A system of beliefs is held by a social system as an acceptable response to the impact of information: a change in the latter *causes* a change in the response. Human history is essentially the history of social adaptations to the changing impact of any new types of information. Therefore, Quine's pragmatic principle may be taken to be an explanation of the changes in a system of beliefs, but only within a system of beliefs in which pragmatism is a basic idea. The neglected point in this interpretation is that in spite of this total dependency of individual beliefs on the systems which they inhabit, Quine's assertion that we are never forced to reject a particular component of a theory is not refuted. Neo-pragmatists still hold that it is to a certain extent up to a society to decide what it wishes to revise, and they prefer moral to scientific grounds for revision. But they also hold that at least in our society there is no unique system of beliefs. Since moral principles, like any other belief, have only to fit *a* system, on what grounds is the moral decision to be made in our society?

In conclusion, the novel anthropological or neo-pragmatist approach in the philosophy of science, raises new problems. On the one hand it claims to provide an objective description of different social systems with their different systems of beliefs, and on the other hand, it denies the possibility to provide *any* objective description on the grounds that the observers are as much prisoners of their own tradition as the observed, and they cannot adopt the necessary neutral attitude for creating such descriptions.

The "first hand" implies that with their anthropological approach these philosophers, or social scientists, claim for themselves the realist objectivity, the neutral attitude, which they deny to the observed members of a community. The "second hand", which consistently denies the possibility of a neutral attitude, implies cultural relativism. An early version of the latter says that each cultural community is a closed system: it creates that type of conception of the world (knowledge) which suits its own needs, while these needs are themselves determined by this conception. The latest version claims to be pluralistic: it denies the existence of a homogeneous community, and therefore the possibility of an intersubjective theory even within one national community.

Since these are the theories of knowledge which compete in our society we face serious questions. For example, can we, as the first possibility implies, retain what we find valuable in modern science without accepting its concept of truth and objectivity? If this possibility is denied, can the social sciences or the study of history do without these concepts altogether? Can we attain social or moral aims without or with a different concept of truth? And if so what does it mean to have a different concept of truth? Finally, is it up to a community to decide which concept of truth is to be used?

In our community, those who believe in the value of science and wish to retain it, need not reject the pragmatist view altogether. The central argument against the prophets of post-modern neo-pragmatism is based on the predictable consequences of their views. After all, the question of choice (as opposed to chance) arises only within a cultural framework in which prediction, even if limited, is taken to be possible, and the wish to control human reality holds a central position. This control may be possible by deciding not only what to revise in theories found false but also what and how to transmit knowledge. Quine's pragmatic principle implies choice concerning revision *within* theories, provided contradictions are not to be expected. This means that the pragmatic, or other social, principles which guide the reorganization of a theory are not included in the theory itself. This inevitable separation between a theory and a metatheory, between a theory and the reflection on what one is doing when constructing it, means that no matter how much science is expanded there will always remain an unbridgeable gap between the explainer and the explained. This seems to be the minimal evidence for the necessity, and not merely the possibility, of choice. It seems, however, that in spite of their declarations to the contrary, both neo-pragmatism and post modern philosophy imply that we do not have a choice. Their view fits a new interpretation of the "invisible hand" which directs all processes (universal or evolutionary) as part of the new version of an information-processing mechanistic view of reality.

For obvious reasons only a few examples can be given here to illustrate the issues raised in this short historical description. They are given in the next two chapters. The first, on the philosophy of science, is elaborated with the purpose of highlighting the consequences of accepting the neo-pragmatist view, and to show that without a deliberate quest for truth the scientific endeavour as we know it will most probably disappear. In the second chapter the possibility is considered that some prerequisites of science are already threatened and their disappearance might be imminent.

14

Truth and Expediency: Some Philosophical Observations Concerning Science

The neo-pragmatist ideas described in the previous chapter developed mainly in the United States. In France the new development arose out of the hermeneutic tradition, mainly as an attempt to revise marxism. Nevertheless, the problems that they have raised, and their essential effect on the conception of truth, are similar. Therefore, Latour's following analysis is chosen for illustrating the anthropological approach to science. A scientific fact, he says, receives its significance only within the socially-structured practice of its study. Crystallography could hardly have evolved without such social institutions as museums in which crystal collections are preserved. In his opinion the question whether crystals would not also exist in nature if they were not collected is irrelevant, or even "illegitimate," because without the institutions which collect them they would remain *unknown*. Similarly, an apparently simple statement that in "naked" nature water freezes at zero degrees centigrade would have remained meaningless without the creation of thermometers and without the incorporation of this so-called fact into our everyday life. It is only the socially-acquired meaning of measuring temperature which turns the statement into an undisputed fact. And again, since 1930 when Pluto was discovered we know of the planet's existence and we know that it had also existed before this date. But this knowledge became significant only because it was brought into our world by further research about its satellites and atmosphere etc. In other words, without becoming part of our socially-organized world all such facts would not have become part of the *phenomena* (which means by definition the observed world) that science purports to describe. To think of crystals, scientific laws or planets existing independently of whether we know about them or not simply repudiates the contribution of scientists to knowledge.

Three claims are made in this short description. First, that human creativity plays a major role in the expansion of our known reality—scientists bring crystals and thermometers into our phenomenal world by placing them in museums and laboratories. Second, that without institutionalized science, an individual's knowledge, or ideas, cannot become a social asset and cannot accumulate—to become significant means not to be dismissed or forgotten. Third, that each new scientific *fact* is constructed rather than discovered. The last claim postulates that the acceptance of any phenomenon as a fact, or its description as true, depends on that knowledge which has become a public asset in relation to which it is interpreted.

Latour's exposition, and in particular the idea that facts are constructed rather than discovered, introduces the paradoxical claim that an objective description of social organizations, like his own description of a scientific community, is possible, but an objective science created by this community is not.

Like pragmatists and structuralists, Latour postulates that science cannot be separated from other types of structured knowledge which help us cope with our environment. And he emphasizes that although our views and motivations are created by our environment, this environment is to a large extent created by ourselves in the light of this structured knowledge. If one adopts this point of view *without reservations* it becomes self-evident that scientists cannot be seen as breaking away from society in order to observe it, or anything else, objectively.

Latour's idea that truth and objectivity are the creations of a society can be illustrated by the following example. In Egypt an ancient goddess was found who had the head of an ibis. The ibis, according to Egyptian mythology, ate snakes. It was thought that without this god-ordained protection the land would be infested by snakes and people would not be able to live there. And in fact, in his *Natural History and the Mythology of the Ibis* (1805), Savigny confirmed that the remains of snakes were found in most stomachs of mummified ibises discovered in Egypt. As Savigny knew that an ibis does not eat snakes, he explained that the snakes must have been inserted in the mummies, adding that the priests who inserted them did not intend to mislead the people but to convey to them a deeper truth. By this deeper truth he presumably meant the idea of the purposeful creation of nature in the service of mankind.

The example supports Quine's claim that the more a principle is central for the interpretation of reality, the more it is immune to revision. Convinced that nature was created for the benefit of mankind, the priests preferred to doubt the evidence of their eyes when confronted with a stomach of an ibis rather than dismiss a principle so central to their interpretation of reality. They treated the missing snakes in their stomachs as accidental events, and considered the insertion of snakes in them as a correction. There is, of course, another possibility. The priests were not interested in truth but in a social cohesion which would give them power. They sought ways to persuade their public and found such ways.

Both possibilities are anachronistically presented here, but they illustrate the two approaches to knowledge characterized by the Greek distinction between philosophy and sophistry. Savigny did not consider the possibility of sophistry. If he was right, Latour's three claims mean, first, that the priests or whoever mummified the birds created the expansion of the ancient Egyptians' known reality by bringing the snake-eating ibis into their phenomenal world through preserving it in the temples. Second, that without the institutionalized priesthood this idea about the function of the ibis as the protector of humanity would not have become part of Egyptian mythology. And third, that the social concern about snakes drove the priests to construct (rather than discover) a fact about the ibis in the light of their genuine belief that the world was created in the service of mankind.

According to the anthropological approach to science, the question then arises how Savigny came to see different *facts* about the ibis. A familiar answer lies in the change which came with the Copernican revolution. Initially the Copernican revolution meant not seeing the earth as the center of the universe, but in time it came to mean a general readiness not to put human interest at the center of attention in the search for knowledge about the natural world. Crystals and birds ceased to be looked upon as having an inherent function for human existence. In the pragmatists' conception this changed approach was the concomitant of a shift toward a new social interest.

In spite of all other changes which occurred between the birth of modern science and the end of the nineteenth century, natural philosophers and scientists took this change of attitude, ceasing to put human interest at the center of attention in the search for knowledge about the natural world, to be the essential aspect of objectivity. Controversies about the relation between science and religion continued. The humanist replacement of God by Man as the center of attention was never complete. But scientists were to be committed to look at the world as it is, and the presupposition behind this was that rational human beings are able to see and understand the world provided they disregard their *personal* interests. The pragmatists' point was that this novel commitment represented a new *socially-determined* interest related to the era's new commercial and industrial activities.

The social determination of this interest can be explained in terms of a socially-endorsed desire to explore the natural properties of things, and a belief widely held in society that the knowledge gained in this way leads best to the utilization of these properties. Crystals were brought into our phenomenal world as raw material for jewels and other purposes before museums existed, just as the ibis was probably known to many Egyptians before they became mythological symbols. But with the new interest and the associated new belief, the function of museums became to display natural objects as they are, independently of common use. The creation of museums reflects a human interest, just as the mummifying of the ibis had done before.

Latour's third claim, that facts are constructed, means more than the dependency of observation-statements on theoretical ones, which as pointed out in the previous chapter was already accepted by the Vienna Circle. His claim is a generalization achieved by dramatizing the idea that, for example, a fact like the measured temperature of water depends on the invented method of measurement and on the validity of the theory on which the invention depends. Ice and the freezing of water were known before such methods were invented, but according to Latour, their very perception changed after these practices had been introduced.

One aspect of Latour's paradoxical claim that an objective description of a scientific community is possible but an objective science created by this community is not, is his attempt to turn the philosophy of science into a social science. Prior to him, behaviorists like Skinner tried to incorporate epistemology in psychology. The difference between Latour and Skinner originated from the idea that the relevant interests and beliefs commonly held in these branches of philosophy are, as pointed out in the previous chapter, social rather than psychological facts. Latour does not reject the requirement to exclude his own personal interests or beliefs when he observes scientists at their work, because he still believes in the utility of disinterested observation. He asserts that as an anthropologist, that is as an external observer, he can find out the principles of science better by observing what scientists do than by asking them what they think these principles are. Whether aware of it or not, he is guided by the principles of modern, realist, anthropology. He disregards the question inherent in his own analysis whether in this case he is not simply following the principles which are still endorsed by his own community, whether his observations can be true in any other sense than a modern convention, perhaps because he takes this relativism for granted. But if so, his own account is no more than a post-modern mythology.

In fact, Latour does not seem to doubt that his own account is not a mere mythology. He accepts the pragmatist (or structuralist) view that an adequate anthropological explanation can neither ignore the common motives of observed people for resolving (for coping with) particular problems in their community, nor ignore their reasons for choosing one way for solving them rather than another. But his interpretation of the role of scientists in the determination of the systems of beliefs applied in the attempt to solve these problems fits the new interpretation of the "invisible hand," an interpretation that replaces the mechanistic determinism of the natural world by a social determinism.

In Latour's opinion, there is no point in asking scientists how they do what they are doing or what they want to do, because what individuals think they are doing is not reliable, and certainly not reliable when we want to know what a social *system* is doing and how it does it. A society, like the universe, simply does not behave intentionally. In spite of his reverence for the scientists' contribution to knowledge, Latour does not regard the scientists' wish to understand their subject matter or their wish to shape their scientific research, and what they believe that they are doing, as a factor in the scientific system.

Like Kuhn, Latour takes *social* reality to be crucial for good science, and both rightly take the methodology employed in science to be part of western cultural reality. The essential difference between their view of scientific method and, for example Popper's, lies in their acceptance of the *deterministic* view in explaining the creation of knowledge and Popper's emphasis of the inevitable separation, mentioned at the end of the previous chapter, between any explanation and the reflection on what one is doing when constructing it.

For Popper the critical attitude, the understanding that a rational person must be aware of the snares in following any method or theory, has since the seventeenth century been a crucial part of successful scientific, social and institutional advancement. Science as serving particular human interests, whether these are general economic interests, as Marx maintained, or more particularly directed to the improvement of technology, as followers of Heidegger maintain, may or may not survive without this critical attitude. But according to Popper if we loose the critical attitude in research, science is unlikely to remain a factor in the shaping of our way of life.

Hermeneutics took this point as a reason for making a distinction between scientific knowledge, which in their opinion evolved to be inherently related to the production of technology, and understanding of human spiritual or cultural activities. By these alone, because of the inclusion of values in the analysis, may we understand the relation between the purposeful human beings that we are, and science and the world.

Habermas turned this view into a distinction between natural and social science. Popper rejected the hermeneutic approach because in his opinion the most important achievements of science were due to the careful separation between facts on the one hand and values, interests, aims and philosophical insights, on the other. This separation does not imply that values, interests or insights cannot be true. It simply protects us not only from fruitless speculation but also from harmful wishful thinking. For him this is the best reason for persevering with the adoption of a narrowly-defined concept of truth in science even if it had been accepted in the first place only as a defence against the influence of religion.

This methodological point is a central argument, for example, in Popper's attack on psychoanalysis. It is not an attack on Freud's insight concerning the existence of subconscious causes of behavior; it may well be a mistake to interpret all behavior in terms of reasons for action which must be conscious and rational from the person's point of view. But Popper objects to Freud's claim that his insight leads to a *scientific* psychology. In his opinion, the opposite is true: only by limiting ourselves to empirically tested statements may we discover some partial real knowledge even in psychology. By adopting Freud's idea we may receive irrefutable answers for all psychological phenomena and thereby lose altogether the possibility of distinguishing between true and false. The arguments Popper employs in his *The Open Society and its Enemies* against Karl Marx are similar.

Of course, the intentional self-imposed limitation on the set of statements allowed into a scientific theory, the limitation of the scope of the concept of truth in science, restricts the possible domains of scientific investigation. In addition to the empirical limitation, two other major constraints were discussed in the previous chapter. In the natural sciences these constraints impose a separation of domains of investigation according to the methods by which theories can be tested, that is by the different methods of assessing what can count as a fact. The study of the structure of atoms, of superconductors, or of neurotransmitters, cannot all be included in one domain of investigation. In other words, even in the natural sciences we remain restricted to finding well-defined islands of knowledge in which a consistent theory describes and explains a limited set of phenomena at the time of investigation. To date, a unified science remains a dream. The important existing unification is the fact that scientists themselves can design the form of their investigation. For example, the idea of *reductionism* is not only an assumption that the world consists only of fundamental particles, or of matter-energy or of any other basic unifying constituents, but it is also a project for research, namely to find out how far we can go by assuming that by passing from one level of organization of these constituents to another (say by passing from physics to chemistry) nothing is added except organization. The question whether properties which emerge with organization are real or merely nominal (that is, categories imposed by the mind), is still controversial, but in the context of the present discussion the important point is that the scientists who explain are the ones who decide what is the best method of inquiry, and their decisions remain outside the world they try to explain.

Popper's objection to the hermeneutic approach should be seen as an insistence on preserving this necessary separation between a science and the scientists' reflections on their own aims and methods, even at the cost of imposing a drastic restriction on the attainment of *scientific* knowledge in psychology and the social sciences, and even at the cost of the remaining philosophical impossibility of including all aspects of human activities in Nature. His objection to the hermeneutic approach did not prevent him from claiming that in order to understand the value of science in human affairs we must take account of its purpose and methods, because he did not think that his analysis was an anthropological observation. Like logical positivists and early pragmatists, Popper saw science as a human creation related to purposes (desires) and beliefs. But unlike neo-pragmatists and Habermas, he did not think that a science can include the reflections on how to create it. This is the inevitable gap between the explainer and the explained, between acting, and reflecting on one's actions.

In contrast to this, when Latour proposes to disregard such reflections of scientists on their science, he thinks he is following a well established scientific approach. He tells us that Poincaré had already shown that we can only understand that world which we have ourselves constructed (for example the world which includes thermometers) and thus emphasizes the conventional aspect of science. And when Latour advises us not to listen to what scientists say that they are doing but look at what they actually do, he claims to rely on Einstein, who gave similar advice. However, neither Poincaré's warning, nor Einstein's reason for this advice, were like Latour's.

Although it is obviously correct to say that the truth of a statement like "water freezes at zero centigrade" depends on the conventional acceptance of this scale in the system of measurement, it is not correct to say that the convention is arbitrary. The numbers-scale is arbitrary and so is the choice of alcohol or mercury as a paradigm for relating the expansion of materials to changes in temperature, but their choice is based on knowledge previously accumulated. The freezing point of water can be found to be at 32 degrees Fahrenheit without making any difference to our understanding of the fact of freezing or to the significance of the measurements. Of course, the inventors of the conventional notation could have made a mistake in assuming that temperature rises uniformly with the expansion of mercury or alcohol in the thermometer. Poincare's warning has more to do with the confusion of what is conventional and what is the knowledge on which the convention is based than with a "revelation" that there is an element of convention in the language of science. Any symbolic notation is arbitrary to some extent, as it is in any language, but it stems from assumed knowledge.

Einstein was not saying that whatever scientists do must characterize science. He knew that scientists wanted to obtain an objective description of the world and believed they were getting it; he thought that he had discovered a mistake in this belief, and was convinced that when his fellow scientists became aware of his arguments they would be ready to discard this cherished belief in "naive realism." As explained in the previous chapter, Einstein persuaded his fellow scientists that they were mistaken in believing that measurements could always be independent of the scientist who does the measuring. He proposed that the dependency of measurements on the coordinate system relative to which they are taken must be taken into account in order to obtain an objective description. Confronted with Latour's ideas Einstein would have certainly rejected the idea that different languages *dictated* conventional views of the world. He would have undoubtedly pointed out that in spite of differences in languages our conventions about method are accepted because they can lead to the desired objective view of the world. Poincaré had a similar purpose in mind when he emphasized the conventional aspect of theories.

Poincaré and Einstein took the social value of objective science for granted. They also took for granted that this, like any other human value, was not part of science. Therefore, they did not even consider the possibility of, and the risk involved in, projecting the mechanistic view of the natural sciences on human affairs, which is the hermeneutics' worry. But they did not take the successful attainment of (maximum) objectivity for granted. They thought that by examining the assumptions underlying objectivity results could be improved. They regarded their philosophical and methodological observations as corrections of mistaken epistemological assumptions which obstructed the attainment of such measure of objectivity as is attainable. They could not have thought that their observations were *corrections* had they not regarded them as true. They certainly did not intend their observations to refer to what scientists do. Similarly, Popper's principle of falsification was not intended as an anthropological description of what scientists always do or think they do, but as a philosophical analysis of what is required to secure validity, from which followed a methodological recommendation.

Poincaré, Einstein and Popper also thought (like Latour) that science is the creation of human minds and therefore free from neither the interests pragmatists attribute to its practitioners, nor the effect of current conceptions inherent in scientific or ordinary language. Because of this they insisted on the need for institutionalized methodological principles to ensure a commitment to a specific conception of truth related to the conception of objectivity explained above. Both Einstein and Popper regarded scientific method as a means of raising the interest in the cultural asset of accumulated objective knowledge, by encouraging a critical attitude in scientists. The principle of replication, the methodological requirement for each experiment to be reported in a manner which enables other scientists to reproduce it, can serve as an example. It is to guarantee the attainment of universal intersubjectivity and to provide a safeguard against possible inclinations on the part of particular scientists to read desired but unwarranted conclusions into an experiment. Both these functions, the attainment of intersubjectivity and the avoidance of unwarranted conclusions, hinge upon social support based on the recognition of the value of science beyond its immediate utility.

What is striking in Latour's or Kuhn's anthropological description of the practice of scientific research is their lack of attention to the scientists' interest in shaping the process by which knowledge is increased. In their mechanistic view of society they think of scientists as operatives, not as intellectuals: only as operatives have they an effect on socially-accepted beliefs, and therefore on social institutions. But at the same time, contrary to the non-predictable results of self-organizing systems associated with this view, they think that because so far the realist point of view has in the pragmatist sense proved itself successful in western society, its success is bound to persist and there is no need to consider the means by which this success is achieved.

For Latour the question whether objectivity is produced by science is as absurd as asking whether milk is produced on dairy farms. He ignores the objectivity which refers to the attitude to research, and this might seem strange for someone who stresses the role of the scientist in producing knowledge. It is in fact as strange as ignoring the role of farmers' interests and knowledge when one comes to assess their success in farming. But Latour's point seems to be that the product of science is *called* objective knowledge just as the product of cows is called milk. Hence the absurdity of the question, in his opinion: as long as there is a social institution that produces theories by conducting research there will be objective knowledge simply because this is how their product is called.

As an example for a change in what is called objective in science, Latour gives Pasteur's refutation of Pauchet's hypothesis of spontaneous generation. Pasteur's ideas, he says, could not have been derived from existing evidence, because all the observed evidence one could have at that time supported Pauchet. But Pasteur constructed the swan-neck flask, an instrument which showed how the entrance of the microbes into the flask could be allowed or prevented. His experiments proved that when entrance was prevented no spontaneous generation occurred. This was a crucial experiment, says Latour, the result of which depended on an invented method, but this result became *objectively true* only because it attained social significance, that is because it introduced the practice of sterilization into hospitals and brought microbes into our world. In other words, it became significant because due to the practices which followed his invention and experiment, the belief in microbes became part of our interpreted phenomenal reality, and spontaneous generation could not be called objective anymore because it ceased to be observed in an institute of research.

What is certainly true in Latour's illustration is that many ingenious experiments may have been forgotten because they were not taken up by the scientific community. Of course, we cannot know of the existence of forgotten inventions or experiments, but we do know that some ideas were accepted because of the social position of their proponents. Such was the acceptance of Newton's theory of corspucles (elementary particles) in preference to Huygens' theory of light-waves, and so is Galileo's experiment, of dropping two balls from the tower of Pisa to prove that their velocities were independent of their weights, which is always reported in history books, although it is not clear whether he carried it out, while the fact that the experiment had actually been conducted earlier by Stevin in Leyden is rarely mentioned. It is also most probably true that had Pasteur's reasons for doubting the possibility of spontaneous generation not stemmed from his adherence to an already existing rival theory (as Kuhn would claim), he would not have thought of his new method. It is certainly true that the method which Pasteur designed introduced a new perceived fact. And his experiment was crucial because hitherto, using the old methods, spontaneous generation seemed to be observed in the laboratory, but with the introduction of Pasteur's new instrument this possibility was ruled out. But the latter agrees with the idea dominant in modern realist science that a theory must be tied to the phenomena. As an anthropologist, Latour should not have missed the fact that Pasteur's attempt to find a new method was motivated by the question how he could test whether apparent spontaneous generation was so in fact. And it is this personal attitude, the wish to find an answer and the incentives to construct an instrument which could help find it, that *is* the most important characteristic of modern science. This is the aspect of objectivity as an attitude which is missing from Latour's description, the readiness to create the means for testing well established "habits of thought."

To Pasteur, as to Einstein and most natural scientists, it was clear that in order to overcome the dependency on the limited and often misleading capacities of the senses, scientists are sometimes forced to resort to ingenuous methodological inventions. In other words, while *measuring* devices are designed to *remove* misleading effects of the external world on our senses, other devices, like the telescope, microscope or the swan-neck flask, are designed to bring some hitherto hidden features of the world into sense perception. In both cases, the purpose of constructing an objective description of the world must be present along with the wish to pursue this purpose. We may add in brackets that the purpose of the invented language of logic, or mathematics, as opposed to natural logical thinking, is similar to the purpose of constructing these instruments. The purpose is to represent a complex system in a perceivable form. But for Latour such considerations of purpose and reflections on its attainment have no place.

Latour contrasts his view with Comte's, who thought that positive science (a concept he introduced) would be completed when all phenomena were represented as different aspects of a unique and comprehensive fact (akin to the conception of absolute truth, discussed at the beginning of the previous chapter: if the world is completely determined by natural laws, then true knowledge must include knowledge of the whole world to its last detail). The idea was certainly taken seriously in the nineteenth century. At about the middle of that century Helmholtz wrote that the purpose of physics was to explain all natural phenomena in terms of unchangeable attractive and repulsive forces whose intensity depended wholly on distance. In his view the vocation of physics would end as soon as the reduction of natural phenomena to simple forces was complete and the proof given that this was the only possible reduction. Comte thought that positive science could also include the human sciences in such project, particularly sociology.

The idea that a scientific understanding of the natural world could be completed does indeed imply a conception of absolute truth which means not only that truths (laws of nature) are eternal but also that they can be known once and for all, in spite of obviously ever-changing human experience. This pre-evolutionary view has not completely disappeared in the modern realist view. Einstein, for example, accepted the idea that Truth is absolute in the domain of physics, but rejected the idea that science, seen as a description of human knowledge, will ever be completed. On this there is no disagreement between modern realists and pragmatists; both think that since science is restricted to the understanding of phenomena it is necessarily restricted to partial knowledge at any particular time. But while Einstein thought that it was the expansion of a known reality which of necessity must from time to time require correction of errors, that is corrections of what had previously seemed to be universally true, pragmatists thought that it was the change of interest, the shift of attention to another aspect of human reality, which is the cause of such corrections.

A central idea of positivism was that the methods established by the natural sciences could apply to psychology and the social sciences as a check on current beliefs. All objections to positivist science cited so far were directed against the assumed complete reliability of this idea. For example, if the current belief is that it is in the nature of Man to seek maximum profit (or pleasure, happiness, utility, power or any other supposedly inherent desire), then the doubts are raised concerning the possibility of testing the truth of this assertion by observation. The impossibility to apply these empirical methods to an inherent (eternal) nature of a human being is obvious. A question whether people in France, the Netherlands or the United States seek any of these goods today may be answered using statistical methods, but then the test is obviously confined to a particular time and place, and its generalization presupposes, and thus imposes an assumption on the test, that it represents essentially a homogeneous population. This is the restriction on the scope of validity of statistical methods (discussed in the previous chapter). Moreover, even with this restriction, the question raised by pragmatists and the hermeneutics remains whether a theory which assumes that,say, people seek the maximization of profit is not itself a factor in the determination of this social fact, thus undermining the reductionist characteristics of Comte's hierarchy, because without universal assumptions about the nature of people and societies, his idea that the laws of psychology and sociology can be known once and for all collapses.

Latour's main objection, however, is not to the inclusion of the social sciences in Comte's project but to the still dominant organization of science in separate disciplines. The logical-positivist idea, that the meaning of truth is its method of verification, is closely related to this organization of science. A generalization of this definition of truth allows that a physicist can, for example, have a different conception of truth when he is dealing with physical research and when participating in a religious or political activity. Latour's objection corresponds to the rejection of the classical mechanistic view, where each part of "the machine" functions independently of any other. He explains that scientists always associate themselves with objects and with other people when they form their conception of the world and thereby affect ours. He tells us that contrary to legend, Galileo did not work in isolation; that in fact he was very well connected; that he created a new science by associating himself with falling bodies and the telescope in new ways which affected his association with the Bible, the Pope and the Church. He explains how power structures changed science at the time of Galileo and how they are changing it today. But he does not worry about the possibility that changes in the power structure nowadays might alter or destroy the nature of science as we know it. The reason for this complacency is the meaning he gives to objectivity as the "product" of science: as long as institutions of research will continue to exist so will objective truth, as he defines it, continue to be produced.

Latour thinks that the distinction between science, as the pursuit of objective truth, and literary creation is arbitrary. According to him the distinction is due to the mistaken belief that the first means the description of nature as it is and the second means the creation of fiction. In his opinion this differentiation is wrong. Science is not the product of an objective mind because no matter how much we try we cannot be neutral observers so as to prevent its fictional character. Science *produces* objectivity because objectivity is only that which a scientific community takes to be objective, and so non-fictional.

In his example of Pasteur's work Latour maintains that the truth of spontaneous generation depended on its being, or not being, perceived as such by the scientific community. The possibility of it being perceived in the one way or the other hinged upon the practices of science and the types of instruments that were in use at the time. These practices and instruments were social facts, which cannot be treated as if they were independent of the social, political or economic system as a whole. Ingenious instruments like Pasteur's were surely regularly invented. His particular invention happened to become a deviation from normal science (in Kuhn's sense) because it occurred at a moment when two theories were competing for recognition. This was the reason for its becoming a crucial experiment. In other words, his description is similar to the new mechanistic view described in the previous chapter: the effect of a new instrument was the new input to the system of beliefs which combined the unusual deviation from accepted beliefs (Pasteur's idea) at a point of bifurcation (where two theories were competing) so that the system is reorganized to meet the challenge. The similarity is in the fact that Latour accepts the view that a system of beliefs is reorganized, but instead of the neo-Lamarckian interpretation of cultural change, which admits a degree of human control on cultural history, he gives it a sociological explanation.

Latour's rejection of Popper's principle of falsifiability fits this description: the principle is a noble belief, he says, but if truth and falsehood are not attributed to independently known facts there is no point in pretending that they are. In other words, if what we call facts are nothing but sentences that we take to be true, if they are nothing but the input to contemporary minds (understood metaphorically as processing machines), then there is nothing against which we can test them except against the set of other beliefs (stored in the machine's memory). But more important, in his opinion, there is no point to pretend that the effect of reflection on actions is different. Pasteur's attitude to research, in his opinion, was crucial for choosing one set of sentences to be true rather than the other, but this choice was not a product of an illusory "power of reflection." This reflection, according to Latour, is like Hume's earlier assertion that philosophical reflections were habits of thoughts, with the pragmatists' explanation that these habits are formed by particular interests.

The question that arises is the following: suppose we, in our present society, still value the achievements of science and think it to be worthwhile to encourage an attitude like the one taken by Pasteur, can we do it? The crucial part of the question is who are the *we* who value science and wish to preserve it. For Einstein or Popper there was no problem because, without denying the need for social support to science, they believed that its universal value may be recognized by all. For Habermas there is also no great problem because he believes that in a truly liberal society all sciences are still held to be the best tool for the emancipation of humanity. For all of them it seemed obvious that ultimately the *we* is humanity as a whole.

But according to Latour, Machiavelli gave a better answer to this question: the alliances made between people in a community determine the *we*, and the alliances are continually changing and with them the social reality. Machiavelli, Latour adds, failed to see that the same applies to natural reality, but the point in the present context is that the *we* who can sustain science today cannot be the scientists alone. If Popper has been right in thinking that science in its present form requires critical skepticism, this attitude can also only be sustained by "an alliance between people," as Machiavelli had observed.

In other words, had Latour considered this question then to his claim that any discovery or belief can only become significant if it becomes part of institutionalized social practices he would have added that the same is true for the required attitudes to research. The point is that if the attitude and the chosen methods are not part of but prerequisites of science, then the dependency of science on other powerful institutions hinges not only upon the widely acknowledged need for funds, as Latour observes, but also on the social recognition of the importance of these prerequisites; the recognition of the role of the interest of individual scientists in shaping their research and the importance of supporting their critical attitude in education (as Dewey, one of the initiators of pragmatism, proposed).

This addition actually follows from the pragmatist basis of the anthropological approach to science. This approach, contrary to the traditional empiricist conviction, does not regard experience as a purely psychological but as a mainly social phenomenon. Nonetheless, individuals, and not a society as a whole, are motivated to act and have reasons for choosing one action rather than another. Therefore if scientists must have a particular attitude to ensure the characteristics of their science it is not sufficient to point out that this attitude is not divorced from attitudes present in other social relations. The question why the concepts of objectivity and truth created by Galileo were rejected by his most influential contemporaries but were later accepted has been addressed by modern (as opposed to post-modern) historians. The question today is why in Pasteur's time this attitude found sufficiently strong social support and is nowadays eroding. Putting the latter differently: why is Latour's view of science so popular today in circles other than those of natural scientists? Why do social scientists feel that the only alternative to copying all methodological aspects of science as they have been in Pasteur's time is to adopt an attitude like Latour's?

Post modern writers emphasize the fact that a modern community is not the homogenous entity that social scientists take it to be but a network of various sub-groups. Therefore, if only in alliance with other power structures in our society scientists are likely to continue to experience the wish to preserve science and to appreciate the value of preserving it, it may also be true that, contrary to Latour's observations, only a new social understanding *may* help us discern which sections of society may constitute such an alliance.

It is of course quite possible that with their new mechanistic approach to anthropology Latour, Kuhn and their followers accurately describe an irreversible change in social attitudes to science. It is quite possible that in fact changing attitudes are exclusively the *result* of changes in a social system; that the mechanisms of social change never involve, or that they are never dependent on, philosophical reflections on what should be done, and therefore that there may be no point in a philosophical analysis which can have no effect. But this surely is an open question.

It is also possible that the extensive dependency on language in the new mechanistic approach is correct; that the new version of the mechanistic model, where people are described as information-processing machines whose crucial inputs are linguistic utterances, is adequate. However this seems less likely if we observe that this model, which is supposed to take the complex whole into account, does in fact take only one factor of change to be dominant, unless the concept "language" (like that of information) is so generalized as to describe a multitude of different phenomena, and thus looses its explanatory power. Ignoring for the moment this lack of precision when talking about language, the question arises whether, Latour's observations are not paradoxical: if they are true, then his own analysis is no more than the product of a socially-institutionalized way of thinking. Alternatively, since by his own analysis (or at least the model he seems to accept) no dominant view is inevitably acceptable as true, and certainly not at a particular time when views are competing, why take his view as the *only* possibility? In fact, this is just a reformulation of the idea that there is an inevitable gap between the explainer and the explained. In this case it is between a reflection on how to approach an inquiry about "how do scientists ought to go about their inquiries" and the observation, doubtless correct, that an approach is usually determined by habitual responses to challenges of various degrees of immediacy. The point is that there are *arguments* for choosing one approach or the other when we reflect on how to do science, and not *evidence*.

It was pointed out in the previous chapter that a central point in post modern neo-pragmatism is the role attributed to a language in shaping people's beliefs. It is therefore worth noting what Wittgenstein had to say about the power of language in philosophical reflection, because in his later work he initiated what Rorty called the "linguistic twist" in philosophy. Like logical positivists, Wittgenstein thought that the analysis of concepts was the only useful task of philosophy. But while logical positivists thought they could sharpen the linguistic tool in order to obtain consistently used concepts, Wittgenstein thought that he could only show the correct social contexts to which particular meanings belonged and thereby prevent their persuasive use in other contexts where they did not belong. Wittgenstein did not deny either the possibility of philosophical reflection or its role in the construction of knowledge, but he interpreted this role as avoiding the trap of mistaken use of language. In the same spirit, but without assigning the whole responsibility for correct reflection to the use of language, William James observed earlier that the tremendous success that a mechanistic approach has had in the domain of engineering persuaded psychologists to adopt this approach also in their research. But in fact, he added, we have neither reason nor evidence for assuming that the same approach is *totally* valid in psychology or in any social domain. His appeal to psychologists was to keep their mind open to the possibility of counter-examples.

In contrast to James, Popper did borrow the idea of social engineering in order to combat the appeal to total ideologies or social theories, such as Marxism. Popper's motive for this recommendation was his fear of totalitarian regimes, which is not very different from the fear of post-modern philosophers that hidden assumptions of universality behind factual diversity lead to the undemocratic suppression of subjective wills and rationalities. But if we consider again Popper's principle of falsifiability, and compare the objections to it within the scientific camp to those of Latour, we see that in fact the first camp is careful not to extend a theory beyond its scope of validity while the post modern camp, represented here by Latour, is not.

The objection to Popper's principle stems from the replacement of the correspondence theory of truth by the coherence theory of truth. The central idea behind the coherence theory of truth, as explained in connection with its acceptance by the Vienna Circle, was that we cannot test any particular statement except in the light of other statements in a theory. And as Quine observed, this means that the discovery of falsity cannot mean more than that something we used to regard as true must be false. Therefore, a commitment to search for truth cannot mean more than a commitment to look for a mistake somewhere in the theory. An example for this interpretation can be found in Einstein's arguments for his relativity theory in which we clearly observe that alternative considerations for possible revisions were sought, but these were strictly confined to the theory itself. The blurring of these confines stems from

Quine's assertion that it is to a certain extent up to us to decide how to revise a theory, and that we do so according to a pragmatic principle. For Quine, the "certain extent" remained within the confines of the theory, but Latour ignores this constraint. For example, according to Quine, if a new set of measurements should contradict the known melting point of copper, this discovery is more likely to be questioned than the theoretical truths on which rests the reliability of the thermometer, because this reliability served us so well in theoretical explanations in the past that it cannot be ignored. But according to Latour, the reason for this preference is that thermometers have become too important in our everyday life to be considered for dismissal. According to him, it is this fact rather than any scientific principle that determines the preference. The argument seems similar to the one used by Quine to explain why we never reject logic, but it extends the applicability of Quine's pragmatic principle beyond any scientific theory.

Scientists who adhere to modern realism do not deny that without social institutions, such as factories which produce thermometers, or the inclusion of logic in education, science could not have become what it is today. But they do not identify the acceptance of truth with a semi-automatic confirmation of what is taken by a society as fact. Nor do they identify it with a semi-automatic acceptance of this extension of Quine's principle. Instead, *truth* is seen as a concept associated with a possible reflection on what we think or do. In science it indicates the purposeful creation of a well-tested conception of reality, where "well-tested" neither provides a guarantee for eternal certainty, nor means the acceptance of persuasive doctrines, as neo-pragmatist post-modern philosophers claim them to be. In fact, the most important difference between pragmatists like Quine and neo-pragmatists, or post modern philosophers like Latour, is in the fact that although all of them see the effect of social practices, including language, on what is considered to be adequate knowledge, Quine and early pragmatists have seen and appreciated the effect of science on social attitudes, while the others abandoned this belief. The objections to Popper's recommendation of the principle of falsification by Latour relies on the extension of the coherence theory of truth to include all our beliefs, in a universal anthropological theory in which the *production* of science has no particular importance.

As explained in the previous chapter, the essence of the *extension* of the coherence theory of truth to all knowledge, is the idea that the basic argument against the correspondence theory of truth is that we cannot distinguish between *statements* of fact and the facts themselves, even when the statements apply to perception. Therefore, the idea that the acceptance of any statement depends on the acceptance of others, must be generalized to all knowledge, including knowing as simple a fact as snow being white. According to this extension of the coherence theory, if our certainty about empirical knowledge is not merely a result of habit, it must be based on another belief, for example the belief that perception is caused by the real world. As D. Davidson puts it, we cannot step outside our skins in order to examine whether or not our perceptions were caused by reality and therefore whether their assumed truth is more reliable than other beliefs. However, Davidson also points out that the same applies to the pragmatist view that takes basic beliefs to be caused by social reality: we cannot step outside ourselves in order to examine whether our basic beliefs were caused by social reality and therefore whether the reliance on them was a guarantee for adaptability, which is the basis for the pragmatist definition of truth. In other words, the neo-pragmatist generalization of the coherence theory of truth says that the dependency of what is accepted as a fact on theory is not confined to each particular theory, but is spread over our whole system of beliefs. And even if, (as Wittgenstein and modern interpreters of the mind as an information processing machine,) we replace *the system* by a network of systems of beliefs, the fact remains that no belief can be tested except by a host of other beliefs.

If this generalization is taken seriously then Latour's rejection of Popper's principle of falsifiability must be directed not only at its application to scientific theories but also against Popper's recommended social engineering, on the grounds that no social fact can be considered a mistake without relating it to a host of other facts. A modern realist, even one who on the whole accepts the new mechanistic model of the mind, will point out that the only way to escape the vast complexity of interacting facts, which we cannot possibly master, is to analyze this complexity as far as possible into separate domains (or practices) describable by logically consistent systems of statements, so that the methods of science can be applied to them. This strategy accommodates a revised principle of falsifiability in science as well as in attempts to solve social problems, which Popper called social engineering. In contrast, Latour and post-modern social scientists must accept complexity as insurmountable. In their opinion, the replacement of "Grand theories" (or "grand stories" as they call them) by a network of applicable theories cannot help because the latter presupposes the possibility of correcting errors locally, irrespective of the complexity of the human world in which everything is related to everything else. Wittgenstein thought that most philosophical problems would disappear if we realized that every social practice has its own language with its own rules of use. Philosophical problems arise, according to him, when concepts designed to be used in one domain are borrowed to be used in another. Latour and other post-modern philosophers think that the borrowing of concepts from one domain for use in another is not due to confusion but to the real intermingling of facts, practices and experiences. It follows from this that if absolute truth, the understanding of the whole complex system to its last detail, is not attainable, then no truth at all is attainable. And if no truth is attainable, on which we can build up our trust in others, then as far as our human phenomenal knowledge is concerned, there is no truth: all our knowledge is our own mental creation. This acceptance of complexity as insurmountable may be the reason for the flight of many social scientists to a new kind of individualism, a belief that one can do no more than attend to one's own affairs, including one's own intellectual interests, and their giving up any attempt to deal meaningfully with social or common affairs.

About Latour's intermingling of facts, practices and experiences, on the grounds that this is an anthropological fact, a modern philosopher may point out that if science is an improvement on common sense, as early pragmatists have maintained, then so is the separation of domains of investigation. What Wittgenstein described as sub-languages which have *combined* to produce a confused natural language, can on the contrary be seen as evolving out of existing natural languages to produce the separate domains of knowledge we can have. This is in fact Davidson's opinion. Davidson agrees with the anthropological view of knowledge, by which one acquires beliefs from one's community through the medium of the common language, and a *common* language implies commonly held beliefs. But he thinks that this view of knowledge implies that a primitive concept of truth must initially apply to all domains of human behavior. According to him, without a primitive notion of truth not only a common language is impossible but any aspect of communicative culture could hardly have emerged. In his opinion, intentional behavior could not exist without the ability to interpret the intentions of others. One acquires different intentions only by encountering the interpreted intentions of others. This is the essence of the social characterization of human experience, on which Rorty's analysis is based. At least, as Davidson himself point out, this follows from the language-dominated view. But unlike Rorty or Latour, Davidson points out the enormous overlapping of accepted truths across cultures and languages. These overlaps are too trivial for raising the interest of anthropologists but nevertheless they undermine the total dependency of facts on distinct theories in different societies, and thus the cultural relativity implied from this dependency. But most important in the present context, his analysis shows how on the basis of overlapping general world view embodied in different ordinary languages, the pragmatists' view of knowledge implies the organization of knowledge in different disciplines, and shows how the recommendation to use different criteria for accepting the truth of scientific statements and accepting the truth of moral beliefs could have emerged.

Wittgenstein's view, on whose ideas Rorty also draws, does not lead to Latour's social determinism. Wittgenstein pointed out that knowing implies being ready to give compelling grounds. "I know p," he says, neither expresses mere subjective certainty about p, nor does it supply a guarantee that p is true. For subjective certainty, expressed by "I am sure" one does not and need not give any grounds. The difference between a *feeling* of certainty and *knowledge*, he adds, applies even to self-knowledge. For example, a person does not necessarily know better than an observer what he is going to do next. The observer may see or know factors of which the subject himself is unaware. This seems to correspond to Latour's proposal to disregard the reflections of scientists on their own work, on the grounds that he can see better than they do what they are actually doing, as opposed to what they think that they are doing. However, Wittgenstein adds that what counts for establishing what is known is the choice of criteria involved in ascertaining, or making sure, whether an interpretation that has hitherto been considered true or natural due to its familiarity, is or is not correct. The crucial question is what kind of criteria we are prepared to accept as decisive. There is nothing unrealistic in claiming that in natural science we *should* trust our senses more than our theoretical "habits of thought," while in moral or social studies we should trust an expected fulfillment of a purpose rather than merely the facts which we perceive, the facts which gave rise to a problem in the first place. The question which economists and other social scientists should consider is whether, or for what type of problems, we can find a way to predict an expected fulfillment of a purpose which will comply with the constraints on the creation of scientific knowledge.

All this does not mean that Latour's anthropological observations are all mistaken. The question is whether his *conclusions* are correct. Latour tells us that in the 18th century, when scientists wanted to free themselves from the power of the church, they constructed new alliances. They created a sub-culture that was to deal only with truth, not with power. Nowadays, he says, since science has become part of our everyday life, its relation to social power can no longer be ignored.

Ignoring the historical truth of this story we may agree that it is indeed quite likely that a social institution devoted to pure science, the search for truths which are remote from immediate problems or needs, is only possible in societies where sub-cultures are free to develop even if their principles are in conflict with more dominant aspects of culture alive in such societies. This may be the essence of Rorty's appeal to pluralism: if loyalty to the procedures of one's fellow participants in any social practice is the very nature of morality, as he maintains, one has to acknowledge that scientific morality, for example the commitment to experimentally-tested truths, is antithetic to the loyalty required in Church practices or in political alliances. Latour's denial of the possibility of separation of loyalties on the ground that science cannot be free from the intervention of those holding political power, may very well be true today even if it need not always have been so, as he claims.

It is quite possible that the erosion of the social or cultural value of science does not so much spring from the rejection of the claim that truth is immutable, universal or independent of the human mind, as from the observation that at least some branches of science, for example those related to defence or to the pharmaceutical industry, have become hostage to existing power structures. To this fear of science, which replaced the old confidence in its progressive element, is added a resentment due to the identification of scientific theories with a view that the nature and behavior of people can only be explained in the same manner as the rest of the universe, namely by turning a person from a subject (i.e. from the learning, reflecting, explaining and deciding individual) into an object (i.e. into the observed, studied, passively determined and theoretically explained object).

Thus Latour explains that Popper wanted to protect science from the invasion of external social interests, and humanists like Habermas, want to protect the subject from the invasion of the mechanistic approach of the natural sciences. But in his opinion neither science nor the subject need protection. Objective science and the condition of being a subject are inseparable: *individually* we are subjects and *collectively* we create (what he calls) objective science.

This, however, is hardly the point. Neither Popper nor Habermas denied that we *can* create intersubjective science and be subjects at the same time. On the contrary, it is clear to them that only subjects, that is only people who are capable of subjectively making choices and decisions, can persuade each other to adopt a particular strategy for achieving a particular aim. For example, only people capable of reflecting on their actions can choose a method that cancels their own tendency to pursue their personal satisfaction when conducting scientific experiments. Popper certainly thought that only rational subjects, including businessmen, could decide that it is useful for them and their society to protect scientific institutions from the power of other institutions such as profit-seeking business enterprises; and Habermas is of the opinion that the enormous social interest in technology, together with the successful contribution of the natural sciences to technology, tempts the social sciences to apply the same approach, and that this threatens the status of people as subjects, and thus is self defeating.

For both Popper and Habermas the distinction between the philosophical reflection needed for the adoption of a strategy of research and the descriptive theory resulting from the adopted strategy is of critical importance. The justification of the recommended strategy in Popper's opinion is that the relativism of Kuhn, in whose tradition Latour's view must be located, is pure nihilism. Nihilism in his use of the word does not mean the wilful destruction of a system, as it meant for Russian anarchists. It means what it meant for Kafka, the acceptance of events as they come, a meaning associated with the emergence of a bureaucratic society where individuals lose their value in the eyes of authorities as well as their own belief in their ability to shape society.

Habermas justifies his recommended strategy of research by pointing out that the methods of research which necessarily look for evidence in existing situations had *not* always been a threat to the subject but have become one now. They had not been a threat when bourgeois liberalism was associated with the rising scientific enterprise; it is only when the mechanistic view of the natural sciences was extended to the social sciences that all observed people lost their status as subjects.

Latour's conception of subjects assigns no significant role to reflection apart from private intellectual satisfaction. But what is common to all methodological corrections, or new suggestions of strategies of research, is an appeal to the reflecting scientist (the subject) to reconsider current strategies. In fact, how else can Latour justify his own strategy of research? What he is trying to tell us is that only his anthropological view of science can explain why the more we connect it to other aspects of society the more we shall understand its true significance and achievements. He says that only this view of science explains how science allows us to modify our life by introducing new elements into our interaction with our environment. And we may ask him: is it an empirical fact that this is the only way? And, of course, we must ask ourselves: is it an empirical fact that we cannot explain how and why microbes were brought into our world, and how and why microbiology was brought into science, without considering Pasteur's reflection on the current strategy of research in his time? If none of these are empirical facts it is because we can neither test them, nor show that they are logically necessary. Nevertheless, only the answer to one of these questions can be true.

Behaviorists like Skinner thought that the completeness of a psychological theory requires that such reflections be included among the strategies for survival described by the theory. Similarly, Latour, Kuhn and neopragmatists think that the justification of a research strategy ought to be included in the common system of beliefs that characterizes the behavior of a society. In contrast to all of them, a suggestion like Popper's is not meant to be an explanation. At best, a sociologist of science can explain his suggestion as a desire to reduce gullibility in order to limit the power of persuasion of those whose interests may induce them to work on the gullibility of others. Similarly, if the objection of Habermas to positivist science is to be explained, it can be seen as an objection to ruling out the possibility that people may, on humanist grounds, choose alternative solutions to prevailing problems in preference to those suggested by the *is* that is. Both views, of Popper and of Habermas, may bring us closer to the *understanding* of the unbridgeable gap between the observer and the observed in the sciences and the role of the explainer in a modern society. It may be this that Rorty has in mind when he proposes to take Habermas' objection as a warning. But a warning, like the suggestion of a strategy, will not be headed unless one thinks that the situation it warns against might actually arise. In other words, unless the analysis on which it is based is believed to be true.

The scientific community *chose* experimental evidence as a crucial criterion of acceptability. The exclusion of philosophical reflection, and perhaps of a large part of the social sciences, from the domains in which this choice is justified does not mean that acceptable persuasion should not rely on a concept of truth. This is so even if we are ready to dilute the idea of a universal mind and acknowledge that a particular type of persuasion is effective only within one's own culture.

Neither the claims of Einstein, Poincaré and Popper about science, nor those of Latour and Kuhn could have any cognitive value if they and those persuaded by them did not think that such claims were true. According to modern realists the theoretical language in each science must fit a particular set of phenomena. Pragmatists say that the theory must allow us to act upon it with confidence. So far in western societies these distinct conceptions of truth coincide in the natural sciences. They coincide due to that chosen criterion for establishing truth in them, and because this criterion *was not* assumed to be a general definition of truth in all areas of knowledge or behavior. On the ground that such a distinction will prevent confusion, we may of course decide to use the *word* truth only for factual descriptions, and use another *word* for other evaluations. However, unless we are prepared to accept the arbitrary *power* of persuasion as a replacement for rationality, we shall still have to search for suitable criteria for acting according to some reasons rather than others. This is the meaning of rationality, and it presupposes reliance on truth.

15

Truth and Expediency: Philosophical Observations Concerning the Humanities

If truth and objectivity are related in the manner explained in chapter 13; and if objectivity is defined as intersubjectivity and nonetheless requires that a variety of subjective observations be "calculated away"; it becomes clear that what is true in human affairs cannot be the same as in the natural sciences. In fact, realist historians and social philosophers have known (even before Habermas explained why) that a social theory which has been intersubjectively accepted at any particular time is not so much incorrect as socially lopsided. Marxist theory, for example, claims to have shown that capitalist economics only describes that part of social reality which is of interest to the dominant class to which the influential intellectuals also belong. According to socialist writers and Habermas a more genuine theory ought to include as well the conditions and social relations that are of interest to other classes. In this vein, a realist sociologist today would insist that a social theory ought to include conditions of interest to women, for example, or to ethnic minorities or homosexuals. With such a perception, which emphasizes the relation between a social science and social reality, the creation of a new theory can be seen as an expansion of the phenomena brought under conscious review in the same way as Einstein saw it with regard to physics. The expansion in social science, as pragmatists and Habermas maintain, means that account must be taken of neglected or suppressed desires and beliefs, of desires and beliefs other than the dominant ones.

The problem which Habermas indicated is the contradictory requirement in the social sciences to describe the behavior of individuals *intentionally* and the methodological assumption that objectivity is attainable only by the removal of differences between the intentions of particular scientists. We have seen how Latour claims to have resolved this contradiction by turning the methodological assumption into a realistic description. In his opinion it is a social fact that in a scientific community only common desires and beliefs of scientists are essential for the description of *any* observed domain of inquiry. Hence by definition their description is objective and true.

Several questions have been raised in the previous chapters which are also relevant concerning the humanities. One question raised is whether science as we know it can remain socially significant, as Latour puts it, only if desires (interests) and beliefs of scientists (like Pasteur) will remain common; whether they can be common only in a society in which liberal individualism is common or socially significant. And if this is so, the question arises whether under a different social system the scientific enterprise will necessarily disappear: can science or the study of history and other cultural phenomena retain the same attitude in a social system based on values like solidarity or other communal principles?

Another question raised is whether a Lamarckian element exists in cultural history. It is argued in these chapters that a conceptual gap necessarily remains between an explanation and a reflection on how and what for the explanation is sought; between knowledge, seen as an adaptive response to a changing (phenomenal) reality and the reflection on any particular type of knowledge—a reflection which is another kind of behavior. The question is whether the latter is determined by social factors as Latour claims, or it enables us to change more rationally whatever we wish to change. As we have seen, since Darwin's theory of evolution (at least in parts of the Western world) the expansion of the domains of science from the physical to the biological world purported to include humanity in nature. But this attempt did not succeed in eliminating the conceptual gap between the act of explaining and the explained phenomena, and therefore did not answer the question whether or not a Lamarckian element exists in cultural history.

An important aspect of the attempt to include humanity in a unified view of nature has been an *assumed* continuity between cultural and natural phenomena, which introduced a tension between the mechanistic approach, dominant in explaining natural phenomena, and the interpretation of science as a rational cultural creation designed for overcoming natural limitations. The important *realistic* question raised by post modern writers is whether this tension and the related emphasis on the gap between the explainer and the explained are not exclusively a product of individualism. In other words, whether the two questions raised above do not represent an ideology typical to our particular culture, or communities. And whether the observed Lamarckian element is not an illusion created by the same ideology.

Within a naturalistic interpretation of humanity the aim of science ceased to be a "mere" desire for understanding. It became functionally explained as a tool for predicting the consequences of anticipated events and for bringing about those events of which the consequences are deemed favorable. The restriction of purpose to a socially defined function of predicting and controlling the environment drastically limited the role of individuals in creating knowledge. But even the little scope which remained for it contradicted the mechanistic, deterministic, conception of natural phenomena within which any *purposeful action* (the limited interpretation of free will) is an illusion.

The enormous role attributed in the last decades to the effect of language on human life may be regarded as an attempt to resolve this tension between the naturalistic explanation (associated with the mechanistic view of the world) and the interpretative culture (which created this scientific approach): the ability to speak and learn a language is certainly a natural property of mankind, but its emergence enlarges the role of interpretation in the determination of behavior.

In the United States, for example, a social critic in the realist tradition could claim that greater attention must be paid to the effect of their slave origins on the mentality of the black minority; to the effect of the variety of cultural backgrounds of immigration groups on their mentality; to the effect of gender conceptions on the mentality of women and on the attitudes of men toward them; and similarly on the attitudes to homosexuals. Such a claim involves a reinterpretation of social reality in the light of a historical rather than an evolutionary approach, but it nevertheless increases the scope of causal explanation. This reinterpretation also implies that truths are more local and transitory than in biology, let alone in physics. "Locality" in the realist view means a lower spatial or temporal range of validity. Einstein explained that we shall never be able to include human and physical events in one theory simply because events that are for us of the utmost importance are mere local fluctuations in physics. As distinct from such realist social scientists' or the Marxist emphasis on objective social and economic "forces" which determine thought, Wittgenstein and Foucault, for example, stressed the conceptual-linguistic component as a constraint on any attempt to change any existing features in a social structure. According to both, a social practice includes a specific vocabulary and rhetorical style as its major determining factor. While this shift of interest may have been intended to articulate the non-naturalist aspect of a culture—the limitation of the scope of rational understanding by a culture rather than by nature—its actual effect has been an anti-realism with a vengeance.

The idea behind the emphasis on language is that its natural evolution gave rise to the emergence of social phenomena which Wittgenstein called language-games, and a social change occurs by creating new language-games. Wittgenstein's notion of language games is similar to Foucault's analysis of the relation between institutions and the central concepts dominant in running them. For example, the institution of psychiatry is described as a network of procedures carried out in a psychiatric hospital or clinic by people whose role in treating the patients is well defined. The procedures depend on the assumption made by the use of the concept "mental *illness*" in the psychiatric discipline that gives doctors the task to restore their patients' mental health, and their conviction that they, and only they, can do so. The rationale of the institution's existence, in this view, is that the phenomenon known as madness in other cultures is redefined as an illness. Only with this assumption can diagnosis be stated and judged true or false, and treatment can be decided upon.

This conception is central and it overrules any extra objections that can be made to the status of patients treated in a hospital or in a clinic. The objection of people considered not-normal to be treated as ill, according to Foucault, can lead to results only by the rejection of this vocabulary and the creation of a new one.

Wittgenstein would add to Foucault's example that we cannot know whether or not a mental deviation is comparable to a physiological deviation we call illness. He emphasized that we do not know, and perhaps cannot know, whether the language involved in a particular social practice reflects any reality external to it. He explained this with regard to the concept "voluntary": the concept was probably invented for distinguishing between lifting our arm and waiting for our increased heart palpitation to subside after running, but this differentiation tells us nothing about the legitimacy of using the concept "voluntary" when we choose a research strategy, or when we describe the behavior of rats in a maze, or when we use the concept of *voluntary unemployment* in economics.

Both Wittgenstein and Foucault thought, however, that by changing the language we can free ourselves from this kind of arbitrary comparisons, although Foucault added that such a liberation does not mean that freedom from one power structure will not bring with it an unpredictable new one. The point is that neither Wittgenstein's nor Foucault's analyses remove the Lamarckian aspect of cultural change. They merely replace its location from intentional behavior to intentional use of language. The possibility that people can choose a policy (or a strategy of research) is replaced by the idea that social change occurs according to the topic that is receiving attention, and receiving attention means being talked about. Modern scientists would point out that the conception of madness as illness, by which it is compared to a physiological deviation from the normal based on the assumption of a universal normality, has been a liberation for mad people earlier removed from society under cruel conditions. Foucault would reply that in fact one power structure was replaced by another. The response of modern scientists could be that indeed within the procedures in a mental institution a doctor may have too complete control over a patient, but at the same time doubt whether it is the *concept* of illness that is responsible for this, and most important, whether a linguistic change would be sufficient for changing the system, or whether it is even possible to bring about such a change at will. But both the sufficiency and the possibility are implied by the language-dominated conception of society and the will.

The pervasive power of a language received an extra boost from the humanities. Not so long ago literary critics attempted to borrow systematic methods of analysis from the sciences. But now the situation is reversed. In the past, the intentions of realist writers, like Balzac, Flaubert, or Tolstoy, could have been compared in some sense to the intentions attributed by Savigny to the ancient Egyptians who mummified ibises. Realist writers attempted to bring to our notice essential features of a social world through descriptions of particular lives without pretending that the evidence (the events in the story) rested on objectively observed facts. These authors thought they were using fiction for illuminating truths about society that were hidden under the multitude of current events. But if, as the new argument goes, there are no objective truths at all then there is no fundamental difference between science, that pretends to bring observable truths to light, and literature that illuminates hidden truths, because both tell fictions. Both are to be judged according to whether they bring to our attention anything we wish to see or see changed, anything that seems important to us—to the writer, the readers or the students of any discipline.

Just as Latour considers *his* own description to be realistic, so do those who replace the assumption of universality by particular language games. A language game purports to explain the role of these fictions in a society. For example, the concept of efficiency is clearly defined within the context of economic activities. Such a definition, according to this view, expresses the writer's subjective point of view. They agree with Wittgenstein that a language is always public. But the scope of public meaning is reduced from being common to all speakers of a natural language to being common to a restricted public which shares a particular vocabulary and the interests served by it, in a particular language game. Hence, while one particular writer can share a definition of efficiency with a group of profit seekers, another writer may point out that the term reflects no more than this profit seeking interest and may propose another meaning. As followers of Derida would say, this particular *constructed* conception called "efficient practice" can be deconstructed.

The replacement of objectivity by intersubjectivity no longer reflects the possibility of knowledge that can on principle be universally acknowledged. Interests, knowledge and a particular type of reasoning (a rhetoric) belong to the groups who share them. Two consequences follow: first, that if there is no way one can define a term like efficiency except from a subjective point of view, there is no way by which one can tell whether an economy is *really* efficient because the concept does not apply to the economy as a whole. Second, that subjects are neither the individuals that liberal empiricists took them to be, nor are they "shaped by *the* society" in which they live: they are products of sub-groups with which they share interests and beliefs which constitute the various language games in which they participate.

The new "linguistic twist" that emerged with the anthropological view of science which stresses the impossibility of having clear-cut distinctions because of the social system's complexity, is different. According to this view, even if such distinctions which define any concept in terms of its opposite may have been formed for specific purposes, these purposes are in fact too involved one with another to make possible the separation of one language game from the next. Hence, applying Rorty's advice to consider Habermas' analysis as a warning to Foucault's criticism must result in an extra warning that any attempt to change an unwanted situation is necessarily made without knowing its outcome in advance.

Yet, although this view seems more deterministic than Wittgenstein's or Foucault's, it too does not do away with the gap between the explainer and the explained. The new model of society as a complex system of interacting individuals admits the pragmatist assertion that it is the fact that, for example, measuring is so central a feature in modern culture that it turned into part of a modern person's cognitive system. Or that the language of logic, in spite of being an invention (one which like that of agriculture irreversibly changed the pattern of culture) came to characterize cognition, at least in the western world. The same applies to the invention of mathematics and statistics. When the model is applied to a system of beliefs it shows that although all these inventions evolved together with the practices in which they were employed, their formulations in independent language-systems helped to represent other complex systems in a perceivable form. And the new information-processing algorithmic models which evolved with the use of computers do the same: they do not simulate naturally existing ways of thinking but are trying to bring within reach phenomena that only this computational invention can represent in a perceivable form. But they do not recognize that the decisions to use these inventions for this purpose (as well as their rejection by many mathematicians and scientists) cannot be included within their invented simulations. The attempt to explain all language-dominated behavior in terms of information-processing algorithms is like earlier attempts to characterize all thinking by logic. Any correct insights gained from this model (as from the anthropological approach to knowledge) are obliterated by the neglect of this point. Similarly, it is the insistence to consider all aspects of thought as linguistic inputs into the same network of language games, producing "built-in" patterns of output, which makes rhetoric and persuasion the only factor of change. It is this emphasis on rhetoric which persuades post-modern philosophers that earlier philosophers mistakenly attributed a *real* role to reflection on the purpose or likely effect of a language game.

By this view the replacement of the Marxist central position of the working class, as the carrier of expected change, by other associations such as the ethnic, racial, homosexual or feminist groups, must be regarded as a result of neither a change in class structure nor of an expansion of social analysis. It must be seen as a result of the fact that at least in the U.S. the ideological rhetoric of social equality *was* successful in *persuading* a large section of workers in the population that class differences do not affect their opportunities, but *was not* successful in persuading the population that ethnic, color or gender differences made no difference to their prospects of social success.

When the shift in attention took place, the members of these groups (blacks, feminists, etc.) did not set out to create a new "normal science" (in Kuhn's sense of the term "normal") in the universities. Their cultural studies appeared in the faculties of art because they regarded the very conception of science as inextricably entangled with the idea of *scientism*, namely with the thought that the only valid knowledge is provided by a science in which only universal statements are true and human beings are characterized by universal properties expressed in the language chosen by white males, and that this makes science an inevitable instrument of white male power. Participants in these studies also took on board the idea that *objectivity* is nothing but the way *some people* study the conditions of others. The point of this idea is that even if the interests of the oppressed were to be taken account of in a scientific manner, this way of studying cannot (as for example Habermas believes) become an emancipatory instrument because the oppressed can only attain their liberation by finding their own identity in a new rhetoric in a new language game. In other words, it is, according to them, the subjective identification with the analysis, and not its objectivity, which counts, and it makes little difference whether or not other scientists find the claims true.

The new attitude in cultural studies is seen as fulfilling a socially therapeutic function rather than an attempt to advance the acquisition of knowledge. Wittgenstein introduced the idea that his philosophy has a "therapeutic function," but its meaning is different. In his *Philosophical Investigations* he argued that by finding the real origins of concepts in their related social practices their projection upon domains where they do not belong will be avoided, and so free us from illusions raised by other philosophers about knowledge that we cannot have. The therapy applies to philosophy, and does not claim to have other liberating functions either for individuals or for groups.

Without using the term "therapeutic function" Spinoza, for example, did assign such a function to his philosophy. He wrote his *Ethics* with the purpose of liberating people from their enslavement to the passions. In his opinion passions were the product of social influences and the only way to overcome them was to obtain knowledge of one's true nature. In his opinion, the freedom of an individual was confined to the ability to reflect on an idea and either accept it or reject it. Hence the liberating function of knowledge was to exercise this power of the mind correctly. This was also the function of the concepts true and false. Similarly Marx, adopting a social approach rather than Spinoza's individualist one, thought that class consciousness is acquired by discovering the real place of working people in creating the wealth of society. It was this acquisition of knowledge which was to provide the working class with the liberating self-confidence required for class struggle. Instead of their need to master their passions came the need to reject the false consciousness imposed on them by the ruling class. There were of course many important developments in the long period which separated Spinoza from Marx, but they shared the idea that true self-consciousness was based on objective knowledge.

Spinoza could still think of an essential nature of the human being, a universally valid essence comparable to essential properties of all things in the universe. The passions could be seen by him as accidental variations, which later scientists would describe as "local" fluctuations that can be ignored. The aim of self-knowledge was the discovery of this essence, and the objectivity of the self-observer meant the removal of local influences (the passions) which obstructed this achievement. Marx wrote when the evolutionary approach was gaining ground. For him the consideration of what was the essence and what were fluctuations was very much dependent on the time and place of the society described. While for Spinoza the liberating power of self-knowledge lay in enabling one to deploy fully one's potential power to control one's peace of mind, for Marx this potential power was to control one's destiny, a power which was different in different positions along the essential (true) path of social evolution. For him the task of philosophy was to describe this historical path, and to hasten the recognition of the potential power of workers in a capitalist society.

The Marxist view, like the view of early pragmatists, attempted to explain cultural phenomena scientifically. Just as Darwin's original theory lacked a description of an objective mechanism explaining natural selection, so did Marx's theory involve a "missing mechanism"—the way by which material social-economic circumstances *determine* self-consciousness. Marx did not think that there was an essential contradiction between the assumption that a deterministic explanation can be offered for social change and that there was a need for class consciousness to bring it about. Like Darwin (concerning evolution) he supposed that this contradiction must be only apparent and would eventually be resolved. He thought his crucial achievement was to establish continuity between history and the theory of evolution, and hence with the natural sciences. He believed that the inevitable victory of the working class was essential for the survival of humanity, and that true self-consciousness, which for him meant class consciousness, was the property selected for survival. He considered that with his theory the universe, the evolution of all species and human history were shown to have a unique evolutionary path. He did not think that observed false ideologies, which obstructed the victory of the working class, rendered his theory unscientific. Nowadays, he would perhaps describe them as mere fluctuations along the inevitable path of history.

But this unique necessary direction of evolution is exactly that which has become questionable after the sought-for mechanism in Darwin's theory has been discovered, where mutations must precede natural selection. A favorable mutation, a deviation from the normally expected, caused by chance at a particular time and place is crucial for the further path of selective survival and therefore for the determination of evolution as a whole. In other words, the idea of an inevitable evolutionary path can be rejected in science's own terms, and is not the invention of the language-dominated view of human affairs.

Concerning cultural history, however, the point is not inevitability but the role, or the very possibility, of human interference in a process that *seems* inevitable. Or the other way round: the possibility that what seems to be a possible choice is in fact inevitable. The latter can be illustrated for example by Sartre's view. His insistence on the existence of human freedom can be explained away in the mechanistic model of reality where complexity and the role of language are predominant. Sartre claimed that the human condition is characterized by being *"condemned* to freedom." He dramatically illustrates this by a person facing a hopeless dilemma: his friends call him to fulfill a task in the resistance, but he knows that his mother who is ill will die if he goes. His choice is between letting his mother die and depriving his friends of a help which may endanger their lives. The description of the dilemma is not unrealistic, but in his diary (written at the beginning of the second world war, when he was a prisoner) Sartre relates the will to a particular type of consciousness: an attitude of distancing oneself and the object of consciousness from immediate action. The idea implies that the dilemma described above is of a person who knows "a tree" of possible actions. To be *condemned* to freedom in the example appears to be a result of the unfortunate effect of any choice, but in general it means that at each point of bifurcation he must choose his path although he cannot tell how it will join later choices to form a complete path in this tree, and thus he cannot tell the consequences of his present choice. Hence his freedom does not mean that he can control his destiny. But once knowledge of the tree of possibilities is denied, and the dilemma is reduced to the particular moment (or moments) when the person must actually decide whether to go or not go with his friends, this freedom may very well disappear because the person no longer faces this abstract "tree of possibilities." If a deterioration in his mother's health requires his immediate presence he will not go; and if at that moment of decision the prospect of being considered a traitor is particularly threatening or vivid on his mind, he will go. The unlikely event that both happen at the very same moment, would place the person in the same situation as Buridan's donkey, and the most likely result would be his psychological collapse.

In his diary Sartre compares his analysis to Spinoza's. His point is that although the actions of the hero of his drama are determined by immediate circumstances, and his personal identity is simply the result of such events which determine the story of his life, his view of himself is part of that level of consciousness in which he distances himself and these events from immediate action. If, after the war, the person lived among people who took the resistance to have been the saving of France, then even if he had stayed with his mother by the force of circumstances he would see himself as a coward if not a traitor. But if he lived among people who judged the resistance as unimportant or a mistake he would judge himself favorably.

In fact, the affinity to Spinoza is greater in the opposite view, that human interference in a process that *seems* inevitable is possible but has very little effect except on the personal level. This too finds its place in the new model of reality, where the possibility of real interference in the reorganization of a given system is caused by the effect of information. When describing a human being or a society, this model includes points of bifurcation, points after which the future path may take more than one direction, and also the possibility is recognized that these points of bifurcation give the opportunity to direct an actual path at will. But although such opportunities may be interpreted as freedom, this freedom is relevant only for an individual's state of mind (as Spinoza thought) but it cannot in reality determine the future life of this individual. This is because every system consists of elements which are themselves systems. Therefore, small changes in the elements may either have no effect at all or may cause large changes in the system higher in the hierarchy so that the future path of the latter is unpredictable (as shown by the example of the evolution of species, and also by Spinoza's death caused by tuberculosis). When the number of bifurcation points is very large the system may collapse, but more often than not it reorganizes itself in an unpredictable way.

In a social system, this model may accentuate the role of human interference in selecting a favorable path, but at the same time undermine the idea of inevitable technological or economical progress, let alone moral progress. Marx, like the early pragmatists, acknowledged cultural factors of change. For example, they saw in the introduction of agriculture a human intervention, in a previously dominant form of organization, which brought with it an irreversible change in human history. Similar, although less universal, was the effect of the industrial revolution. A way back seems inconceivable. But these are retrospective judgments. The present urgent problems, like the pollution of air and the water, as well as growing unemployment and other social ills, are visible "points of bifurcation" that may well reverse, or destroy, the imagined inevitable path of progress. We cannot regard these phenomena as unimportant fluctuations, but the question remains whether we can correctly predict the effect of our interference.

Foucault's view may be interpreted in a similar manner. He thought that he could fight for the emancipation of, say, homosexuals, but warned that getting rid of one institutional power could not prevent the probable emergence of another. In other words, he emphasized that a predictable change in a system causes non-predictable changes in a higher or in another level of organization. However, those who are now taking part in the *new culture studies* in the belief that their studies are part of a struggle for social emancipation do not accept this interpretation. If they were following Foucault, they would claim that by participating in their groups' activities they can attain their own emancipation *now*, without bothering about a future they anyhow cannot control. But this is not what they claim.

The difference seems not so much to be due to their rejection of the idea of progress as to the way it can be achieved. In particular, they reject the idea that progress is achieved by the spreading or the enlarging of knowledge. That this belief is still common among natural scientists can be seen, for example, in Steven Weinberg's article in the *Scientific American* of October 1994. In his opinion even if science is interpreted as a particular creation of western culture it is quite possible that "what we learn about why the world is the way it is will become part of everyone's intellectual heritage," and this possibility hinges on the universal recognition of its value. But according to the new neo-pragmatist interpretation of knowledge the only way through which knowledge can spread, for example that a concept like mass or space could become intersubjective as Weinberg suggests, would be if the interests and rhetoric of physicists concerning the physical universe became common to all by the latter's power of persuasion. According to neo-pragmatists, this is not necessarily the case even in our own culture because the acceptance of the scientific view depends on a variety of other factors (forming the social alliances, as Latour explains), and communities with other cultures may or may not choose to share this heritage. But the main cause of the recent "cultural revolution" is not this interpretation of the place of knowledge in human history but the cultural relativism that sprang from it.

This relativism, like other post modern ideas, also fits the view of the world as a hierarchy of complex systems, where a person's brain is a processor of information, and the mind is its functioning "software" which gets its input data from the human environment. The emphasis on language, or on the fact that the human environment is a cultural reality based on communication of information, is compared to the fact that different software can function on the same hardware. With or without this metaphor, this emphasis brought with it a generalization of the term "language" to include all communicative media. The very concept of culture changed. It includes anything that has a communicative function, from the theory of relativity to the comic strip, from Beethoven's sonatas to pop music, in fact everything that has or may have an effect on behavior and on finding one's place in society.

In the past, nature was contrasted with culture because it was held that while nature was given, culture was a human creation. But just as fluctuations in natural phenomena were dismissed, the traditional view of culture paid little attention to local differences in science, philosophy or art. Only the cultural phenomena which were supposed to change (often interpreted as enrich) human experience permanently and which went beyond everyday life were thought worthy of attention. The test of their value was survival: at the time they are produced it may not be possible to determine which ideas or works of art are of true value but with the passage of time they are sifted by history. Only those which have a lasting effect are true cultural assets. The analogy with Darwin's natural selection is obvious, and Weinberg's view fits it. This conception of culture excludes a-priori most journalism, caricatures, popular literature and music etc., which are all essentially related to current local issues or fashions. If, however, one looks for those products of language (or communication) that have a direct effect on particular people's thoughts and behavior, and which determine what is called "a personal identity," this exclusion is unjustified. In relation to this direct effect the impact of the local and temporary is in fact much more important than any long term or universal effect.

The new version of culture associated with personal identity finds its counterpart in the post-modern interest in language. A cultural branch of real value in the modern-realist sense has always been recognized as one that has its own language, which needs to be mastered in order to gain the benefits arising out of that branch. This is true for logic and mathematics, musical notation, and any other technical vocabulary designed to clarify issues by making the language more precise. But concentrating on these sub-languages the role of ordinary language in shaping a culture has been neglected in scientific circles. The interest in ordinary language as a factor of social control (as opposed to interest in it as a central cognitive faculty) was accentuated by the actual proliferation of specialization in social organization as well as in science. This may have been the source of Wittgenstein's idea of "language games" and of Foucault's parallel analysis. The modern social structure accentuated the fact that for the uninitiated the development of specialized terminologies in the various fields of interest became a barrier to understanding. The resentment of the uninitiated of these barriers is seldom directed toward mathematics or musical notation (without which the domains in which they are in use have become unthinkable) but toward languages associated more closely with common social communication. Medicine and legal procedures are good examples of the sort of domains where a language barrier to understanding constitutes an immediate state of dependency, and is therefore experienced as an instrument of power.

The effect of the scientific differentiation of domains of inquiry on social relations is undeniable in the case of medicine. Having one's stomach treated as if it was detached from the rest of one's body, let alone one's person, often causes resentment even when one does not question the validity of the physiological theories applied by doctors. A realist may accept this fact as an inevitable evil, but the language barrier deepens the resentment because it adds a feeling of helpless dependency, of being excluded from decisions about one's own life. This resentment remains even when one knows that the development of a technical language is necessary for advancing a correct interpretation of illness which serves everyone's interest and not only the interests of the experts who understand the language. Together with some disappointment in a medical institution, as a result of earlier high expectations that it should overcome all causes of illness, these resentments contribute to the flight of a large number of people toward alternative medicine. But the main post-modern contribution is due to the idea that the language is the main source of evil, because if true, there is in fact no reason to judge any approach to medicine except by one's personal "participation" in the treatment.

Such a radical and exaggerated rejection of modern science is now leaving its mark on arts-faculties in many universities. It means more than the refusal to read classical "white male" literature, just as the flight to alternative medicine means more than a rejection of being talked to in an incomprehensible language (or *"rhetoric,"* as the term is now commonly misused). Criticism of this radical rejection of science does not mean that the resentment against the control attained through rhetorical devices by experts, and very often by politicians who pretend to be experts, is not a real social issue. The same sort of criticism levelled against the use of language as an instrument of power may exist without putting the entire scientific enterprise in jeopardy.

A particularly good example of this is the work of Noam Chomsky. As linguist he looks for the universal aspects of language, for a common property of the human species. He takes linguistics to be a natural science in the realist empirical sense. As distinct from Wittgenstein, whose observations apply to the *use* of language, Chomsky postulates that, since the ability to speak is a natural phenomenon, an ordinary language must have some universal features which are common to the human species, and which make its acquisition possible. But just as science, or any other knowledge, can be used for good and evil purposes (as traditional scientists have always acknowledged) so can knowledge of the properties of a natural language serve both ends. Chomsky never tires of warning his public that apart from his postulated *syntactic* common features of all languages, the distinct use of words, or dialects, reflect the heterogeneity of society in normal life, and that more often than not rhetorical devices become instruments of power.

Chomsky is chosen here to illustrate the point because he is no less radical in his opposition to established means of control, including the power of rhetoric, than the post-modern proponents of cultural diversity. The difference is that while Chomsky warns that among other ill effects of succumbing to this power of rhetoric the achievements of science may be destroyed, post-modern analyses accept this power as inevitable: it is, in their opinion the essential source of power, to the exclusion of all other factors, for better or for worse. The post-modern approach is reminiscent of the Marxist exclusion of all but economic factors in determining the social superstructure, against which post modernism in France developed in the first place. But now it simply replaces economic forces by the force of language. It is this exaggerated attention to language which gave rise to relativism.

This can be illustrated by the common post modern statement that a text can be understood only by placing it in its proper context. Any competent historian will accept this claim. Every historian is aware of the risk of reading his or her own interpretation of the world into a text, as well as a possible misleading interpretation of events by the author of the text. Every historian knows that to understand a text correctly the intentions of its writer and the circumstances under which it was produced must be taken into account. This is the meaning of objectivity even if, unlike in the natural sciences, one cannot in this case literally "calculate away" these personal points of view. In fact the very use of the term "point of view" suggests the analogy. The search for a true interpretation is the search for the phenomenal reality of the past, from which the phenomenal experience and the interpretations of contemporary writers is not meant to be excluded. Historians are not unaware that they cannot escape the influences of their own time and mind even with careful reading, but they hope that by reading the interpretations of others they may be alerted to the possibility of misrepresentation. Every historian is also aware that the risk of misinterpretation is particularly great with an old text where the words may have changed their meanings since it was written in ways which may easily go unnoticed when there is no other source of knowledge for comparison. For realist historians, scientific method means to rely on as much contemporary evidence as is possible, which often mean mainly contemporary documents. The method is a standard norm, and is pursued with full knowledge of its difficulties. It is even acknowledged that the task is often too difficult to be achieved in full.

But this is *not* what post-modern critics mean when they speak of "placing a text in its correct context." They only *start* from the claim that all texts are interpretations of other texts and that interpreters can never know the intentions of other authors. They generalize the term "text," just as the term language has been generalized: archeological finds, for example, are also texts. They cannot provide evidence for texts because they are interpreted by archaeologists as part of their story. They conclude that because we can rely on nothing but texts, and these are always re-interpretations of earlier texts, written with ever different purposes in mind, any attempt to extract true facts from historical texts, the so-called evidence, can never be anything but an illusion. In other words, the post-modern historical conception is that because historians always write and have always written history according to their own concerns, there simply is no such thing as historical truth or a past reality. Post-modern historians ignore the pitfalls of interpretation which modern historians warn against for the same reason that Latour rejects Popper's principle of falsifiability: if there is no authentic evidence to be found there is no point in looking for it. And the radical view dominant in cultural studies concludes from this that putting a text in its context means to put it in the context of today's power structure, to unmask the hidden intentions of their teachers or the present persuasive power of the text in their hands, irrespective of its meaning and the intentions of its author in the past. The same applies to literary studies. Students believe that they may be able to escape the persuasive power of some "oppressive" texts simply by not reading them. But as they cannot escape the effects of texts they are taught, they find it important either to insist on reading those texts which are closest to their heart, or to expose the hidden power of the others.

Post-modern students do not argue with realists. From their point of view the concept of truth, as it is related to realism, belongs to the ideological rhetoric of modern social structures within which, as early pragmatists indicated, people thought that it was useful to describe things as they were, independently of human interest. But this is the ideology from which they wish to free themselves. The purpose of reading a text is to get out of it whatever can be *useful* for the reader here and now. Reading historical or literary texts may have its uses because they may contain helpful suggestions, but their authors' original intentions or the reality they describe are not only impossible to know but irrelevant for this purpose. The licence to read a text as we wish does not stem merely from the impossibility of knowing the writer's intentions; its main justification is the possibility that by changing the use of a word (which means changing its meaning, or changing its significance in the rhetoric of the argument) one can change the power structure it represents.

Whatever is true of reading a text is true of writing one. There is no fundamental difference between writing scientific history and writing a fictional description of a period. The former as the latter are mere interpretations; basically both are fiction. This then is a general feature of post-modern cultural studies: they blur the boundaries between fact and fiction, between science and art, between philosophy and literature, and between logical argument and rhetorical persuasion.

The idea is similar to Latour's about science, with an extra emphasis on "local" effects of language. A social struggle can be carried out by calling the opponent a terrorist. All the opponent needs to do to parry this attack is to reinterpret the word "terrorist" to mean a freedom fighter. As Latour's appeal to Machiavelli says, who will win the struggle in the end depends on what social alliances will be formed. But whereas a realist thinks that the alliances which decide the winner will also determine which meaning of the word will stay in the language, the premises of the new culturalists imply that the interpretation of the word that will win will determine the outcome of the struggle.

This post-modern view gives an anti-realist interpretation to the latest information-processing machine model. People can use any observed detail in their natural or cultural environment as a bit of information, as raw material for creating or changing their specific environment. The world itself is a text from which we receive information. The world is the phenomenal world, where the "phenomenal" gets its language-dominated interpretation. The "book of nature" is not written in the language of mathematics, as Galileo thought, but has been written by men and women in the past and continues to be written by them today in a variety of languages. It is a creative work of art. And like all works of art, the conceived world which we take to be reality is an imaginative creation guided by contemporary values (other bits of information) and not by a non-existent objectivity. By this view the writing of modernist texts has been informed by a *value* called "truth," where the inverted commas are intended to indicate that like all values the particular meaning of truth is an invention of a particular culture with little natural or universal about it. But other values tell us what is (politically) correct today.

Again it must be emphasized that the notion of truth applies to a cultural creation also in the modern realist view: a *theory* can be true or false, not reality. But even the realization (as Poincaré saw it) that most terms used in science are conventional did not do away with realism and truth because a language was not seen as an arbitrary invention. The evolution of a language was supposed to rest on an assumption of continuity between a perceived and a conceived natural world and, at least to some extent, between a traditional conception of the world and any new conceptual creation. This view was held by Einstein. He did not think that his view replaced Newton's theory because the latter was wrong but because it was shown to be a good approximate description of the world as it was known in his time. The replacement of the correspondence theory of truth by a coherence theory of truth presupposed that the creation of any theory is an extension of a natural tendency of people to give structure to their perceived world. The difference between a theory and a common sense interpretation of phenomena is a difference in the immediacy of experience. Perceived facts in everyday experience are structured conceptions where the structuring is done by ordinary language. When the use of language is understood in this way, the difference between sense perception and variable conceptions is narrowed down, at least with regard to some statements which we call facts. This is the reason why, for example Donald Davidson, who sees himself as a follower of Quine, still writes in the tradition of early pragmatists who did not reject science but claimed to place it in its social-cultural context, while Rorty, who rejects any "naturalistic" relation between a language and a reality it claims to represent, is an anti-realist in spite of his reliance upon Davidson.

Any view of science must recognize its social character—the dependency of its development on the institutions which support it. Any view of science must admit that if it is a *recommendation* of a modern scientist to associate the conception of truth to the way it is ascertained then the related scientific practice is a cultural creation. And no view of science denies that ultimate uncertainty remains. But what is avoided by realist science, by early pragmatism and even by Davidson and to some extent by Wittgenstein is crucial: if political, moral, and scientific correctness are all fiction, depending on the language we *choose* to use, then there are no grounds to object to those who assert the natural necessity of poverty, unemployment or any social evil, and there are also no grounds to refute those who deny the factual historical occurrence of the Holocaust. Moreover, it is quite possible that had the Nazis won the war a generation of pupils and readers would have come to believe in both the truth and the moral virtue of all their "theories." What we should ask Rorty, post-modern historians, or students of the related cultural studies is whether, in their opinion, a moral argument for change in a society with or without any analysis of true possibilities in its support, *must* have the same persuasive power; whether a moral story, like a novel describing atrocities, must have the same effect on our assessment of the inhumanity of a particular ideology, culture, or form of social organization (or perhaps of our species) as has the *knowledge* that such atrocities were actually committed. In short, given that invented stories have the power they claim for them, and given that their claimed purpose is to create a culture where people care about and are more tolerant toward each other, does the post-modern rejection of the value of truth really serve their purpose?

The point is that the description given in these three chapters suggests that the claims of post-modernism may look like little more than the exaggeration of problems which have been recognized long before. But the effect of these exaggerations can be far-reaching. The need for imagination and creativity in order to make sense of any aspect of the world, as well as for bringing to life an understanding of history, cannot be denied. But is it morally right, or useful, to be imaginative and creative *instead* of being careful with the facts? Free creativity, like wishful thinking, can be as dangerous an instrument of power as the rigid requirements of the mechanistic view which claims to accept observed facts alone.

A disturbing possibility which follows from the same description is that the ideas expressed by post-modernists are not *arbitrary* exaggerations. They often look very much like a realistic mirror of our present social reality in which advertising in marketing and similar devices in the rhetoric of public relations agencies have become powerful institutionalized practices. Advertising has become more important in our market economy than the true quality of the advertised products. And the intellectual "language game" is seen as a market place where ideas are treated as products. Since advertising is more efficient in controlling markets than the actual demand for and supply of products, persuasive rhetoric is now also being recommended as the best vehicle to sell ideas. Wittgenstein's warnings are forgotten.

Initially positivists recommended that moral decisions should be made on the basis of true knowledge, but they failed to take into account that in the social sciences human aspirations are moral facts. Their moral commitment to the value of truth eventually led many of them to assume that *"is"* means *"ought,"* without realizing that by their own views what is true when associated with "ought" ought to be judged by what we want to achieve, and not by the *is*. Post-modern criticism appears to follow a similar road. It began by following their predecessors' notice of this omission in positive science as well as the neglect of the role and the power of language in modern analysis. But its devotees failed to realize that their exaggerated attention to the latter, which they turned into "rhetorical determination," reflects a new social development. The result is that replacing the conception of a fact by a "cultural creation" makes it easier to accept the new social practices as they come. As Jane Rossetti explains in her *Economics as Discourse*, the term "persuasion" does not mean that by their doctrine persuasion means that anything goes, or the effect of a stronger vocabulary, but how well a theoretical interpretation redefines or reinterprets a community's stable existing perceptions. So again the *is* means *ought*. Popper's warning against the nihilism implicit in Kuhn's description of science seems to be vindicated.

Not all post modern writers embrace this result. The tension between accepting the "no choice" attitude as an inevitable social fact, as suggested by Latour, and the belief in the possibility to control *our* future lives remains. This is the tension between accepting the new mechanistic view and dismissing the need or even the possibility of interfering in the working of this universal information-processing machine, and seeing a Lamarckian factor in cultural history, namely a possibility of interfering and controlling its path, if being aware of the limitations of such possibilities, as suggested by Foucault. Both interpretations are found in post-modern views. But when the latter is held in cultural studies, it gets a peculiar twist which results from the exaggerated accentuation of the power of language. They seem to think that by the mere expression of wishful thinking, by merely changing a present or historical interpretation they can change the world. It is as if they trust that it is sufficient to invent a history in which the place of women, blacks, homosexuals, or any other discriminated group, is described as having been central, to effectuate an actual improvement in the present day conditions of such a group.

Similarly, the new relativism which is often presented as multi-culturalism or pluralism, is not taken to mean a recognition of the actual existence of different, and often contradictory, values, as for example the not full compatibility of securing the essential needs of everybody and rewarding personal (competitive) achievement. It is not meant as respect of the fact that, as a result of such contradictions, some social groups may prefer one value rather than its contrary. It is not meant to be a liberal ideology, a recommendation of tolerance toward the arguments offered in support of these preferences (toward their different rhetorical styles, as these are described). Instead, this relativism is seen as a positive power in its own right, a power which can be employed by every interest group in its own way and can replace any other form of struggle, and thus "automatically" *create* a liberal, tolerant society. Those holding this belief assume that the recognition that winning social struggles is, and can be, brought about by rhetorical innovations implies that, being verbal, it has a greater chance of creating mutual tolerance than other, more violent, sorts of confrontations. This is also Rorty's idea. Relying on Dewey, he maintains that one of the benefits of culture is that it replaces real war by arguments. But if all languages are instruments of power, and if there are no other criteria for choosing between arguments except persuasive rhetoric, whence comes this optimism? After all, even if strife is replaced by a verbal contest, access to the means of persuasion is not equally open to all. Dewey certainly did not think that argument meant merely verbal contest. He believed in the power of education, and in particular of scientific education.

There is, of course, a genuine difficulty with the requirement to stick to the truth. When we find some criteria for distinguishing between true and false, this is always related to a specific branch of knowledge, or in the post modern terms, to a specific domain of interpretation. Reflection on any of these criteria may form a new domain of interpretation. We may find moral reasons for accepting the chosen criteria, or as pragmatists explained, we may turn to an anthropological explanation why different societies accept different statements as knowledge, and thus understand our own choice. But then we are confronted with a new set of criteria for ascertaining what is a true moral value or a true explanation of social choice. In the last resort we are always left with no criteria. We are left with the merely intuitive notion of truth. This difficulty is the often emphasized unbridgeable gap between the explainer and the explained. There is no way out.

16

The Political Dimension

What have been described here in economics and in philosophy are the symptoms of a loss of direction; the engine has stopped, the boat is drifting. For centuries the West, and particularly the west of the West from which intellectual changes spread, had turned its eyes to the morrow and eagerly embraced change, and by this it marked itself off from earlier and alternative cultures. From Wagner's *Zukunftsmusik* through Rimbaud's cry *"Il faut être absolument moderne"* and a papal *Rerum Novarum* the new, the revolutionary, the forward-looking, indeed the future-hailing was the common theme of otherwise quite disparate movements. By the 1890s these were fully fledged; symbolically, Walter Crane's Hope greeted the rising sun with outstretched arms. By the 1920s they were everywhere triumphing, and not only among the young. The names they had given rise to were affirmative, all-embracing, programmatic; Positivism and Futurism, *L'Humanité* and *Vorwärts*, beyond-the-real Surréalisme, Cubism and Vorticism, Modern Dance, Modern Linguistics, Modern Architecture, Free Schools, and free love.

Hitler himself was obliged to lay claim to 1000 years of a Socialist future, but the rest, however, diverse, he consigned to a collective cultural Bolshevism (and all were indeed revolutionary in spirit), the work of Cosmopolitan Jewry—and indeed multi-cultural Jews like Einstein had made a noble contribution, out of all proportion to their numbers, to that roaring wind of original thinking which we now call Modernism. As was to be expected, from the 1950s onwards much of this intellectual energy spent itself in practical Modernist achievements, from town planning to the Welfare State, and the millennarian banners were flaunted more rarely. Whatever else Existentialism was, it was clearly not a cause to die for.

The subsequent loss of momentum is revealed by the chosen names of the movements we have been discussing. Neoclassicism defines itself by reference to a system of thought that reigned for a century from the late 1770s, and if Post-modernism is moving forwards at all, it is with its eyes fixed on the rear-view mirror. The astonishing claim, on the collapse of actual Bolshevism, of the "End of History," might well have been greeted with a sigh of relief if it meant that movement had stopped and passengers might now alight from intellectual vehicles driven so dangerously.

That claim was a cry of triumph not so much over a fallen political enemy, for few equated the Soviet Union with "history," but over Modernism itself, a brutal declaration that movements of whatever inspiration will not change the future, that we must submit to what comes. And away from the abstractions of the present pages, in the everyday world of ordinary people, many today have the impression that the wheel is motionless at least temporarily, at top dead center or bottom dead center before its real motion carries them upwards, as few now dare hope, or downwards, as they try not to fear. So they immerse themselves in their daily business and immediate circle, and turn their back on the political parties who until now claimed to command the levers of change. In these doldrums, in Britain for instance 80% of the population reject a grey prime minister, a greedy top management and greasy politicians familiar with the slush-fund and the sleaze of pocket-filling deals. In this atony, this dystrophy of civil society, people live materially from day to day and intellectually from hand to mouth.

In the dark days of World War II, in a broadcast-recording for the Science Conference in London on September 28th, 1941, Albert Einstein declared that in his view to ask what hopes and fears the scientific method implies was not the right way to put the question. In his opinion, "whatever this tool in the hand of man will produce depends entirely on the nature of the goals alive in this mankind. Once these goals exist, the scientific method furnishes means to realize them. Yet it cannot furnish the very goals. The scientific method itself would not have led anywhere, it would not even have been born without a passionate striving for clear understanding. But perfection of means and confusion of goals seem to characterize the age. If we desire sincerely and passionately the safety, the welfare, and the free development of the talents of all men, we shall not be in want of the means to approach such a state."

Einstein's statement is as true today as it had been when he made it; nobody is against safety, welfare, and the development of talents, but events have given these desires a different meaning from the one which he had supposed to be self-evident. The goals of a society are a matter of culture, and a narrowly materialistic individualistic community perceives safety, welfare, and talent differently from a community moved by compassion, solidarity and the search for truth.

The director of an atomic energy generating plant may be very much concerned for his and his family's safety but less troubled by hazards facing the rest of the community. He will move his home as far as possible from his enterprise but not shut it down because other families which do not have this option are living in its immediate vicinity. Nor will the state (barring extreme circumstances) close down the power-plant if it is deemed necessary for maintaining the country's economic competitive position. Similarly, irrespective of class and social status, many people will deplore cuts in social benefits, but they will not be prepared to reduce their own income even if they are or can be convinced that this is the only way to secure the welfare of society as a whole and in the long run possibly also their own. Economists will develop their talent, and advance their status in the eyes of their peers, by filling professional journals with sophisticated mathematical formulas which, as Wassily Leontief says, are "leading the reader from sets of more or less plausible but entirely arbitrary assumptions to precisely stated but irrelevant theoretical conclusions." Worse than this, most economists never ask themselves what purpose and whose they are serving, except perhaps to promote their own status or to satisfy a whimsical interest in mathematical games.

The point is that values and goals are the ever-changing historical product of societies, and a society nurtured on individualistic materialism is ill equipped to choose goals and pursue policies designed to promote *social* safety, *social* welfare and the *free* development of talent; and a scientific community which regards *expediency* as its guiding principle is ill equipped to deal with truth. The values which determine an individual's behavior at any given time are a much better indicator of the real values governing the society than the values its members may sincerely think they adhere to, or claim they do.

Sociological research done in the Netherlands during the 1970s has shown that most workers when asked the abstract question whether they are in favor of equal pay for everyone answered affirmatively. But the same respondents separated the workers into those deserving better and poorer wages when asked the more specific question whether all employees in their enterprise ought to receive the same remuneration. This division was clear in spite of the fact that the question was formulated in a manner which did not imply a reduction of the higher earnings but a raising of the lower incomes to obtain the proposed equality. Similarly, the question whether dangerous, dirty and physically demanding work deserves the same remuneration as safer, cleaner and less physically exerting but very responsible work also received an affirmative reply, while the more direct question whether a coal miner ought to receive the same pay as a minor company executive was answered in the negative by almost all who were asked except the miners.

In the 1980s, probably under the influence of the reduced time allocated to the humanities in education curricula, and of the media campaign in favor of free market competition, the climate of opinion underwent a change. The answer to the abstract question about equality of pay no longer received an almost unanimous positive reply, and even the answers to questions about equal pay for equal work became more differentiated, particularly with regard to women. Social status became more directly related to income, and the power to command people became the hallmark of distinction and a deciding factor in the justification for income differentials. In the economic sphere efficiency and acumen remained important but yielded pride of place to hierarchy, and in politics social responsibility and ideology gave way to access to the media. The point is that people are capable of thinking about theoretical situations divorced from their concrete reality. They abstract some essential elements from their social system and consider them independently of the concrete relations which are associated with these elements. This is what Rowls suggests and what the research done 20 years ago has illustrated with regard to people's attitude toward equality. What was neglected was the effect which with the passage of time the concrete attitudes have on the theoretical outlook. People today have simply become less favorably inclined toward equality.

Unlike the depression of the 1930s, which affected the lives and hopes of millions of people from almost all classes, the depression of the 1980s had a discriminatory effect. The incomes of the employed did not diminish, as had been the case in the 1930s, but separated society into reasonably well remunerated employed people and the unemployed, poor and destitute members of the community. In the USA it led to ghettos and "no go" areas. In most countries of western Europe the disintegration of society was delayed by the social security system of the Welfare State, but is now rapidly moving in the same direction. With the collapse of the Soviet Union and the spreading of reliable information about her dismal economic performance and depraved record in the sphere of human liberties, the fear of revolution which lurked behind some measures to alleviate the distress of the poorest in the 1930s also disappeared. As a result of these developments ideas like the *New Deal* lost their attraction for politicians. Ideas like these can no longer secure them an electoral majority. They realize that even if all the unemployed were to cast their votes for an updated similar proposition the total number of their votes would not suffice to balance those of the employed.

Even an unlikely combination of environmentalists, communists, old-age pensioners, the unemployed and their dependents, and the genuinely religious-motivated supporters of a less profit-centered policy would together not muster more than 20 per cent of the votes in the Netherlands. In the USA, where most of the deprived do not even bother to register for elections, the percentage would probably be smaller.

Worse than this, the virtual monopoly of the establishment over the media of public information now makes the presentation of *alternatives* to the "received" recipe for solving the unemployment problem, as the New Deal had purported to be, practically impossible. There is nothing sinister in this and there is no conspiracy to hide the truth, but there is the simple fact that the information given to the public is usually selected by people who do not consider themselves experts in the field of knowledge they report, and that they rely for their information on what they believe to be the best established sources. The very nature of their work allows them little time to analyze the press releases and government communiqués which they receive. Their task is to report the news, and an official press release is news. In the Gulf war reporters were in fact prevented from obtaining first-hand information, and had to rely only on press releases, and this practice is not confined to matters of defence alone. Often reporters also do not know the *true origins* of the news they are reporting, and the measure of its import on the public mind. For example, if they report information provided by an international organizations such as the OECD, they may not even be aware that it is based on the material supplied to the organization by member governments and therefore reflects no more than these governments' official policy. But by broadcasting the news the media are creating the impression that they convey independent international confirmation for the ruling point of view. The public, learning of the OECD report, finds that it conforms with what their government is saying, and concludes that what the experts have been telling them is right. The public stops thinking. If the "experts" and everyone else agree that the world is flat, it must be true. Even the ministers and experts who originally supplied the material upon which the international report is based forget the doubts they may initially have had, and feel that their views have been confirmed.

The essential problem is, however, not the control and the power of the media but the waning of critical thought. People brought up in a culture which relies on authorities and puts little store by criticism are not equipped to question "received truth." An education programme which is primarily directed to serve industry by imparting to students practical learning, though this may well be the best available technological knowledge, without encouraging them to be skeptical as a matter of principle with regard to validity and premisses, cannot but lead to stagnation and loss of humanism. An education system which does not extol independent thought and does not disseminate values which transcend narrow materialistic competitive self-interest is doomed to destroy the very objectives it is claiming to preserve, even if it genuinely wishes to preserve them. The rise of capitalism had been closely associated with the development of a critical attitude toward established truths. Copernicus, Kepler, and Galileo, and later the entire movement of the Enlightenment, broke with the hegemony of the established conceptions and opened the door to new ideas. But the new trend in education, which stresses techniques at the expense of critical thought and a formalist methodology at the cost of the humanities, is reversing this process and is leading us back to a kind of medieval blind reliance on authority.

Taking economics as an example it is easy to illustrate how the modern professional establishment has canonized the underlying premises of "received theories" and transformed scientific argument into scholastic dispute. It vested certain ideas with an axiomatic status and made all theory begin from there. The fact that any axiom is self-evident by definition makes an examination of its empirical validity superfluous or impossible. Consequently a great deal of economic debate is based on what may well be metaphysical premises. The most obvious of these is the accepted premise that an invisible hand directs self-interest toward the common good. Ricardo was wary of this postulate and so were Marx and Keynes. Friedman, in his *Nobel Lecture*, adopts a pragmatic attitude. For him such economic "axioms" are unnecessary hypotheses because he believes that there is no certain substantive knowledge in either economics or in the natural sciences. But he adheres to the idea of equilibrium and therefore, like most of the rest of the economics profession, tacitly takes on board the *invisible hand*. If observable reality does not corroborate the postulate this is none of his concern, because all that matters is that the predictions come out right. The rest of the profession which does believe in theory accepts the axioms and evades their examination by proclaiming the unaccommodating *reality* a "special case," as it did with Keynes' general theory. In other words, the profession turns economics into scholastics and declares heretic and excommunicate all who question its basic premises. For the materialistically ambitious young such excommunication is no light penalty. It deprives the victim of all the advantages the "church" has to offer to its converts. It denies him or her tenured appointment at respected universities, funds for research and for attending conferences and symposia, as well as the opportunity to be given work for influential institutions.

A recent illustration of this thought-stifling process and of the effect of the new feudalism on the functioning of large organizations has been given by Susan George and Fabrizio Sabelli. In their book *Faith and Credit—the World Bank's Secular Empire*, they describe the World Bank as an organization akin to the Mafia, the Church and the Soviet Communist Party. Asked by a *de Volkskrant* reporter, Susan George explained that the World Bank had developed into a club which propagates a set of values, beliefs, traditions, and fundamentalist doctrines. These are expounded by its "saints" and reinforced by an *esprit de corps* which taking its inspiration from an intellectual leadership which permits no deviation from its own "true" teaching. Next to this the organisation is beset by personal pyramids with everyone dependent on his direct boss; hence nobody dares to open his mouth. In this situation, Susan George says, the president, and certainly the current president Preston, cannot exert real influence because in such a structure the bureaucracy cannot be overruled. The reason why such an organization can survive is that everyone wants to be employed and that those who are employed wish to retain their jobs.

To join the organization aspiring candidates must first do a lot of work for it and learn to keep their criticism to themselves. They must show respect for the objectives of the Bank and refrain from voicing independent opinions. The main avenue to advancement passes through the World Bank's *Young Professionals programme*. This programme is tailored to the transformation of people into ardent supporters. Each year between twenty and thirty out of five thousand candidates are allowed to participate in it. More than ninety percent of the selected aspirants studied at Harvard, MIT, Oxford or the London School of Economics. But not all the participants are assured of obtaining a post at the end of the course; there follows an experimental year of apprenticeship during which the candidate must prove himself worthy of an appointment. Once appointed, whoever dares to argue about or question the ideological premises or the functioning of the Bank is passed over in promotions or posted to some hot and far-off Gulag.

The process of silencing dissent was finalized in 1987 during the Bank's reorganization. At that time 600 jobs (ten percent of the total number of the Bank's employees) were scrapped and this provided an excellent opportunity to eliminate any remaining vestiges of dissension and to reward compliance. After the reorganization, which was disastrous for morale and for work climate, the rank and file became very silent indeed. The result of this, according to Susan George, was "absence of originality and creativity, and hence of new ideas; and a total unwillingness to innovate or make old practices more efficient."

External criticism of the Bank's ideology and practice is regarded as an image-problem and treated as a public relations obstacle which can be solved by publicity campaigns. The point of departure for these campaigns is the announcement that all critics are wrong because their appraisal is based on erroneous data. If this does not help the Bank has a second line of defence: it creates a new department. If critics claim that too little attention is paid to women's problems a department "women and development" is established; if the critics complain about too little attention to the environment, an "environment portfolio" is established. But no sooner are these new organs created than they are encapsulated in the Bank's culture and their objectives become subordinate to the organization's higher goals.

No doubt Lewis Preston meant what he said when on taking office in 1991 as the Bank's president he proclaimed that the World Bank's prime objective was the struggle against long-term poverty. But in fact it is not he but the bureaucrats below him who really call the tune. Most of them have already held their offices for thirty years and have little wish to adjust their *laissez-faire* ideology. The fact that many scientists, politicians, members of the Club of Rome and of Unicef have indicated the risks involved in allowing the free market to rule supreme leaves them unmoved.

An extreme example of this *"economism"* is Larry Summers' "poison memorandum" of 1992. Larry Summers, the American Secretary of State who might well have succeed Preston on his retirement in 1996 as the head of the World Bank, had not Rubin stopped him in order to help to solve the Mexican economic and financial crisis. In this memorandum Summers asked himself whether the Bank should not stimulate the displacement of environmentally undesirable industries to the Third World. Summers is an economist, and in terms of purely economic calculations this idea makes perfect sense. Later Summers claimed that the memorandum was merely a discussion paper. But the authors of *Faith and Credit—the World Bank's Secular Empire* feel certain that this approach is typical. They believe that the World Bank is committed to the idea of the market and blind to its shortcomings.

The point is that this climate, in which people are treated as tools instead of ends, is hardly restricted to the World Bank. As suggested in an earlier chapter (The New Feudalism and Managerial Oligarchy) it is spreading from business to politics and education. When to reduce the cost of Dutch university education the length of studies was shortened the courses in ethics were the first to be abolished in several medical faculties. The primacy of practical professional studies seemed self-evident. But is it? It deprives medicine of its social purpose and strips the medical profession of the values it requires for playing the humane progressive role which were traditionally assigned to it. It makes patients suspicious of doctors, and some doctors sometimes more concerned with their own material improvement than with their patients' health. The techniques developed for organ transplantation are of course laudable; but will they remain so when physicians buy organs from the poor to save the lives of the rich? Presently such practices are still rare and illegal but there is no reason why they should remain beyond the pale. If ethics is taken out of the educational curriculum and the market, and individual freedom with a market interpretation is all pervasive, no reason remains to forbid such practices. After all, individual freedom includes the freedom to dispose of one's assets for a market price; so why not human organs if the price seems to the poorest very generous? That such reckoning is not wildly fanciful can be seen from the steadily increasing newspaper reports about needy Asians who are lured to dubious clinics to donate kidneys for what appears to them lavish rewards.

Although this example is extreme it does illuminate a problem. Recently a Harley street doctor was in fact struck off the medical register for this reason. He could not be successfully prosecuted in England, but medical ethics succeeded where law failed. But from the free market's point of view the transaction is perfectly justified—it is a legitimate market transaction. Looking at it from a purely economic point of view the buying and the selling of a kidney is logical and not different from any other kind of trade. The purchaser pays a price to save his life without necessarily causing the donor to loose his. The physician may take the same view. The ethical objection is that it grants those with much money a right to life which it denies to those with little money or with none. But this is not very far removed from many other market practices and herein lies the crux of the matter. If society wants to sustain humane values it cannot allow the logic of the market to be the final arbiter of conduct. It must sustain or create some countervailing forces, and for this education is essential. In other words, society must allow sufficient room in the educational curricula for the humanities. Just as a critical attitude to knowledge is essential to sustain scientific and technological innovation, so is a good familiarity with the humane and aesthetic values of our intellectual heritage necessary to maintain the social consensus upon which the functioning of an enlightened market system depends. But there is the rub: if the sale of human organs is placed beyond the market because it is considered inhumane where does humanity begin and end? On the same grounds, should not minimum wages and social security allowances also be excluded from the logic of the market place? The point is that a reasonable balance needs to be maintained between the logic of the market and the welfare of society, and that without acknowledging the role of liberal education this cannot be achieved.

It follows that education is an essential issue in the struggle for sustaining the economic as well as the other positive achievements of the western world. Fortunately it is also an issue where those wishing to preserve these achievements may still have prospects of success because sooner or later even those most committed to reducing government expenditure will recognize that without fundamental research and innovation and without a good measure of social consensus the industrially advanced nations have no chance of surviving the competitive onslaught from Third World countries like the Asian tigers. This means that the recent pressures which transform education into vocational training and deprive it of its critical qualities may eventually be resisted not only by part of the new generation of students, liberals and by the Churches, but also by some of the top leaders of large industrial corporations.

Indications for a development in this direction are discernible. Already there is a certain measure of apprehension among university students about the contents and quality of their education and among big business leaders about the lack of managerial sagacity and the stagnation in the sphere of fundamental research and innovation. In the Netherlands, the catastrophic results of the policy of reducing the cost of higher education and of separating teaching from research, though still denied by the political establishment, are already obvious to some major industrialists. The universities, which since the late 1980s have been turned into institutions for vocational training and have been placed under the management of a host of bureaucrats who bestow upon themselves professorial titles, are now in fact less places of learning than schools where students absorb little else but received theory from secondary texts. The situation in the research schools is more varied, but the reduced number of students accepted into them is drastically limiting the range of the talent which will be available for innovation in the future. In many, though not in all, of these schools the leading professors are appointed by bureaucrats with little concern for science but with much regard for publicity and its effect on the recruitment of funds. The result is an emphasis on short-term, and from the government's point of view "politically correct," research and little concern for new long-term fundamental scientific insight. The bureaucracy can live with this, but for how long can industry do so?

Naturally all this is disguised by favorably formulated statistical presentations which show a sharp increase in the number of publications and research reports. But a closer scrutiny of the quality of the publications soon shows that many of them are of little value and mere reiterations of things already elaborated in the authors' doctoral dissertations or in earlier discussions on the subject. After all, if one's tenure and status depends on the *number* of publications and not on their real innovative contents few scholars will not be tempted to publish just for the sake of publishing. It goes without saying that there are also many excellent scientists in Dutch universities and research schools, but their work is greatly hampered by the lack of support for whatever does not immediately lend itself to glossy publicity and does not provide the bureaucracy with an opportunity to assign the researchers' achievements to themselves. The official statistics may well show a large improvement in academic output, but this cannot hide the real debilitating consequences of the policy for society and its economy. It is for this reason that it is not inconceivable that a tacit political alliance of forces may already be developing which unites various groups, each for its particular reasons, in an effort to restore to education its old value. But the coming to fruition of such a coalition is still far off and may well never materialize until the fundamental changes in the class hierarchy in the industrial countries is recognized.

Earlier in this book, in the discussion of the rise of the new managerial oligarchy, the point was made that a new strata of society has come into existence which has deprived the capitalist class of its unchallenged leading position in the industrial hierarchy. The examples cited in this chapter show that the rise of the new strata is not confined to industry. They show that the industrial managerial oligarchy is sharing power with a fairly large political oligarchy sustained by a submissive bureaucracy. Like the industrial managerial oligarchy, the political oligarchy and its bureaucracy have their own interests, ideology and spheres of dominance. Like the industrial oligarchy, which is only marginally controlled by the shareholding owners of the enterprises it is managing, the state oligarchy is only marginally controlled by the public it is supposed to serve. Classical and Marxian economics embraced a class conception of society which either accepted as an inevitable fact of life or illuminated the conflicting interests of the classes. It divided society into capitalists and workers and assigned to the former the "love of gain" and to the later the fear of destitution as the motive for their conduct in the economic sphere. This is no longer a true reflection of reality. In its rise the new strata which is increasingly replacing capitalists at the top of the social ladder has different objectives and a different method for attaining them. It is not that great riches no longer bestow considerable privileges and power, but they no longer confer the same social esteem and power they previously did. Relying on a compliant bureaucracy, which is held together by a kind of feudal nexus which makes each member dependent on his direct superior for advancement, the new oligarchy imposes on society laws and regulations that serve its own immediate interests. Like the new captains of industry, the political oligarchy is not entirely free from supervision. Like the former, who have to satisfy their shareholders, it too has to take account of periodical elections. But between elections the leading members have time to pursue their own particular ends and to arrange matters in a way which maximizes their re-election chances without hindering the pursuit of these interests.

In a recent survey of the literature about political economic interaction models, B. Snels finds them dividing into two categories, *political business cycle models* and *partisan cycle models*. In the models of the first type political parties, once they obtain control of government, are all seen to have the same objective, namely to stay in power. The result of this is that the economic policy of one government hardly differs from that of another. The parties manipulate the economy with the objective of maximizing their votes. In the second type of model political parties have dissimilar objectives, and Snels believes that a change of government engenders a change of policy. Snels attaches importance to this distinction with regard to the recent efforts to bring about the European economic integration. But if the analysis of the changes in the social structure as they were suggested in this chapter is correct, Snels' division of the political spectrum is irrelevant. Though the personalities involved may be different, and one party may present to the public an ideological image of itself different from that of another party, they all remain "vote-maximizing" and therefore once in power they find themselves obliged to pursue similar economic policies. Irrespective of ideology they follow what they believe to assure them of an election majority; and if this "interest" is in conflict with their proclaimed ideology it is "excused" by simply attributing the deviation from the election programme to forces beyond their control or beyond human control altogether, "to the real world we have to live in" as the British Labour Party says. Moreover, as political leaders depend for information on an established (permanent) bureaucracy and on advisory bodies of experts, whose memberships also rarely change with changes of government, their decisions seldom differ irrespective of which party they belong to.

The present government of the Netherlands, a coalition of the Labour Party with the conservative Liberal Party, may serve as an example. In all matters of economic and social policy it simply continues precisely where the previous governments left off. Even the arguments given for reducing social cost and wage rates have remained the same. The reason for this is obvious: the majority of people still live fairly comfortably in the Netherlands and having constantly been told by "experts" that conditions will improve they feel no need to bother with alternatives. The leaders on the right of the political spectrum have no reason to want a change of policy, and the leaders on the left can hardly tell their voters that they have been wrong ever since the late 1970s when they began supporting the policy. One can hardly expect a political leadership to choose to swim against a torrent of public opinion which it itself helped to create in the course of its efforts to justify and excuse the abandonment of its declared basic party principles.

All this is not to say that all politicians are unprincipled and that there are no ideological differences between parties, but in government these principles and ideological commitments become secondary to the wish to stay in power. Not all but at least some leaders of large parties genuinely wish to implement their party programmes but, like Lewis Preston of the World Bank in the example given above, find themselves hamstrung and misinformed by the bureaucracy below them and by the need to watch the public opinion polls in spite of their being aware that public opinion is a created artifact. However, the most debilitating factors are self-delusion and the adaptation of leaders to the milieu they enter once they have obtained their coveted positions of leadership. Wishing to retain their status they convince themselves of the need to hold government office in order to achieve their political ends in the long run, or of the necessity to make compromises for avoiding the implementation of even worse policies. Moreover, by holding high office their contacts become increasingly limited to a strata of society of powerful people who see the world from their own perspective, which reflects their particular strata's interests. Consequently, even if the high officeholder's own background may, as often is the case, not have been that of the powerful he is gradually converted to their opinions which become his "truth." For example, they forget that interest rates are at least partly determined by the Central Bank and investment funds are not solely dependent on the rate of interest; and that a government deficit can be eliminated by raising taxes. But as tax increases are unpopular and usually fall upon the better-off, who are still the majority in the industrialized countries, the raising of taxes is simply not considered and instead a song and dance is performed about the ill-effects of a state deficit.

Intuitively the student movement of the late 1960s was aware of this but did not understand it. Their call for a "march through the institutions" was a true reflection of public resentment. But public resentment was not against the cause of the malaise, namely the rise of the new oligarchy, but against its manifestation, the way its rule presented itself to the general public in its day-to-day contacts with bureaucracy. The same was true of the student movement. It missed the recognition of the new reality. What its leaders did not comprehend was that the new political oligarchy and its bureaucracy are no longer the handmaidens of a powerful capitalist class but have become a "class" by itself, a class which sometimes shares power with the traditional class of capitalists but more often overrules it. Therefore the student movement's attack on Capitalism was at least in part misguided. Its primitive Marxism alienated the religious poor, the liberal middle class, a good part of the rich who had accepted the Keynesian compromise: in fact it alienated many who should have been its natural allies. Emotionally the movement was rooted in a mixture of Jewish-Christian ethical conceptions of justice and compassion for the underprivileged, and in a resentment of arbitrariness and arrogant authority in general. Politically it took up arms against a Capitalism which was no longer the prime enemy. It did not recognize that by the end of the 1960s poverty, the curse of the old era of capitalism, was no longer the main issue in the industrially most advanced countries, and had been replaced by the arbitrary abuse of power which is the hallmark of the new oligarchy and bureaucracy. It also did not see, and at the time could perhaps not see, how this abuse of power might bring back the poverty which by the end of the 1960s had been so dramatically reduced.

To be sure, no complex society can exist without an organizing factor a bureaucracy. But it is the culture of a society which determines the character of its bureaucracy and settles the way in which it functions. A self-serving political oligarchy cannot but impose upon its administration a set of rules which makes it uncritical and inflexible. It must impose rules to fit all circumstances with which an administrator may or may not ever be confronted. In other words, it must eliminate individual judgement and replace common sense by rigid rules. But reality is far too complex for such rules to suit all cases and events, and the public, as well as the administrator who must apply the rules, becomes increasingly frustrated by nonsensical decisions. The unfortunate result of this is that it leads to a resentment of *regulation* rather than to a resentment of the climate in which the administrative bodies which apply the regulations are obliged to work.

This brings the discussion back to the problem of education. A community which regards people as it does computers which react in the way they are programmed to without common sense to make decisions by themselves, can simply not do without rigid regulation, nor can a community which is morally corrupt or has lost a certain measure of propriety. Such a community can not avoid absurd judgments which either cause even more resentment or lead to the introduction of "corrections" which increase the number of rules and regulations *ad infinitum*. In other words the survival of the achievements of the Western World crucially depends on education, but the new oligarchy has most to lose and least to gain from it. Education, as distinct from training, is anathema to obedience and compliance, and these are the attributes the new oligarchy requires to ensure its hegemony. It is in this that "political correctness" become the involuntary partner of the system. The denial of the traditional role of the study of history and literature in the widening of the concept of "humanity" simply ignores progress. If the term human progress can be given any meaning at all it means the extension of equal rights to an increasing number of people. Ancient Rome regarded slaves as "speaking instruments"; Feudal society distinguished between people with blue and red blood; early Capitalism abolished slavery and "blood" distinctions but transformed workers into "hands"; and late capitalism allowed workers to rise on the basis of individual competitive ability but did not provide them with equal opportunities; Democracy promoted equal rights for all irrespective of color, religion and sex, though unfortunately they were never fully attained. The same is true of modernist science which has searched for the unifying principle behind events. In short, the hallmark of progress is the search for what is equal in mankind, and the hallmark of reaction, as distinct from conservatism, is the stressing of differences. Nazi Germany separated mankind into superior and inferior races, as has always been done by all who do not wish to see others equal to themselves, the new oligarchy does so by claiming for itself a superior understanding which it denies to others. Striving for equality is not antithetical to individuality. The contrary is true: equal rights provide the basis for the opportunity to realize individual aims and desires.

It is true that each of the early achievements of liberal society was related to its contemporary economic background, but it was also the steady advancement of liberal education which gave them their direction. The assumption that the improvement of the position of women and minority groups runs contrary to modernist thought is therefore simply wrong. And the negation of all the traditional elements in education and the severance of the links with the cultural heritage from the age of the Enlightenment can hardly serve to advance society toward a wider conception of mankind. But it does help the new oligarchy to introduce a new hierarchical division. It introduces a distinction between takers of decisions and those obliged to live by them. But this is what the new "class" needs for its controlling power, and this is the reason why critical thought and liberal education is replaced by greater practical competence.

Objecting to this turn of events does not contradict the striving for women's rights or for the emancipation of minorities. The modernist cultural heritage is not all "white male dominance" but a mixed bag of élitism with emancipatory tendencies. To negate this, *after* they set a new agenda, does not really serve the cause of women or discrimination against minorities; at best it can achieve the inclusion of some of their members in the new "class" while the rest will join the new army of those discriminated against, namely the majority of people. Worse than this, the single issue groups are not only divisive in their approach but bound to fail in their efforts where it does not suit the oligarchy. After all, those holding power have better access to the media of "information" and more power to convince the public of their views than the single issue groups. For the elimination of discrimination raising awareness among sufferers and the public at large may perhaps suffice, yet those in power, unless they are restricted by the cultural heritage and by critical thought, are far more likely than the oppressed to succeed in subverting beliefs which are undesirable to them.

The point is that the culture of a society, its beliefs, customs and arts, determines its goals, and that a society which places too much emphasis on competition, when competition has lost its true role, only destroys its solidarity and coherence. It encourages people "to do their own thing," to pursue individual short-term advantage, which it makes them lose sight of the long-term consequences of their choices and of the limitations imposed on them by the general framework within which they are made. But the tendency for everyone to pursue his own immediate interest, in the belief that this gives a better chance for advancement than the protracted and difficult collective effort to obtain general improvements, sets society adrift. It deprives it of a sense of direction, and in such a society the goal which Einstein and modernists regarded as self-evident is lost.

In the past, the opposition of the working class to the hardships which accompanied the industrialization of the western world gave birth to trade unions and to the socialist movement. Though initially their objectives were to meet the material needs and desires of individuals in achieving these objectives their methods were collective. In the process they produced a new social conception of *solidarity*. Unlike the old conception, such as solidarity within the family, the church and the nation state, the new conception held a promise of material improvement for individual members of society on earth here now and in the future. It combined the immediate wishes of individuals for economic betterment with the progress of society in general. It repudiated the "trickling down effect" of the identification willy-nilly of the enrichment of one group of people with the welfare of the nation as a whole, and by spreading the idea of mankind's unity, provided a realistic and practicable instrument for the reducing of the hardships of the lower strata of society.

Again this was not entirely new; for centuries the church had preached compassion and the idea of caring for the infirm and the poor had been for long part of western culture. But earlier practice was divisive; it transformed compassion into charity, the free gift from "betters" to the "deserving" or "undeserving" poor below them. The new conception of solidarity introduced a sense of equality which looked upon the fair distribution of the fruit of economic progress as a *right* and not as an act of altruism, and it suggested collective action, solidarity, as the means for obtaining it.

It is this element of modern culture which is now threatened. The new-style Thatcherite Liberal market-ideology creates a climate of "each for himself" which is not confined to economics but penetrates almost all spheres of social life. The result is that people no longer intuitively rush to assist a person beset by hooligans in a street but stop to consider first if it is safe to get involved. They turn a blind eye to unfair treatment of fellow workers in the work-place, weighing first the repercussions of involvement for their own position. They prefer to make individual deals with bosses in the (usually vain) hope that this provides them with a better chance for advancement than collective action. They condone the fading out of ethical and aesthetical values from educational curricula without thinking about the long-term consequences of this process. To be sure, all these tendencies were also present in the past but their impact was diminished by public disapproval, but the new hyper-competitive culture removes this powerful constraint.

This transformation can perhaps be illustrated by what is now happening to values like *courage* and *pride in excellence*. Traditional literature gave *courage* a specific connotation which was linked to public service. Such public service was of course variously conceived at different times, but at any time *courage* was only regarded with approbation when it was shown in a socially desired context. The personal display of courage by a soldier in the service of his nation or by a citizen defending the weak was usually respected, but similar courage shown by a gangster in the pursuit of his objectives was normally ignored or regarded with opprobrium. However, once taken out of this cultural context, which was imparted to the young by literature and by their social environment, courage became an object in itself. This can be seen now particularly in the poorer urban areas where many young people demonstrate their courage by joining street-gangs or committing hideous crimes for no reason but to prove themselves courageous.

Something similar is happening to *pride in excellence*. Traditionally competition held the connotation of "let the best man win." In sport it was not unusual, when the referee had missed a player's foul, for the perpetrator himself to draw attention to it. This at least was the behavior expected from a sportsman and a gentleman. It might have lost him the game, but the public loved and appreciated a sportsman who conducted himself in this manner. Few wanted to win unfairly; such a victory was not appreciated. Even in business most who engaged in foul play did their best to keep this from the public eye. The new spirit of competition is different. Only victory counts, and as long as breaking the rules or laws remains formally unchallenged the victory is valid. Many businessmen though unprepared to break the letter of the law are quite willing to ignore its intention, and take pride in finding loopholes in the law which enable them to evade paying their taxes. In other words, it is no longer only the *best*, but also the *slyest*, who can win and carry off the laurels or the profit with public approbation.

It is in this context that the recent clamor for more "individual responsibility" must be evaluated. Lacking the old sense of decorum and the sensitivity which in the past had been an important part of a good education, incompetent members of the new managerial oligarchy try to obtain efficiency from those in their employ by competition rather than good will and cooperation. Usually the result is a demotivated work-force. Often this kind of competition is economically debilitating because more and more labour is employed in services where motivation plays a major role and efficiency is seldom directly measurable. Since the work-rhythm in most service activities is not set by conveyer-belts it frequently depends on the individual worker's application and commitment to the task whether the gains from automation are obtained or seriously diminished by the workers' lack of dedication. Worse than this, the climate created by divisive competition in the work-place tends to contaminate other spheres of life and generates a general mood of distrust, despondency, disinterest in other people, deficient solidarity, and eventually absence of social coherence.

In the political sphere the ranking of *decorum* inferior to success, and the turning of success itself into a kind of vindication of almost all means by which it is obtained, is also becoming more evident from day to day. Hardly a week goes by without the newspapers reporting some new political scandal. In the USA, Senators and even Presidents are deservedly or undeservedly reported to be or to have been involved in financial or sex scandals. In Britain, the term *sleaze* has practically become a byword for politics. In Belgium, Willy Claes is accused of accepting bribes to finance the advancement of his party. In Italy the country's seven times prime minister Andreotti is charged with links with top Mafia boss Toto Riina. In Holland, when large scale reorganizations are taking place even Trade Union leaders are suspected of making arrangements in favor of their members by circumventing the law of last in first out. The public figures whose involvement in scandals is spreading distrust in politics are too many to be mentioned here by name, but a few will suffice to illustrate the drift. In Britain the names of Jeffrey Archer, Neil Hamilton and Tim Smith spring to mind; in Italy Silvio Berlisconi, Bettino Craxi, Francesco de Lorenzo; in France Alain Carignon, Henri Emmanuel, Gerard Longuet, Michel Roussin, Bernard Tapié; in Belgium the Vice Prime Minister F. Vandenbroucke, Guy Coëme, Guy Mathot, Guy Spitaels; in Spain Alfonso Guerra, Mariano Rubio; and in Germany Jürgen Möllemann, Franz Steinkühler and Max Streibel.

Once again there is nothing new in the fact that politicians are corruptible; and it is a good sign that the press still finds corruption in high places newsworthy, because it indicates that decorum is not yet altogether dead. What is new is that in the public's mind high office is increasingly becoming synonymous with corruption. And herein lies the real danger for the future. Distrust in politicians is leading to distrust in politics and hence to disbelief in the possibility of obtaining desired ends by means of the ballot-box. It encourages extra-parliamentary action, resort to individual efforts to obtain desired ends, or to resignation, the feeling that whatever will be, will be, because there is little which can be done about it. Consequently the new market liberalism is either leading to social instability, or to a "running on the spot" which is leading society nowhere in particular, since the improvement of the life of one person is only attained at the cost of another. But a political élite can only lead a nation toward a desired future when it has a vision of this future and commands the public's confidence; this is precisely what most party leaderships lack. It is this absence of ideology and absence of faith in leaderships that furthers the spread of Post-Modernism, disbelief in politics, and the rise particularly of division among the single issue groups, and of "political correctness."

But it is not only sleaze which undermines the public's confidence. To obtain power in a democracy a party must win elections or have at least sufficiently good election results to be influential. This places politicians in a dilemma. On the one hand they often cannot permit themselves to stand by the principles which initially may well have encouraged them to engage in politics, because to obtain power or hold on to it they are forced to make compromises. On the other hand, when they compromise they fear to lose the support of their more principled constituents. Therefore, those politicians at least who have made politics their career and who have no other profession to fall back on resort to subterfuge. They do not take their electorate into their confidence, but dress their decisions in plausible arguments and, like the sophists of antiquity and some economists of recent times, place their trust in rhetoric rather than in truth. The result of this is that people lose confidence in politics as an instrument of change. Moreover, this also influences the politicians themselves. Seeing that they can convince people with false arguments and explanations they develop a kind of arrogance which makes them believe that they are more intelligent than their followers. Their attitude toward their constituents becomes increasingly dictatorial, their party organization becomes more and more bureaucratic, and their party membership is gradually eliminated from decision-making processes. In the end the party leader and the party élite remain the only decision-making organ.

This is one reason why all major parties prefer to lull the large middle class into false confidence and do not alert it to its impending fate. For a long time this middle class, which nowadays comprises the great majority of all the gainfully employed, was *the* beneficiary of the Welfare State. Even those able to pay for it themselves enjoyed government-assisted housing, free health care and education, unemployment pay and many other material advantages. Many European sociologists believed this middle class interest a safeguard against a return to the pre-war misery. Their confidence was misplaced. Since the late 1970s increasing unemployment has progressively, salami-like, sliced off the lower tiers of the middle class and thereby increased the number of people no longer merely enjoying but actually depending on the social arrangements of the Welfare State. At the same time, fewer and fewer working members of the class were obliged to pay more and more for sustaining those sliced off from the bottom tiers of the salami. The politicians of the Left refused to look this process in the eye. Instead of taking the public into their confidence and telling it that this process was in progress, and in place of taking the unpopular stand that the taxation of the working population must be raised to sustain the growing need for government expenditure to fill the gap in employment where private enterprise cannot or will not provide it, they simply took the easy way out. They did not warn the decreasing number of employed, who make up the majority of the middle class, of the risk of approaching unemployment, and they did not encourage the unemployed to resist the slashing of their social benefits. Instead they used a whole array of plausible half-truths borrowed from the right wing of the political spectrum to convince the public that the malaise is only temporary, or that it is a kind of unavoidable natural disaster. In fact, they took on board the entire self-interest-dominated ideology of those who always objected to the "featherbedding" of the poor, because it seemed the easiest way to retain the vote of the as yet employed majority.

Given that the tax-paying employed still make up the majority of voters this is of course hardly surprising. For a political élite vying for votes it is naturally more rewarding not to mention the salami-slicing process and the need for higher taxes than to speak of a measure of wage-restraint and of reducing the money doled out to those who cannot earn it. This is particularly so when "better no wage demands than the dole" is made more palatable by powerful propaganda from political adversaries such as the employers organizations, and presented as "less *more* earnings rather than less earnings altogether," as a Dutch government did in the early 1980s, and when incompetent state supervision has made misuse of social security funds obvious to all. It is in this light that all the commotion about state deficits, the loss of jobs to Third World countries, the influx of immigrants, technological innovation, as well as the fear of an aging population must be seen. The truth is that state deficits are the *result* and not the cause of unemployment, that in many countries, for example in the Netherlands, exports exceed imports, that immigrants when they are employed add more than they cost to the national product, that technological innovation raises productivity and when its proceeds are properly distributed increases incomes and therefore creates more rather than less employment, and that the continued rise in productivity allows fewer people to produce more and thereby compensate for relative shifts in the age composition of a society with a growing number of retired. It all hinges upon the *distribution* of the national product, and distribution is a political problem that can only be resolved by political means.

Another reason why political parties have lost people's confidence is that even honest and well-intentioned leaders cannot escape the climate in which they operate, nor the conceptions held by their peers and their advisers. A Prime Minister who repeatedly proclaims that "jobs, jobs and again more jobs" is the mainstay of his policy may well be voicing his genuine desire to fight the persisting or growing unemployment in his country. But, imprisoned in the Free Market atmosphere, and advised by economic technocrats educated in this climate, he can simply not see any alternative to the policies dictated by the latest fad. In this way such a call for more work is transformed into something which may be furthest from his mind. Like compassion into charity earlier, the *right* to work is turned into a kind of benefit granted by employers to the unemployed, into a socially divisive element in the cultural framework of the society. It revives the old conceptions that unemployment is a kind of natural calamity or the result of labourers' immoderate wage claims, and it ignores the lessons from the 1930s, the work of Keynes, and the humanism of the early post-war era which for a time turned governments from night watch-man guarding against thieves, fires and foreign enemies, into active agents of social emancipation responsible for full employment. The old-new position still allows governments to decide the route of a new road, the division of the education budget, the creation of a few jobs in the public sector, decisions important in themselves, but it leads them to ignore the *structural* impedi-ments to the attainment and sustainment of full employment and the need for social emancipation.

However, as long as there is no real shift of policy to address such struc-tural issues, the salami-slicing process will continue. And as the number of the unemployed continues to increase and the number of those able to sustain them to diminish, a choice will eventually be forced upon industrial society. It will either have to accept South American conditions, that is its separation into a small group of affluent citizens and a large majority of poor and destitute people, or it will have to take collective political action. And herein lie the great risks in allowing the new political élite to go its way. For centuries the first alternative was normal. Most historians are in agreement that even Spartacus regarded it as such, and that his uprising was not directed against the institution of slavery but his and his followers position within this institu-tion. The same is said about the various peasant revolts throughout the Middle Ages, they were not against Feudalism as a system but against the wrongs which they felt were done by infringement of the rules of the prevailing system. Marxism, which was the one challenge to a system as such, failed precisely because most people preferred to improve their lot within the old system rather than experiment with an unknown future. Post-war democracy achieved a mental revolution. It professed the unity of mankind and therefore the *right* of *everyone* to share in whatever riches society was able to produce. It also pro-vided the means to render effective this right by letting each citizen vote for the political programme which best suited his needs and aspirations. It did not postulate equality but it provided all strata of society, including the economi-cally and socially least well endowed, with a means of protecting their inter-ests by peaceful means. But all this hinged on confidence and valid information. It depended on the belief that parties felt committed to their programmes, and that the information upon which these programmes were based was true. Nowa-days confidence is shaken. People trust neither politicians to stick to their election programmes, nor the information presented to them as true. Many members of the lower strata of society feel that democracy has become sham, and they turn away from politics because they no longer see it as a means for protecting their most vital interests. They cast their votes, if they go to vote at all, not *for* the parties they elect but *against* the parties they do not wish to be in power. It is this turning away from politics which has become a crucial factor in the prolongation of the present economic difficulties. It deprives so-

The Political Dimension   195

ciety of the non-violent means for finding redress to its current economic and social ills and it prevents it finding an answer to the looming danger of a South Americanization of the economic and social relations in the western world.

A third reason for loss of public confidence in politics was the abuse of the social and economic security offered by the Welfare State. Not that prior to the Welfare State there were no corrupt capitalists and dishonest workers, but none would have wished to be known as such or would have regarded it as a socially acceptable practice. No "captain of industry" would have publicly proclaimed that "under certain circumstances, bribery is quite respectable," as the chairman of the Dutch Liberal Party in the Senate did in 1976; or that "there is no absolute universal ethic because morals, habits, values and principles are everywhere different, and that we must adjust to them," for the reason that "all the rest is nonsense," as the ex-chief of Gulf declared in the same year. But the loss of social disapprobation of corruption did not affect the upper class alone. Working men took undue advantage of social security arrangements, office workers made personal use of their employers' stationery, postage stamps and telephone. Garages submitted to their customers bills for work which was not done. Dentists dispensed with tooth fillings and provided patients with much more expensive full or partial crowns. Persons receiving unemployment benefit conspired to work illicitly for employers unwilling to pay the taxes and the insurance legally required for their personnel. At one time or another everybody came face to face with these phenomena and people working honestly began to wonder if the system was not favoring corruption and penalizing decency. They began thinking that without the old fears of loss of job and destitution the economy could not adequately function and society disintegrates. The result was Thatcherism in its various specific national guises.

Again it was the politicians who must be held responsible for this turn of events. The new élite was simply not interested in the reversal of the trend. It had little to gain from change. The traditional parties of the right, though not happy with the drift toward the moral disintegration, were too scared of a powerful revival of the left to consider any other measures to contain it, and adopted policies which they hoped would bring back the pre-war capital-labour relations which had assured the hegemony of capital. But the real culprits were the Labour Parties. Unwilling to admit that not only capitalists but also workers can be corrupt, they simply ignored the problem. Instead of spending much effort and money to devise ways to stop the drift, they either belittled it or tried to convince the public that with the passage of time it would just disappear by itself. To the more dogmatic radicals it seemed self-evident that man being decent by nature would abandon bad practices once the conditions that had given rise to them were no longer there. If Marx was right in thinking that the economic infrastructure determines all facets of the superstructure, then it could only be a matter of time before the malpractices were abandoned once the economic fears which had produced them had become irrelevant.

Whether this is a correct interpretation of Marx's point of view or not, it served as an excuse for those who, out of probably unjustified fear of alienating working-class voters, did little if anything to stem the drift toward corruption among common people.

In reality economic conditions influence the conduct of society and the conduct of society influences the economy, but how economic conditions influence the conduct of society is no foregone conclusion, at least not in the short run. A society which has for generations been impressed with the fact that private property conveys economic security and social status will not easily abandon this belief. Even if other ways to feel sure of one's livelihood and to obtain esteem become apparent, old tendencies linger on. Aristocratic titles still command respect in many places even though in reality they have long lost their singular position and advantage. All this means that to be successful any attempt to revive the progressive economic policies called Keynesian must take note of the possible effect on people's conduct. Economic security without deliberate, powerful and costly state efforts to restrict corruption is an illusion. It is certainly not enough to introduce half-heartedly some legislation to prevent corruption. But to fight the abuses of the economic security provided by the Welfare State by its abandonment, as the Thatcherites attempted to do, can only end in social and economic disaster. After all, few modern people would accept that the best way to fight rape is to forbid women to go into the street at night or to remain alone at home without protection. What is required is a clear policy to make the young abhor corruption and inhumanity, and to prevent their elders from succumbing to temptation. To introduce such a policy without infringing on people's individual rights is difficult and expensive, but it can be done. If this is well explained and honestly pursued most people would accept it.

17

Conclusions

What then can we do? The writers of these pages do not presume to offer a route map of the way out of this wasteland of the spirit. So far they have been describing the charts which have been used to shepherd us into it, and the dangers of continuing to use them. All they can now do is to point to a possible exit and hope to persuade people to move in a body towards it.

The first thing to realize is that the era in which *economic growth* engendered more employment has passed. Economists must be made to understand that the time when unskilled labour could quickly be absorbed into the industrial labour force by on the job training is gone. Second it must be acknowledged that the modern mode of production requires a growing volume of ancillary services which have a public rather than a private character. The obvious examples are the construction and maintenance of communication systems and the protection of the natural environment. Third it must be understood that there are services which can be and services which cannot be made less costly by technological innovations. The latter are the services whose quality depends on the simultaneous attendance of the provider and receiver, like physicians and patients and teachers and students. Such services may be improved by technology but not made cheaper.

When these changes are taken into account it becomes self-evident that economic policy needs reconstruction. The prime objective of economics in the highly industrialized countries must not be *growth* as it had been in the 1950s and 1960, or *financial stability* as it is since the 1970s, but *full employment* in the conventional sense of this term. Instead of holding on to the idea that economic growth provides employment, and "small government" is good for financial stability, it must be recognized that growing employment produces economic growth and that financial stability depends on the judicious regulation of income distribution. People need to realize that economic growth is no more than a statistical representation of a positive change in certain economic indicators such as the National Product. It represents the money-earnings and spending of a community during a determined length of time. It tells nothing about the activities from which the money was earned and what goods and services it was spent on. An increase in the National Product may just as much reflect an increase in the number of factories producing sweets, as the increase in the number of dentists employed to repair the tooth decay caused by the sweets.

Taking this as their point of departure, governments will have to create employment; they will have to make investment where private enterprise fails to meet this need and it is in the long run public interest to do so. As a result new incomes and savings will be generated and effective demand for goods and services in the private sector will also be increased. The investments in the public sector will improve the functioning of the private sector and reduce some of its costs, and the savings on social security together with the additional tax revenue from the greater volume of employment will reduce government deficits. The state must make low-interest finance available for innovating enterprises, and reveal to the large middle class that it risks South Americanization unless it is prepared to accept tax increases if such increases should become necessary. It must explain to those still gainfully employed that such a levy is then not merely a matter of solidarity (though the revival of solidarity is also important in itself) but that it is perhaps the only way to prevent the "salami-slicing" process continuing and slicing off more and more employed workers and therefore bringing the risk of unemployment and misery closer to everyone.

All this requires careful planning. Governments must make choices, and if they want to sustain welfare and social and political stability, and preserve the measure of social justice the West has attained, and advance it further, they must plan for full employment and turn their attention to the measures which will become necessary to meet the new problems the pursuit of full employment will entail. In spite of the bad name state planning has received from the experience of the Soviet Empire, it remains part of our life. A housewife plans the next meal, teachers plan their lessons, (at least they should), a family plans its holidays, a general his campaigns, and a multinational enterprise plans its production targets sometimes for decades ahead. The same is true for governments. To allow things to drift in the belief that some metaphysical power will lead the economy toward growth, social justice and stability, is an illusion. And a government which adopts a position of helplessness, saying that things must follow their course because nothing of great influence can be done, is merely shedding its responsibilities. To live up to its public obligations a government must make a careful analysis of the work which those who are presently unemployed can do and find out which useful tasks correspond with their abilities; assess the *real* extra cost and gains from such employment; and calculate the distribution of the tax-burden economically most desirable. It must meticulously examine the spending and saving patterns of the various income groups, and evaluate the impact of increasing employment and taxation on the demand for domestic and for foreign goods and services and the expected influence of changes on the volume of consumer and company savings, and seek ways to restrain inflation by tackling its social causes rather than their monetary consequences. It must promote open government by providing truthful information to trade unions and employers' organizations about its own intentions, and oblige large firms to disclose their financial position and investment requirements. In short, government must try to restore public confidence, engage in *long term* planning, and systematically gather and correlate information about the many probable consequences of a policy of state-assisted full employment, and seek new ways to deal with the monetary and fiscal consequences of the policies it envisages.

If all this is not to remain a *fantasy* all who are objectively threatened by the demise of the achievements of modern western civilization need to be identified and recruited. The poor, along with all but the most privileged members of the middle class and churches, socialists and many intellectuals and students must be encouraged to become politically engaged in a common effort to save the humane elements which are part of our heritage. The interest of the poor and unemployed in such an effort is obvious, and so is that of many members of the middle class who already feel the ground quaking under their feet. The churches, or at least a great number of priests and ministers, are extremely worried about the loss of morality and about increasing poverty. Socialists have always been committed to mutual support and equitable sharing, and many intellectuals know that integrity is threatened by the new social and economic establishment. The new generation of young people is showing concern about its studies and future, and like every new generation resents the false values of its elders. Old people are worried about their pensions and the cost of health care. In some countries they have already formed political pressure groups. The other single issue movements, for equal opportunity for women, for the protection of the environment, for the improvement of the conditions of black people in the USA and of other minorities, have not yet seen that struggling in isolation cannot really solve their problems. They need to understand that only full employment can remove the *economic fears* which are the main stumbling blocks on their road to success. But to achieve this all who have an *objective* reason for demanding change must act to revive the economic aims and the moral values of western civilization as they were postulated in the early post-war period, and strive to improve on them in order to break with the many old and new habits of mind.

The poor and the workers, as well as the socialists, must recognize that their *main* adversary is no longer the capitalist, but speculators, bankers, the new captain of industry and many leading members of the political establishment—the new class of top managers and bureaucrats. Real capitalists, the shareholders, are already beginning to recognize this. They are increasingly aware of their loss of power and status, and see the conflict of interest between themselves and this new class. In the USA shareholders have begun organizing in order to obtain seats on managerial boards with the explicit object of protecting themselves against the predatory instincts of their enterprises' managers. In Britain, the high salaries which managers grant themselves even in inefficient firms have recently caused uproar and not among shareholders alone. In the Netherlands, Fokker corporation lost 449 million guilders in 1994. While 1760 workers lost their jobs managers' salaries increased from 2.4 to 7.5 million guilders. And the insensitive and high-handed behavior of public servants has not only alienated the poor but practically everyone who has no access to persons in high places. But the majority of people have not yet recognized the nature of the new class constellation, and have not yet learned to employ the power they have to resist its worst excesses.

It follows that the task at hand is to make socialists and churchgoers perceive that nowadays more unites them than divides them; they have in common the cultural heritage of socialism, Judaism and Christianity. Judaism has upheld the principle of justice, Christianity of compassion, and Socialism of solidarity. Christianity is no longer a tool in the hands of capital to lull workers into accepting a life of misery on earth by the promise of a better "life" hereafter. Christianity is a force which, though not always wisely, admonishes people to adhere to values little different from those postulated by socialists and by Marx himself. There are indeed differences, but they are secondary to the present need for changes in the social climate. Perhaps the most important task of the churches at this time is to resist the neo-fundamentalists who are preaching the kind of individualist faith which goes together with the postmodern "each for himself."

Intellectuals too have no substantial quarrel with either Church or socialism. The time when Galileo was excommunicated is long gone, and with few exceptions which do not worry the Church alone (such as genetic manipulation and abortion) religion puts little restriction on scientific research. In their rise socialism and scientific positivism were interlocked. It is not the Church that should worry true intellectuals, but the abandonment of the search for truth in favor of expediency, and the funding of research which is likely to be financially rewarding for certain people rather than serving mankind's needs. What intellectuals ought to be weary of is the intrusion of false advertising into their domains which sows a climate of public distrust in science and in the integrity of scientists.

We have to show the young that there is a future, that there is real hope for a better and fairer world if they will help to build it. That they will be able to receive recognition for ability and excellence once they have got rid of the hegemony of the new social and political establishment and its perverted values, and of the rigid new hierarchic system by which it sustains itself and prevents advancement by merit rather than by subterfuge. They need to be shown that the conversion of truth into expediency, and the transformation of "good connections" into a source of personal advancement rather than excellence, is not "the way of the world" but the product of the culture which a perverted establishment imposes on society. They ought to be convinced that all this can really be changed if they are ready to fight for such a change. The question whether human conduct is more influenced by genetic factors than by the social environment is a red herring. It is enough to accept the obvious, that at least part of human conduct is environmentally determined, and since human environment is basically social environment, it can therefore be swayed to serve the common good.

To the elderly it needs to be explained that the economy is not "a zero sum game," where everyone's gain is somebody else's *real* loss. It is clear to them that if an economy is growing, as it has done for decades and thanks to technological progress continues to do, it is the distribution of the *added* output they need to be concerned about, and not the ability of the economic system as a whole to sustain a larger so-called inactive population. Since the 19th century increasing productivity has in practically all the industrialized countries made a shorter working day and working week possible without loss of output. This shows that for as long as productivity continues to increase, and working hours are no further reduced, there is no reason to fear that the relative rise in the "inactive" part of the population must cause an actual diminution in the welfare of the gainfully employed. It only means that the active receive less of *more*, but not less in absolute terms. The real problem is therefore not the growing burden of an aging population but how this *more* must be divided between profit, wages and transfer payments. In other words the problem is how to assure sufficient investment to sustain innovation and growth into the future. But this is part of the general problem of distribution which was discussed earlier in this book and is not specific to the aged. After all, the current scare about the cost of an aging population was formerly raised over the introduction of shorter working hours and over the loss of child labour to compulsory education.

The single issue groups ought to be reminded that their objectives are better served by common effort with all the others whose vital interests are adversely affected by the current trend than pursued in isolation. The issue of the emancipation of women is too complex and too important to be addressed in detail here, but it ought to be said that focusing attention on their problems to the exclusion of all others' is not the most promising way to solve them. As a single issue movement, women can achieve high positions for *some* women, and raise certain *legal* obstacles to advancement, but this will not really solve the problem for women as a whole. To conduct the struggle in a climate of *them* (men) and *us* (women) not only alienates a large number of potential supporters, but does not help to create the climate necessary for achieving true equality and mutual respect between the sexes. It introduces a whole spectrum of unnecessary divisive and debilitating factors into the struggle and provides numerous openings for opponents to exploit. As long as there is poverty and unemployment, employers (including women) will always find specious arguments justifying sex-discrimination, such as difficulty and cost in finding temporary replacements for the pregnant, which evaporate in times of full employment. In the 1960s large enterprises, like Philips, established crêches next to their factories to look after children while their mothers were at work, and there was little if any talk about the extra cost of pregnant women. But since the 1980s, when massive unemployment re-emerged, these arguments have been revived and have sounded convincing to male workers fearing for their jobs. This then has provided employers with a mass support for the revival of discriminatory practices against women lacking during the time of full employment. This culture of discrimination has been reinforced by arguments that working women neglect their children, and that it is in the public interest to exclude married women from the labour market. It also has given governments unwilling to raise taxes the opportunity to stigmatize divorced or unmarried mothers so as to save on state allowances. It is of course a fact that in some countries unmarried mothers present a real problem, but it is also true that without adequate child-care they simply cannot go to work and therefore gain little from other women achieving equal employment opportunities. Their children's welfare depends on solidarity, on a consensus that they need *by right* and not by charity to be provided for out of the public purse. But this requires a return to the welfare principle, not well served by women's movements which insist on dividing society into *them* and *us*.

In other words, the emancipation of women requires not only women's solidarity but solidarity of both sexes and a concerted effort to eradicate many old entrenched prejudices which affect more than the position of women. But this can only be achieved when men are free from the fear of unemployment, and when a sense of communality (of real human rights) takes precedence over sectoral interests.

All this is also true of the black minority and other groups suffering discrimination and also of the efforts to protect our natural environment. As long as the pursuit of private profit dominates the social climate, making people scared of losing their jobs, environmentalists can achieve some *corrective* goals but not eliminate the causes of the ills they wish to avert, and certainly not in a manner acceptable to all. . For example, they can succeed in reducing traffic pollution, or in restricting the use of cars by adding to their cost of maintenance, so that in the end only the rich will be able to afford one. But they cannot cause industry to make serious efforts to search for a non-pollutant motor. The power of the motor-car manufacturing and fuel-producing industries is much too strong for this. The American government was able to place a man on the moon because the military-industrial complex saw in such a scheme new opportunities for making profits. But a law to allow only non-polluting engines on the roads would at present meet with their resistance. The motor and fuel industries would have to write off enormous investments and make costly new investments, without much hope of the demand for cars increasing beyond the current level. In other words, it would not be a profitable exercise. Therefore, while in theory a government can pass such a law, it can in practice only promulgate it if it is able to rally sufficient support to overcome the opposition of the industrial power structure. For this no single pressure group is powerful enough. The struggle to eliminate the real sources of our environmental hazards can only be successful if it is part of a much wider struggle, namely the struggle for restoring to the people the control of government.

Again, the environmental movement is important, it generates and spreads awareness of the problem, but to book real success it must unite with other forces who are equally in need of emancipated government. The movement for the protection of our natural habitat must cease to allow itself to be mislead into regarding *economic growth* as an adversary, and learn to understand that it is not economic growth which needs controlling but the *direction* it is taking. It should note that a rise in the GNP may reflect an increase in the number of air and water polluting factories as well as an increase in the number of new installations to purify the water and the air. It may reflect the construction of more energy generating plants which may cause global warming or reflect the employment of more researchers to find a substitute for them. In fact, it may even only reflect that certain jobs which had previously been done without money changing hands are now being paid for in cash. It is therefore not economic growth which wants watching but the specific character of the growth.

Without economic growth the Third World is doomed to poverty and the rich countries are condemned to continual unemployment. This is what the environmentalists must understand. The manner in which such growth is effectuated is a different matter. To influence this matter the environmental movement must lend a helping hand to all others who are struggling to reform the social climate and to return the control of government to the people, so that the long term public interest will take precedence over the pursuit of private gain. The environmental movement must see that without removing the fear of unemployment and destitution it will always remain "corrective" after the event, and alienated from the great majority of the people whose current needs and fears are greater than their anxiety about the catastrophe which may befall them in the future.

What all the movements mentioned earlier have in common is that they have grievances. Each of them has good reasons for being discontented, but discontent alone is dangerous. It tends to create a climate in which the *symptoms* of ills become the focus of attention while the underlying causes are ignored. Worse than that, discontent precipitates conditions which can be exploited just as well by reactionary forces as by those who are genuinely committed to elimination of the ills. The rise of Nazi Germany and the coming of the Welfare State illustrate the two outcomes. Nazism did not solve the problems which gave rise to discontent in pre-war Germany, but it diverted attention from its sources which it was neither able nor willing to remove. It offered surrogate answers to the symptoms of the ills and presented them as solutions. To members of the middle class it presented the illusion of deliverance from fear of loss of status, and gave the hope of enrichment by ridding them of Jewish competitors in business and in the professions; to working class people it provided an escape from job loss, and the delusion of sharing in the "grand mission" of their nation compensated them for low wages; to the unemployed and destitute it gave bread and Storm Troop uniforms which provided them with spurious self-esteem and social status; and to the industrialists it gave the mass support they needed to fend off social reforms or revolution, greater work discipline and "devotion to duty" from their labour force, and a market for military hardware. When it turned out that all these were sham solutions, it was too late. The Nazis in control of government had established a machinery of terror to quash all manifestation of discontent and no longer needed to provide solutions for the causes of the discontent which had brought them to power. By controlling education and the media of information they could indoctrinate the masses and create a state of mind which transformed discontent into "sedition" and the discontented into "asocial elements and criminals." Only the major catastrophe brought people back to their senses—a catastrophe that cost the lives of millions and left Germany in ruins.

Returning to the subject of single issue movements the point to be noted is that by concentrating on single issues people become oblivious to the fundamental reasons from which the troubles with these issues emanate. Such movements may achieve some measure of success but hardly ever positive long term solutions. But take out fear of unemployment and the solution of many and perhaps most of their problems becomes more practicable. As Adam Smith had noted, "in what constitutes the real happiness of human life beggars may in no respect be inferior to those who would seem so much above them." No one denies this, but also nobody who experienced long unemployment and dire poverty will deny that these are a major causes of *unhappiness* and discontent. Hence, in spite of the new fashion of telling people that happiness comes first and that it is independent of employment, or, as in circles close to the British government where it is nowadays the practice to avoid speaking of unemployment and talk of "consumer choice," implying (but not saying) the jobless are still "consumers," discontent will continue spreading. In fact not unemployment, but fear of loss of job leads to action—the jobless cannot strike. But, as said, discontent does not guarantee changes for the better. It can just as well lead to hopelessness and resignation as to action, and when it leads to action it may just as well engender fascism and reaction as it may promote democracy and the assertion of human dignity and rights.

Today both these tendencies are well discernible in most parts of the western world. One hears people speak of the "end of history" and the "end of the great stories." In the ideological sphere philosophies like post-modernism deny the unity of science and of mankind and preach that "anything goes," and that truth is no more than good rhetoric. In the material sphere the rich remove their homes to regions where they are separated from the rest of society, and hire private security guards to protect their houses and their businesses. Solidarity among workers is transformed into passive membership of Trade Unions, and political engagement becomes a visit to the ballot-box every few years, to cast a vote *against* some party or politician whom one dislikes, rather than *for* a party programme which holds a promise of real change. Increasingly the poor and unemployed are written off as "losers" and "free riders" who deserve no better than their lot, and the rich and employed regard themselves as the only valid members of society and shamefully exploited by taxation to support them. And while all this is taking place post-modern philosophers speak of a tolerant society where each individual should be able to do his or her "own thing."

But there are also manifestations of a different kind. The very existence of the single issue groups, and the growing anxiety of churches and humanists about the loss of "norms and values," reflect the other tendency. In the USA President Clinton, in his election campaign, promised to make health-care more accessible. He did not manage to implement it, but the fact that he made the promise shows that the majority of American people favor it. Though the old and the poor were only a small segment of its traditional electorate, the Labour Party of the Netherlands lost a very considerable part of its traditional support and was practically wiped out when it ceased to care for them. Even in Britain, where the process of social disintegration is the most advanced in Europe, Lady Thatcher had massive media support for her handling of the miners' strike and for the dissolution of the Welfare State particularly from characters like Maxwell, but since then has been deliberately turned into a non-person to try to save her party. All in all, though badly battered, the early post-war conception of proper human conduct is not altogether gone and there are signs of its revival with the young. Even the persistent concern for Third World populations and for refugees from overtly terrorist regimes and ethnic massacres bears witness to the fact that old-fashioned decorum is not yet extinct.

In the 1960s, when there was a labour shortage, there had been few complaints when thousands of foreign workers were attracted to various European countries. There were none in the Netherlands, a few in the United Kingdom, some about Algerians in France. Now people complain about the flood of immigrants, and governments, unable to solve the unemployment problem, exploit these protests to veil their impotence. And yet they do not dare to stop the flow. Too many of their followers would still regard it as inhuman. In spite of the large state deficits foreign aid continues, and not only because of the pressure to continue it from those who in the rich countries benefit by it themselves.

The essence of all this is that the fate of the humane values of western civilization is still in the balance—the battle for a more decent world is not yet lost. What is required to stop the drift toward despondency and patchwork remedies is a plausible positive *alternative*. Discontent, and efforts to correct specific wrongs alone, cannot reverse the trend. A realistic alternative, the vision of a future worthy to be struggled for, is indispensable. Without it discontentment breeds despondency, reaction and disaster. But given an alternative people find *hope*, and hope is the great antidote to despondency and fear.

For this reason it is absolutely necessary to make clear that it is not mankind's objective *inability* to sustain full employment and abundance for all but perverted institutions which prevent it. We have wonderful new technologies capable of providing plenty, and marvelous media of information with the facility of spreading knowledge to all corners of the earth, but a distorted social and economic system keeps the greater part of humanity in poverty and ignorance. Obviously, the social and economic system to which we have become accustomed, and whose assumedly inevitable laws we take for granted, is based on misconceptions.

Since the year 400 BC, or even earlier, people have seen kites gliding through the air; in 1232, during a siege, the Chinese used kites to send messages behind the Mongol lines; in 1589, Giambattista della Porta observed a kite-flying and theorized about it; and in 1894 Baden-Powell used kites to lift human beings into the air. But in spite of birds and kites people took it for granted that Man could not fly. Those who dared to try made themselves wings and flapped them up and down imitating the motions of the birds. Their efforts failed because they were looking in the wrong direction. But Man *can* fly. When George Cayley, Otto Lilienthal and Octave Chanute abandoned the old state of mind and cast their eyes in the right direction, they proved it. Once they ceased flapping wings, they were soon able to see that the leading edge of the slightly concave wings of the birds is rather sharp and that its feathers are small and close-fitting so that a streamlined surface meets the air; that on the trailing edge of each wing the interlocking of larger feathers forms a surface that stimulates the action of the movable back edge of the wings. They were able to notice that in flight-flapping, soaring and gliding, the bird's flight feathers overlap so that air pressure on the underside of the wing causes feathers to form an airtight surface, and that on upstroke feathers part sufficiently to permit some air to pass through and reduce the pressure against which the wings must work, and aerodynamics was born. The myth that people cannot fly was dead, and in 1903 the Wright brothers' first 59-second flight proved it.

It can be argued that the coming of flight was more complicated than this example may suggest. It involved both lift and motion, and a constant intricate feed back between technology, culture and conflict, which makes a paradigm shift as tricky a matter to understand as hurricanes. All this is true but does not invalidate the essential point, namely that before people abandon their old misconceptions they cannot see things they could have seen which remained unnoticed or appeared to be irrelevant. Therefore, as long as people persist in the belief that the market provides the best mechanism for promoting economic growth and equitable distribution, they simply ignore alternatives. Like those who had attempted to fly by flapping wings, their efforts to "correct" the economic system will land them flat upon their faces. When they discover that there are things beside the market which determine the flow of the economy they will be able to resolve the problems which cannot have a solution within a market system. David Ricardo saw long ago that the *distribution* of the economic product of society is inextricably related to its growth, and must not be ignored or relegated to the functioning of some assumedly self-validating mechanism. This does not mean that on the microeconomic level there is no market mechanism which adjusts supply to demand by the variation of prices and profits, but it means that on the macroeconomic level there are also other, and sometimes more important, forces determining the long run fate of the economy which are beyond the regulating mechanism of the market. These forces are in the sphere of *distribution*, namely the distribution of the national product between consumption and investment, between the public and the private sectors, between the supply of goods and of services, and between the satisfaction of present wants and aspirations for a better future. All these distribution problems cannot be solved by current market forces; their solution requires decisions which cannot be left to individuals whose immediate requirements prevent them from acting upon considerations of the collective long-term fate of the society in which they live.

The conclusion from the above must be that the economic process functions in two separate sectors, the private sector where markets determine wages, prices and the allocation of resources, and the public sector where decisions determining the long term future of the society are made. The former sector is endowed with a self-regulating mechanism, the latter sector has no such mechanism and depends on the culture of societies—on their aspirations and political power structure. The only *objective* factor which limits its freedom of decision-making is the society's level of technology. The rest depends on *values* and on the political will to sustain and improve desirable institutions and abolish or adjust those which hinder progress toward responsible economic growth and greater social stability and equity. For this reason the protection of the humane values in our heritage and the encouragement of political engagement are imperative. Political power must be removed from unimaginative short-sighted politicians and humdrum insensitive bureaucrats, and handed to persons who think for themselves and lead the public rather than follow current fashions. It must be given to governments which have the courage to determine the division of the national income with an eye to the future, and which care for the humane notions of decorum which are still alive in the hearts of most members of society. Under the present circumstances it seems almost impossible that such governments can be elected, but it can and must be done. Democracy and universal suffrage have given us the means for it. All that is needed is that our real desires be made explicit and we demonstrate their power to revive the public's political engagement. Perhaps the new media of communication (like e-mail), can make this possible. The spreading of ideas by the new information technology is less expensive for its user than the printing of books and articles, and it may be one of the instruments enabling us to break the near-monopoly of information or misinformation of the ruling social and economic power structure. Moreover, not only those afflicted by the present state of affairs, and those who are increasingly fearing the prospect of becoming afflicted by it, are longing for change. Many members of the establishment also feel that things must not be allowed to drift toward the moral void and the social and economic disaster to which the present policies are steering us. Even among the most docile bureaucrats many feel frustrated with the rules and regulations that deprive them of using common sense for solving problems and make them seem insensitive in their daily contacts with the public. It is therefore more than likely that as soon as we the people will decide to move against the new-fangled political morality we shall find many allies even among those who are now inert, or have little to gain from change, or seem to be the enemies of social and economic progress toward greater equity.

Our social and economic system is in the process of reorganisation, and the final outcome of any system's reorganisation is always unpredictable. But throughout the process there are points of bifurcation at which decisions must be taken which influence its future. Let us not miss these opportunities to try to build a better world.

"If Winter comes, can Spring be far behind?"

Glossary of Terms

The glossary is based on the dictionaries and the glossaries in the textbooks listed below. The present authors have however adjusted several of them to suit the specific meaning in which the concept was employed in the context of this book.

Acceleration principle: The principle hypothesizes that the level of aggregate net investment depends on the expected change in demand. It is based on the assumption that firms maintain a fixed ratio of capital stock to output. In Keynesian economics this means that changes in the demand for consumer goods bring about even larger variations in the demand for capital equipment which is necessary to make them. Paul Samuelson describes the acceleration principle as "a theory of investment spending which holds that the level of investment will be governed by the rate of increase in GNP. That is, there will be positive (or high) net investment when GNP is rising, and there will be zero (or low) net investment when GNP is just holding steady (even if GNP is already very high).

Administered prices: Prices which are determined by the conscious decisions of the managers of a firm or by a public authority, rather than by market forces. This is generally possible where the seller is a monopolist. (See also **Administered Monopoly**).

Almagest: Book written by the Greek astronomer Claudius Ptolemaeus (Ptolemy) in the second century AD, who systematized the data and doctrines known to Alexandrian scientists in his time. It influenced European astronomy until Copernicus revised the image of the universe. In Ptolemy's work the earth was spherical and stationary at the center, with the sun, moon and planets revolving about it.

Behaviorism: The doctrine that mental states are reducible to dispositions to behave in certain ways. In psychology this means that a scientific description of behavior need not rely on knowledge of mental states, because these can always be described in terms of observable behavior. The philosophical assumption underlying this methodological approach is a rejection of dualism, the consideration of mind and matter as independent substances. A scientific assumption is that the aim of psychology, as of all science, is to produce predictions of behavior in order to control it. Because dispositions to behave are determined by external stimuli, control of behavior is to be obtained by controlling the stimuli.

Berufsverbote: Regulations excluding suspected "subversives" such as Communists from public service in post-war Germany.

Business cycles (conventional business cycles): Business cycles are alternating periods of trade boom and depression occurring at fairly regular intervals. During the boom employment, wages, prices, profits and production are rising, and in the ensuing slump they are falling. The business cycle, (also known as the **Trade Cycle**) is a fluctuation in the level of economic activity, (usually proxied by national income) which appears to have a regular pattern: expansion of activity, contraction, and further expansion about a long-run secular trend of economic growth. Many economists believe that the long-run trend is also subjected to cyclical variations of different length. Samuelson remarks that in modern parlance, business cycles are said to occur when actual GNP rises relative to potential GNP (an expansion) or falls relative to potential GNP (a contraction or recession). There are several theories attempting to explain this phenomenon. Some of these explanations relate it to "Real Causes" and others to psychological or monetary causes, or to over-production and under-consumption and to saving-investment disequilibria.

Capital: In economics the term capital usually relates to goods in use as a factor of production, i.e. produced goods which are factor inputs for further production. For example, machinery, tools and equipment, buildings and stocks of partly or wholly finished goods. When the term capital is used in this sense, it is often called **real capital** to distinguish it from its use in accounting and finance where it means the total amount of money subscribed by the share-holder-owners of a corporation.

Capital goods: Goods, like machines, which are not directly enjoyed by their owner but indirectly through their contribution to the more efficient production of other goods. (See also definition of **Capital**)

Capital stock adjustment principle: A theory suggesting that the level of net investment is a proportion of the difference between the desired capital stock and the actual capital stock, reflecting the possibility of imperfect adjustment to an optimal level in any finite period of time. (See also Acceleration Principle). [Pearce]

Causality: The principle that everything has a cause. A causal relation between two given events or two given situations holds when the occurrence of one is inevitably followed by the other. When the principle is applied to perception a **causal theory** holds that a causal relation holds between an external object and perceiving it. When applied to memory, the theory holds that remembering an object or an event is to be in a state similar to its original occurrence. When applied to the meanings of words it holds that there is a causal relations between a thing and the word which refers to it, or between a situation or event and the sentence which refers to it. A difficulty with this theory is that many, if not most, linguistic expressions do not have a clear reference.

One way out of the difficulty is an anthropological explanation. The simplest example is of proper names: nobody can remember the causal relation between Adam Smith and his name, but the relation was transmitted from his generation to ours.

Classical Economics: Although not a school in the sense of an alliance of persons, a community of ideas, an acknowledged authority and a combination in purpose, they were, however, united by a general similarity of principles and methods. Adam Smith is considered the founder of the school. The basic principles, which are common to all are the postulates that liberty and property are the keystones of every rational economic order and the claim that political economy resembles a natural science in the universal applicability of its laws. The most outstanding representatives of this school were Adam Smith, David Ricardo, James Mill, John Stuart Mill, John Elliott Cairnes and (in France) Jean-Baptiste Say.

Comparative advantages: The relative advantage for a nation from specializing in producing and exporting those commodities which it can produce at relatively lower costs, and importing those goods in which it is a relatively less cost efficient.
The principle holds that under certain circumstances the increased product obtainable from specialization and exchange is greater than the one obtainable when each country produces all it needs itself.

Consumer goods and services: Goods and services desired for their own sake to satisfy current wants.

Contextualism: The proposition that the meaning of a word can be understood only in the context of its utterance; that the significance of any action depends on and can be understood only within the particular circumstances of its performance; that the truth of a statement depends on the context within which it is stated, for example the theory in which it appears.

Core activities: The activities in which a corporation has specialized and gained one or several major advantages in comparison with other corporations. This advantage may be due to well established markets for its particular produce, technological experience and know-how, the ownership or use of expensive capital equipment which is not or not yet available to competitors or would be competitors. More loosely the term is also applied to the main branch of production of a firm.

Correspondence theory of truth: The idea that the truth of some propositions can be tested directly by confronting them with facts. In particular, that the basic statements of a theory can be so tested one by one, without reference to the truth of other theorems in that theory.

Crowding out effect: A fall in private consumption or investment due to a rise in government expenditure. The assumption is that government borrowing reduces the volume of savings and hence raises interest rates. This causes private investment to diminish so that government investment does not add to total investment but merely replaces private investment.

Deficit financing: A situation in which government expenditure exceeds its revenue, and deliberately finances activities by going into debt or printing money. Keynes was the first to suggest this as an instrument to revive the economy during recessions. He hoped to alleviate a depression by the state spending more than is received in revenue, and using the borrowed funds on public works of some kind, in the hope that the state, as an employer, will increase the purchasing power of the community and generate economic activity and through the **multiplier** regain more taxes to repay the money it borrowed. In the 1930s, this policy was called in the USA "pump-priming".

Effective demand: Aggregate demand for goods and services which is backed up with the resources to pay for them. This is to be distinguished from notional demand which refers to a desire for goods and services, which is unsupported by the ability to pay, and can thus not be communicated to suppliers through the price mechanism. [Pearce]

Epistemology: The theory of knowledge. Deals with the origin of knowledge; with the place of experience and reason in generating knowledge; with the possibility of error and the relation between knowledge, certainty and skepticism. Theories about the nature of truth and about the acquisition of knowledge are closely related. The correspondence theory of truth is associated with the logical-empirical idea that knowledge is built up like a pyramid. The central problem of epistemology in this case is to identify the secure foundations of the pyramid and a sound method for constructing its higher layers. The coherence theory of truth is associated with the idea that the creation of new knowledge is like repairing a boat one lives in without the possibility to get out. The central problem of epistemology then is to secure the stability of the boat provided by its interlocking parts. Of particular importance to this book is the concept of naturalized epistemology, the study of the actual formation of human knowledge. By this conception epistemology becomes part of the psychology of learning. This excludes the possibility of having any philosophical reflections about the processes of learning described in this science that might question their validity. Alternatively, epistemology becomes just another science in the history of science. The result is the same: it ceases to be a philosophical reflection on the validity of knowledge.

Frictional unemployment: The amount of unemployment which corresponds to job vacancies in the same local labour market and occupation. As it takes time to match workers and jobs, unemployment and unfilled vacancies can exist side by side. Some economists also include speculative and precautionary unemployment elements in frictional unemployment on the assumption that the labour market always tends to full employment. Milton Friedman suggested the term **Natural unemployment** which covers frictional unemployment. He described natural unemployment as follows: "the level that would not be ground out by the Walrasian system of general equilibrium equations provided there is embedded in them the actual structural characteristics of the labour and commodity markets, including market imperfections, stochastic variability in demand and supplies, the cost of gathering information about job vacancies and labour availabilities, the cost of mobility and so on". [quoted here from Pearce].

Fiscal measures (of control): The use of taxation and government expenditure to regulate the aggregate level of economic activity. This implies reducing taxes and increasing government expenditure to stimulate effective demand if unemployment is excessive, and raising taxes and reducing government expenditure to lessen effective demand in order to contain inflation if it considered excessive.

Globalization: The development of a global economy in which multi-national firms specialize in the production of commodities or parts of commodities in which they have internationally a technological or other advantage over other firms or posses market control. In common usage it often refers to the internationalization of the market.

GNP (Gross National Product): = Gross National Income. A measure of the money value of the goods and services becoming available to the nation from economic activity. There are three approaches to measuring this: first, as a sum of the incomes derived from economic activity, i.e. profits + incomes from employment; second, as the sum of expenditures, i.e. expenditures on consumption and investment; third, the sum of the products of the various industries. [Pearce] It is necessary to note that only economic transactions, i.e. transactions in which money changes hands are involved; and that as no money can be received without money being spent the total sum of incomes must always be equal to the total sum of expenditure.

Hermeneutics: (From the Greek hermeneus meaning interpreter). A doctrine originated in German theology by which each generation can find an interpretation of the Bible addressing its own concerns. The idea as an approach to history was introduced by Giambattista Vico (1668–1744) who rejected the rising influence of the Cartesian view of his time that the source of knowledge is in clear and distinct ideas. His objection was to Descartes' conviction that such ideas do not change with time. In Vico's opinion we can understand the ideas held by people in the past only by entering their modes of consciousness, and this can be done by relating their language, myths, traditions and actions together. The idea was used by various German thinkers (including Weber and Heidegger) to contrast the understanding of the human condition to that of scientific knowledge. Irrespective of the possibility to achieve the latter's aim, to describe the world independently of the human mind, the aim of the former is to understand the human condition at a particular time by understanding the mental attitudes of the time. The central difficulty with the approach is its circularity, that we can understand the past only in the light of the present, and we can understand the present only in the light of the past, in the light of traditionally transmitted interpretations of the world. This difficulty is common to Hermeneutics and to Anglo-American holism.

Holism: Any doctrine that emphasizes the priority of the whole over its parts. In a theory of knowledge such a doctrine claims that in order to understand the whole it is not sufficient to know the parts. In science the doctrine means that the meaning and truth of particular statements depend on the whole theory to which they belong. Radical holism means that such network of inter-related statements (or beliefs) is all we have, thus undermining the empirical nature of science. Quine's view, known as the Quine-Duhem thesis, admits that statements cannot be tested one by one, but claims that some statements are more testable than others, for example some kinds of experience. This fact vindicates the validity of science, even if it undermines claims of certainty. (See also **Reductionism**).

Human capital: Investment in human resources to raise productivity. It includes formal education and training as well as health care and any other cost which may improve the productivity of labour which is related to the person himself or herself. The difficulty with the cost of human capital is that one cannot always distinguish which part of it is directly related to the efficiency of production and which is simply welfare improving.

IMF: International Monetary Fond

Income effect: The effect of a change in real income on the effective demand for goods and services. (See also **Price Effect**)

ISLM model, ISLM Diagram: A model or diagram detailing the simultaneous determination of equilibrium of the interest rate and the level of national income as a result of conditions in both the goods and the money markets. This combination of the real and the monetary sectors of the economic system is supposedly revealing the conditions of macroeconomic equilibrium. The model which was intended to add to Keynes's General Theory a monetary sector distorts the Keynesian basic conception and returns his theory into the fold of equilibrium theory as a special case, something Keynes himself clearly rejected in his book.

Logical positivism: A doctrine developed by the Vienna Circle (see item). The doctrine inherited the Radical Empiricism of the physicist-philosopher Ernst Mach (1838–1916). According to Mach the mind knew only its own sensations, and a theory was nothing but an instrument for predicting under what circumstances these sensations would occur. Mach maintained that only insisting on the logical structure of a theory could overcome the idealist-subjective implications of this empiricist view. The aim of the discussions in the

Vienna Circle was to find the correct principles of scientific method that would establish what Popper later called the demarcation line between science and any speculations which had wrongly obtained the status of knowledge. Central to logical positivism is its principle of verification, the claim that the meaning of a statement is its method of verification. The idea is that a statement which cannot be verified provides no knowledge (has no cognitive content), and therefore is meaningless. It follows that a metaphysical statement is not merely deprived of a scientific status but is found meaningless. If science was to construct and test true theories, the positive task of philosophy was the analysis of the language of science and the construction of a valid formal logic that would guarantee correct inference from statements that had been empirically verified. Several problems raised during the circle's discussions led eventually to a modification, if not rejection, of its original doctrine. One was the failure to reduce experience to sense data. Under Neurath's influence this led to the replacement of Radical Empiricism by Physicalism, in which physical objects and their perception (phenomenalism) took the place of sense data as the basic elements of knowledge. Another question raised by the principle of verification was whether the truth of an empirical statement could be confirmed by an observed fact; whether the observed fact could be known independently of the language in which it was expressed. The realisation that this was impossible led (again under the influence of Neurath) to a holistic epistemological approach, by which it was acknowledged that each statement could be verified only by other, known, statements in the same or related theory. The coherence theory of truth replaced the correspondence theory. In addition, however, this has shown that each science had its own language, doubts arose about the possibility to construct a common logical language for all science. The impossibility to do so undermined the declared aim of the group to prove the unity of science. It appeared that the doctrine could not be established except by a leap of faith. This meant that a metaphysical assumption crept back into science. But most damaging to the demarkation of science from other human activities proved to be the idea that logical truths were conventions. This led eventually to the idea that all meaning is use, turning science into just another language-game, guided by Hume's "habits of thought". Finally, followers of the doctrine could not decide whether probability should be interpreted as variability in confirmation-instances or as real variability, as measuring degrees of belief or as describing real frequency distributions.

Marginal propensity to consume or save: That fraction of an additional dollar of disposable income which a family or community would spend (or save) on additional consumption (or additional saving). It is not the same as the average propensity to consume (or save), which is the ratio of total consumption (or saving to total disposable income. [Samuelson]

Mark-up: That proportion of price which the seller adds onto average variable costs in order to cover overheads and yield a net profit margin. [Pearce]. The amount added to cost to determine price. [Lipsey] According to Kalecki the height of the mark-up reveals a firm's measure of monopoly power.

Mercantilism: Mercantilism, originally a term of opprobrium and lacking a clearly defined meaning, came in time to be understood as the expression of a striving after economic power for political purposes. It was the predominant way of thinking about economic policy from the 16th to the 18th century in England. Relying upon strong state regulation to promote an export surplus, Mercantilists believed that high profits would stimulate and high wages dissuade people from economic activity. They argued that low wages help to augment the labour force by the fuller employment of women and children who would be left with no choice but to seek employment in order to supplement the men's insufficient incomes. This would reduce the cost of production of manufactured goods and lessen domestic demand and thus improve the export trade and as a result strengthen the country politically. They postulated that the economy was best served by stimulating the entrepreneur through the promise of good profits and workers by the cold fear of starvation.

Modernism: See **Positivism** and **Post Modernism.**

Monopoly, Monopsony: **Monopoly** assumes a market in which there is only one seller of a commodity. That is, where there is single control over the supply of a good or service, and that control can be maintained. **Monopsony** is a buyer's monopoly, i.e. when there is only one buyer. [Taylor]. **Administered monopoly**: A monopoly with administered prices, that is, with a monopoly which administers or sets a price by conscious decision of the seller rather than by the impersonal forces of demand and supply. [Samuelson]

Monetary measures (of control): Government measures attempting to achieve objectives like full employment, a stable price level, a balance in external payments, by controlling the monetary system through the money supply and by influencing interest rates and credit.

Multiplier: The ratio of the change in national income to the change in autonomous expenditure that brought it about. [Lipsey]

National debt: The current volume of outstanding government debt. The debt of a central government incurred by expenditure which could not be met out of ordinary revenue. When combined with the debts of local government the total is sometimes referred to the **Public Debt.**

Natural monopoly: An industry characterized by economies of scale sufficiently large that one firm can most efficiently supply the entire market demand. [Lipsey]

A monopoly which arose out of the normal growth of the business without the need to compete. For example a firm controlling a natural resource which is not available to anyone else, or a firm already possessing an installation which is so expensive to construct that no other firm would find it attractive to enter with it in competition for sharing a limited market.

Negative savings: Using up for current spending earlier accumulated resources.

Neoclassical Economics: The contribution of neoclassical economics to the apparatus of economic analysis was the addition of the concept of utility as an integral part of it, and the introduction of the idea of maximization, i.e. of the utilitarian philosophy and psychology, and later, of the study of the preferences displayed in the market, as a normative approach to the study of political economy. In this way the neoclassicists provided the alternative to the classical "labour cost" theory, opposing it to and supplementing it with a "scarcity-utility theory. Important members of this school were W.S. Jevons, K. Menger, F.Y. Edgeworth, A. Marshall, J.B. Clark, L. Walras, V. Pareto, P.H. Wicksteed, I. Fisher, K. Wicksell and A.C. Pigou. Their method was deductive. They constructed micro-static models of equilibrium, and studied the responses, of the system of interrelated variables which they constructed, under impact from variables they labelled exogenous.They eventually also introduced the use of mathematical techniques for the development of theorems of empirical importance, which to a certain extent made economics into an empirical and normative study. The term Neoclassical economics is usually related to the **Marginalists** approach to the analysis of pricing in competitive markets.

Neoclassical synthesis: An attempted synthesis of the Keynesian real sector of the economy, and monetary sectors, to show the simultaneous determination of money income and the interest rate, and to demonstrate that the classical views that the tendency to full employment equilibrium could only be thwarted by rigidities in the system. (See also **ISLM model**). However, many economists have challenged this line as an incorrect interpretation of Keynes. The synthesis is based on the idea that Keynes's theory is only valid when money wages are rigid, and there is an unemployment equilibrium. In other words that Keynes's General Theory is in fact no more than a special case of the general classical theory. Keynes himself denied this and emphasized the role of expectations and the inherent instability of the capitalist economic system, claiming that the classical assumption of full employment must be regarded as a special case.

Neo-pragmatism: Modern pragmatists find that their predecessors, in spite of their rejection of traditional realism, still hold the concept of truth central to their theories (see **pragmatism**). They think that the question what makes a sentence true is part of an attempt to find secure foundations to philosophy and should be discarded as a pseudo-problem. They think that the correct evolutionary approach of pragmatists implies that natural selection made us cognitive creatures (creatures who produce knowledge), and all knowledge should be seen as an attitude related to successful action. No distinction should be made between having a belief and holding a sentence to be true, irrespective of the domain of action in relation to which knowledge had been created.

Nomenklatura: A Russian term meaning the privileged members of the government and party establishment of the Soviet Union.

Numéraire: A unit of account, or expression of a standard of value, by which other values can be compared. For example, money.

Oligopoly: Partial monopoly. A situation in which there are only a few sellers and their pricing and output policies are strongly mutually influenced. A situation of imperfect competition.

Ontology. A branch of metaphysics concerned with existence, with what really exists as opposed to that which appears to exist. A traditional ontological problem was whether one could show the logical necessity of the existence of entities that were not accessible to sense perception. The existence of God was **The** ontological problem. But the same appeal to logic applied, for example, to Kant's **things in themselves** (the noumena). Another central question was whether abstract entities, like numbers or universals (redness, humanity) really existed. Did they represent different categories of existence? Kant tried to show that there was a fixed set of categories (or conceptual framework) that every rational mind must adopt in order to understand the world. This set of categories was itself an addition to ontology: it demonstrated the nature of the real (existing) mind. Questions that followed were whether the conceptual framework varied with time and from culture to culture; were there fundamental **natural kinds** to be discovered or were they classifications invented by the human mind, the product of particular conceptual schemes? Were different conceptual schemes identical to different languages? Logical positivists (Carnap) claimed that the distinction between objects and attributes was a grammatical distinction between noun and adjective, or between subject and predicate. Hence the idea that universals like "beauty" "redness" or "humanity" existed was the result of the linguistic possibility to transform an adjective into a noun. A logical language could dispose of such entities by translating such transformations "back" into sentences including bound variables like "there is an x such that x is beautiful, (red, human)", or "all x such that x is a man implies that x is human". Quine concluded that ontology as a metaphysical theory can be replaced by what he called **the principle of ontological commitment:** to be is to be the value of a bound variable in a logically organized (scientific) theory. An accepted ontology does not tell us what things really exist, but how to determine what things a theory claims to exist, or what is the set of entities which we must assume to exist if we take a theory to be true. The reductionist view holds that most objects can be "eliminated" from existence in this way because what appears to exist can be conceived as some complex whose constituents are the things that really exist, namely the things that cannot be eliminated by analysis. This (nominalist) view takes only the basic constituents of the universe to exist and change has no real significance. In contrast to this, the non-reductionist view takes events and processes to characterize existence, and therefore that change is both real and significant (see **epistemology**).

Opportunity cost: The value of the next best use (or opportunity) for an economic good, or the value of the sacrificed alternative. [Samuelson]. For example, the purchase of a share for $10 which yields $2, instead of purchasing a share of $10 which yields $4, incurs an opportunity cost loss of $2.

Overproduction: When more of a commodity or service is produced than is required for consumption. That is, when supply is greater than demand, and the supply can only be disposed of at a lower market price, which may mean a loss to the producer. [Taylor]

Physiocrats: French 18th century economic thinkers who believed that land was the only real source of wealth, and agriculture the only wealth-producing occupation. Their reason was that agriculture alone produces a tangible net surplus, because manufacture merely altered the shape of a produce. For example, a farmer has sheep; they provide wool and also multiply. Hence they make an addition to the volume of tangible goods. A tailor merely transforms one stock of goods into another. In the process of tailoring the wool or cloth is consumed and thus adds nothing to the volume of produce. Similarly, land is the only source of savings for investment. Land is limited in supply and therefore rents must have a tendency to rise with population accretion. Consequently land owners can save and accumulate resources. Manufacturers compete and are therefore forced by their competitors to sell as close to cost as possible and cannot save.

Pigou effect: This is the name sometimes given to results expected from changes in the general level of prices. If prices go up or down the real purchasing power of money changes. If prices go down people may spend more and if prices go up they spend less. Hence, if unemployment leads to less income and purchasing power, prices will fall and the purchasing power of those still working will increase. Consequently they will spend more and thus raise demand which will, after stocks are depleted, be followed by the revival of employment. (See also **Real Balance Effect**).

Points of bifurcation: Complex systems are continually fluctuating. At times, a single fluctuation or a combination of them may become so powerful, as a result of positive feedback, that it shatters the preexisting organization. This revolutionary point is called a bifurcation point. [Alvin Toffler's definition in the introduction to Order out of Chaos by I.Prigogine' and I. Stengers].

Positivism: The philosophy of Auguste Comte (1798–1857). Comte believed that there were three stages in the history of science, the theological, the metaphysical and the positive, and the method of each depended on the type of society in which it had developed. The a-priori method of Descartes' rationalism belonged to a previous epoch, superseded by the scientific method achieved in industrial society. Comte believed that the highest, if not the only, form of knowledge was the description of sensory phenomena. The scientific approach was called positive because it confined itself to that type of knowledge which was positively given, avoiding all speculation. Positivism reflected also an attitude, a rejection of idealism and skepticism associated with traditional empiricism. It was associated with optimism about the scope of scientific knowledge that could be achieved, and in particular with the possibility to extend the scientific method to sociology, which Compte placed at the top of the expected hierarchy of knowledge. In the 19th century, positivism became associated with evolutionary theory and with a naturalistic treatment of human affairs. (See also **Logical Positivism**).

Post-modernism: Just as there is no unique definition of modernism, so there is none of post-modernism. Post-modernism is usually seen as a reaction against a naive confidence in objective or scientific truth and against a confidence in progress, which have characterised modernism. In philosophy it implies a mistrust of the "grand stories" of modern "system-builders" like Kant, Hegel and Marx. In the philosophy of science it rejects the view that the theory of evolution implies progress. In political philosophy it implies a mistrust of the possibility to improve the human condition through education in, and the application of, science. Modern structuralists are opposed by the post-structuralist aspect of post-modernism, which includes a denial of any fixed meaning, or any correspondence between language and the world. Post-modernism denies the possibility to distinguish between a true theory and the facts or the reality it describes. Objectivity is seen as a disguise for power or authority in the academy, and often as the last fortress of white male privilege. Logical or rational thought is seen as one rhetorical style favoured by academics and imposed on the flux of all events. Some post-modern writers think that their rejection of objectivity leads to a liberating political radicalism. For some, post-modernism allows the denial of any event, such as the second World War or the Holocaust, leading to an intellectual and political attitude of "anything goes". And for others, such as Rorty (Contingency, Irony and Solidarity, 1989) it licenses a retreat to a detached individualism, to an aesthetic, ironic, and playful attitude to one's own beliefs and to the march of events which they call nihilism. The post-modern frame of mind charted by Jean-Francois Lyotard (The Post Modern Condition, 1984) seems to depend on a cavalier dismissal of any success of science in generating human improvements, on an exaggeration of the fallibility (admitted by modern scientists) of any attempt to gain knowledge in the humane disciplines, and on ignoring that while the history of modern knowledge admits no final description, it admits more or less accurate ones (which is all modern realist science claims).

Pragmatism: A philosophical view developed in the United States, initiated by Charles S. Peirce (1839–1914), William James (1842–1910) and John Dewey (1859–1952). Peirce introduces the idea that the meaning of a proposition is determined by the difference it would make whether the proposition was true or false. (In recent theories of language it is said that the meaning of sentences is determined by its conditions of truth). He maintained that the quest for certainty, the idea that truth has to be established once and for all, could only lead either to dogmatism or to total skepticism, and both were scientifically harmful. For science to fulfill its true aim, to provide predictions which lead to the satisfaction of human needs, fallible propositions were sufficient, and anyhow all we can get. He believed, however, that by following suitable processes of inquiry we would replace confused beliefs that seem to satisfy our needs by better ones, and in this way we should approach truth in the traditional sense of the word. Truth in this traditional sense is a limit of knowledge, scientific effort bringing us ever nearer to the Truth which is never to be reached. As with **logical positivism** this conception of truth could not extend to non-empirical propositions. James purported to fill the gap by postulating that metaphysical or moral beliefs could also satisfy human needs. Any proposition is true if it works, if the practical effect of adopting it satisfies a need. Peirce saw in this attempt a confusion between thought and action. The meaning of a non-verifiable proposition, of a non-empirical conception, was determined by considering the conceivable effect this conception might have on the thinker's beliefs. His point was that such practical considerations were the sole (cognitive) content of beliefs. But unlike the suitable processes of inquiry, which applied to science in action, non-empirical beliefs remained in the realm of pure thought. James's definition of truth laid it open to fierce criticism. It could be interpreted as saying that anything can be considered true if it was useful, but surely a false belief could be useful and a true one harmful to different people. An objection to this is that individuals are indeed subject to this confusion but truth and falsity are publicly determined, and in the long run adaptation to circumstances depends on beliefs being true. Russell's objection to this version was that we would have to wait indefinitely in order to decide whether a theory worked in the long run. The point of James's inclusion of metaphysical beliefs in his definition was that some conceptions were essential to our lives even if we suspected them to be false. As Wittgenstein was to point out later, we are forced to attribute a soul (or an independent mind) to another even if we suspect that our bodies function like machines. The practical value of beliefs was emphasized also by Dewey's instrumental interpretation of knowledge. Theories were not the product of disinterested intellectual curiosity but were instruments for action. According to Willard van Orman Quine (1908–), the reason for choosing the pragmatists' criterion of acceptability is that Peirce's conceptual considerations allow competing intellectual products. There are always several mutually inconsistent theories each of which being compatible with the known empirical data (the evidence). This means that the choice of one theory rather than another at any time must involve considerations other than truth. Concepts, for example, are largely conventional. But most important in Quine's opinion was the impossibility to distinguish between empirical (synthetic) and logical (analytic) propositions, as suggested by logical positivists. His holistic epistemology and theory of language introduced indeterminacy to mutual understanding. This is made explicit when a visitor to a foreign community is forced to interpret the behavior, language and beliefs of its members all at once. Since translation is never unique more than one interpretation of the lot is always possible. However, although epistemology, in his opinion, should be naturalized, as pragmatism requires, this does not mean that any observed acceptance of beliefs as knowledge is equally valid. It also means that since science proved to be the best knowledge we have it should provide the model for all pursuit of knowledge. (See also **logical positivism, holism, neo-pragmatism**).

Price effect: The change in the demand for a good that comes about because of a change in the price of that good. [Pearce]

Price competition: Competition by reducing the price of a firm's product to capture some of the sales from other producers of the same or of a close substitute product. This distinguishes price competition from competition by advertising and providing better quality, or better service etc.

Product innovation, process innovation: **Product innovation** means an addition to a firm's saleable output. **Process innovation** means a change in a firm's mode of production usually to reduce costs. The latter may be the result of the application of new technology or better organization. A change from labour working on a conveyer-belt to automation is an example of process innovation.

Proxy variables, Instrumental variables: Variables used in regression analysis to replace or "stand in for" another theoretically more satisfactory variable in cases where either data are not available on the latter, or the latter is unobservable (e.g. "desired" levels of consumption or permanent income). An instrumental variable is one used to replace actual explanatory variables as weights in regression analysis. [Pearce]

Rationalist: One who believes in **Rationalism,** in the major role of reason, or rationality, and logic in the acquisition of knowledge. The rationalists' major problem concerns the origin of the first premises, those beliefs that are self evident (see **Rationality**), from which other beliefs can be derived. Plato held that these were known by intuition and were innate. The discovery of this source of a-priori knowledge, knowledge which did not require experiential evidence, was the best knowledge we could have. Aristotelian logic was basically derived from an analysis of the knowledge hidden in the structure of the language. In the 17th century, with the increasing role of mathematics in natural philosophy, rationalists like Descartes, Leibniz and Spinoza, came to consider the grasp of mathematics as the paradigm of a-priori knowledge, hidden in human intuition as a gift of God, an ability to discover the grand design in God's creation. These rationalists did not deny the role of sense perception, or of empirical knowledge, but assigned to it a minor role. Similarly, the British empiricists did not deny the role of reason in creating knowledge but assigned it a minor role, mainly because, as Hume put it, reason was a slave of the passions. Spinoza actually anticipated Hume in this pessimistic judgement of human reason but believed that a person was capable of overcoming this slavery. The argument between empiricists and rationalists introduced the dichotomy between synthetic (empirical) and analytic (rational) knowledge. Kant denied that mathematics was a purely analytic knowledge in spite of its being a-priori, and Quine denied the dichotomy altogether (see **pragmatism**). A parallel controversy about the intuitive and the empirical basis of knowledge has applied to language, grammar and logic throughout history. Today, Chomsky for example, still maintains that he is a Cartesian because he attributes innate knowledge of grammatical principles to the mind. But he does not extend this innateness to other types of knowledge.

Rationality: A mental activity, a strategy of behavior or a policy, are described as rational if shown to be required, or be guided by, an acknowledged goal. This definition includes subconscious motives or habitual actions, and allows the attribution of thought to animals. A narrower definition restricts rational behavior to actions justified by reasons, or arguments, and a rational belief to a belief justified by other beliefs, themselves rational or self evident. This definition seems to be dependent on a language and thus restricts rationality to humans. But it excludes the possibility of non-linguistic rational human thought, such as finding a way to take a wide table through a narrow door.

Real-balance effect: A term generally used to describe the situation where there is a change in demand for commodities as a result of a change in the quantity of real money balances. It is the increase in the demand for commodities for consumption as a result of portfolio adjustments by individuals following a change in real money balances. [Pearce] (See also **Pigou effect**).

Real wages: Wages measured in terms of the goods and services they can buy. Wages may rise but their purchasing power diminish, for example during an inflation. A distinction needs therefore be made between real wages and nominal or money wages.

Reciprocal demand: The demand by one country, in terms of its own goods offered, for the goods of another country. The concept was introduced by J.S. Mill to explain how the exact international terms of trade would be established between two closed economy equilibrium price ratios between two commodities by means of the strength of reciprocal demand in each country. This situation Mill described as the equation of international demand. [Pearce]

Reductionism: The systematic practice of reduction, the process whereby concepts or statements that apply to one domain of knowledge are redefined in terms of concepts, or analyzed in terms of statements, of another domain regarded as more elementary. Reductionism is usually opposed to holism. However, the opposition can be understood ontologically or epistemologically. The ontology of a theory is the set of things to which this theory ascribes existence on the grounds that the domain of inquiry cannot be understood without it. For example, reductionist biologists claim that organisms are ontologically reducible to physical systems, that no entities have to be postulated for understanding their behavior in addition to their chemical and physical constituents. Vitalists have denied this view on the grounds that the former's mechanistic explanations cannot account for the behavior of living organisms without attributing to them an entity they described as a vital spirit, or force. They are holists because they maintain that an organism is more than all its parts. Vitalists may or may not agree with reductionists about the basic constituents of the universe. They may claim that the vital spirit is a fundamental constituent of the world, but they also may claim that it is an emergent property, a property that is real but emerges as a result of the organization of physical entities. Reductionists respond to this claim with the concept of supervenience, which is essentially an epistemological notion: they agree that biological properties cannot be satisfactorily described purely by understanding the chemical and physical processes in organisms, but claim that if the existence of any biological property requires the existence of a set of physical entities and processes, and this existence always manifests the biological property, it means that we simply do not know how to reduce the latter to the former, and not that we must postulate the existence of an entity for which we have no independent evidence. The vitalist claim is that the notion of emerging property excludes the possibility of having independent evidence, but the constant manifestation of the property is sufficient evidence. The epistemological opposition of reductionism and holism concerns whether we can or cannot explain one domain of knowledge in terms of another. Positivist biologists, for example, are reductionist in the ontological sense. However, they agree that a tendency to behave is a holistic notion because it names a property that in spite of being a mere summary of a host of physical and chemical processes it cannot be explained in terms of the concepts used for the latter. The concept (or the name) is a logical construction. Holism in this case applies to the organization of knowledge not the world.

Regulated capitalism: A market economy in which the state controls certain key variables mainly to regulate the volume of employment. The Welfare State may serve as an example.

Say's Law: Simply stated this law means that supply creates its own demand. First money is spent on wages etc. to produce the goods which can only later be sold. Hence, earnings are created before the products are for sale. The earnings determine the prices of the total of the goods. If they are above the previously generated incomes, goods cannot be sold and prices fall to their true level. If the prices are below the total value of earnings, then the producers would be selling at a loss and would desist from producing. Hence, supply determines both demand and prices. Consequently there cannot be a general glut of commodities and no long term massive unemployment.

Services: Functions for which there is a market demand and a price. They are intangible goods usually consumed at the point of production and cannot be stored or resold at a different price.

Sophists: Although the term originally applied to generally wise men, it was applied by Plato to various teachers of whom he disapproved, including Protagoras, Gorgias, Thrasimachus, and Hippias of Elis. Plato generally treats them as charlatans who talked purely for victory and took money for teaching the technique. In fact their general stance seems to have been not unlike that of

Socrates, with a reasonably skeptical attitude to speculative cosmologies, such as those of the Eleatics (Parmenides or Zeno), and a reasonable insistence on going to the foundations of morality and epistemology. [Blackburn].

Sticky wages: Wages which because of Trade Union intervention or for other reasons do not fall in spite of unemployment.

Stochastic shocks: The error term in a regression equation, which is designed to capture all of the residual effects on the dependent variable, which are not explicitly taken into account by the explanatory variables. In common usage stochastic means subject to random variation. Thus for example the oil crisis in the 1970s was regarded as a stochastic shock.

Technostructure: A term introduced by J.K. Galbraith to designate the managerial élite and technological experts who control and plan modern industrial production.

Underconsumption: An inadequate volume of consumption in an economy in relation to the volume of production. [Taylor]

Vienna Circle: A seminar founded at the university of Vienna by the physicist Schlick in 1924 (see **logical Positivism**). The discussions were designed to formulate the correct principles of scientific method in order to find what Popper later called the demarcation line between science and speculation. In spite of sharing the Circle's interests Popper never joined the group. Among the scientists and philosophers who participated in it were Bergman, Carnap, Feigl, Neurath, and Weismann. The American pragmatist Quine took part in some discussions, and so did the English-educated philosopher Ayer who brought the group's ideas to Oxford, and whose book Language, Truth and Logic (1936) was influential in spreading logical positivism. Wittgenstein never joined the group in spite of his close personal contacts with Schlick and Weismann, but his Tractatus had great influence on the Circle's discussions. Similarly, although Russell's theory of logical construction was designed to reduce phenomenalism to sensations, and therefore was influential in the group's attempt to develop Mach's radical empiricism, Russell distanced himself from the Circle's logical positivism. The group's activities ended with Sclick's murder in 1936 and most of its member's flight from Nazism. However, Carnap's emigration to the United States prolonged the influence of the group beyond its dissolution.

Wage-fund: This is a doctrine widely held in the 19th century which assumed that a given fund of money exists for the payment of wages, so that if some workers receive more, others are bound to get less. The doctrine postulated that it was futile for workers to raise wages because it would only cause other workers to receive less.

Wealth: Anything that has a market value and can be exchanged for money or goods. Wealth is assumed to have the property of generating income. But wealth is a stock concept and income a flow concept. It also must not to be confused with welfare which means well-being, comfort and happiness.

Wealth effect: An increase in aggregate expenditure due to a fall in the price level and interest rates. It postulates that any fall in aggregate demand by the induced effects of falls in the price level and interest rates will be reversed.

Blackburn = Simon Blackburn, The Oxford Dictionary of Philosophy, Oxford University Press, Oxford New York, 1994.
Bullock = Alan Bullock and Oliver Stallybrass (eds), The Fontana Dictionary of Modern Thought, Fontana/Collins, London, 1977.
Gilpin = A. Gilpin Dictionary of Economic Terms, Butterworths, London 1970
Lipsey = R.G. Lipsey, P.O. Steiner & D.D. Purvis, Economics, Harper & Row, New York 1984, 7th edition.
Pearce = D.W. Pearce (ed.), The Dictionary of Modern Economics, Macmillan, London, 1981
Seldon = A. Seldon, F.G. Pennance, Everyman's Dictionary of Economics, Dent & Sons, London, 1965.
Samuelson = P.A. Samuelson & W.D. Nordhaus, Economics, McGraw-Hill, New York 1985, 12th edition.
Taylor = P. Taylor, A New Dictionary of Economics, Routledge & Kegan Paul, London, 1966

Literature Cited

Arrow K.J. and L. Hurwicz
"On the Stability of the Competitive Equilibrium," *Econometrica*, 26, 1958
Arrow K.J. and F.H. Hahn
General Competitive Analysis, Holden Day, San Francisco, 1971
Arrow K.J.
"Social Responsibility and Economic Efficiency," *Public Policy*, 21, 1973
Becker G.
"A Theory of Marriage," *Journal of Political Economy*, Vol.81, 1973 and Vol.82, 1974
Blair D.D.H., G.A. Bordes, J.S. Kelly and K. Suzumura
"Impossibility Theorems without Collective Rationality," *Journal of Economic Theory*, 13,3, 1976
Blair D.H. and R.A. Pollak
"Rational Collective Choice," *Scientific American*, August 1983
Brenner-Golomb N.
"R.A. Fisher's Philosophical Approach to Inductive Inference," in G. Keren and C. Lewis. *A Handbook for Data Analysis in the Behavioral Sciences: Methodological Issues*, Lawrence Erlbaum, New Jersey, 1993
Brenner Y.S.
A Short History of Economic Progress, Frank Cass, London, 1969
Brenner Y.S.
Agriculture and the Economic Development of Low Income Countries, Mouton, the Hague & Paris, 1971
Brenner Y.S.
Looking into the Seeds of Time, Van Gorcum, Assen, 1979
Brenner Y.S.
"Sources of Inflation: Old and New," in N. Schmukler and E. Marcus (eds), *Inflation Through the Ages, Social, Psychological and Historical Aspects*, Columbia University Press, New York, 1983
Brenner Y.S.
Capitalism, Competition and Economic Crisis, Wheatsheaf, Szabo, Brighton & Washington, 1984
Brenner Y.S.
The Rise and Fall of Capitalism, Edward Elgar, Aldershot, 1991
Brenner Y.S.
"What Went Wrong with Communism," *International Journal of Social Economics*, Vol 20, Number 5–7, 1993

Bronfenbrenner M.
"Cross section studies in the Cobb-Douglas function," *Journal of Political Economy*, Vol.47, 1939
Bronfenbrenner M. and F.D. Holzman
"Inflation Theory," *American Economic Review*, Vol.53, 1963
Bronowski J.
The Common Sense of Science, Penguin, Harmondsworth, 1968
Chase R.X.
"Production Theory," in A.S. Eichner (ed), *A Guide to Post-Keynesian Economics*. Sharpe, New York, 1979
Chomsky N.
Knowledge of Language, its nature, origin and use, Praeger Publisher, New York, 1986
Comte A.
The Positive Philosophy of August Comte, Trubner & Co., London, 1875
Coombs R.
"Automation, Management Strategies and the Labour Process change," in D. Knights et.al. *Job Redesign*, Gower, 1985
Darwin C.
On the Origin of Species, Modern Library, Random House inc., New York, [s.a.]
Davidson D.
Inquiries into Truth and Interpretation, Clarendon Press, Oxford, 1984
de Marchi, N. (ed)
Non-Natural Social Sciences: Reflecting on the Enterprise of More Heat than Light, Duke University Press, Durham NC, 1993
de Volkskrant:
Items on March 6, 1995; November 14, 1994; February 23, 1995; March 15, 1995; January 14, 1995; January 21, 1995; December 17, 1994; December 19, 1994; February 23, 1995; February 22, 1995; December 24, 1994; February 25, 1995; March 11, 1995
Dewey J.
Reconstruction in Philosophy, Beacon Press, Boston, 1957
Domar E.D.
"Capital expansion, rate of growth and employment," *Econometrica*, Vol.14, 1946
Domar E.D.
"Expansion and Employment," *The American Economic Review*, Vol.37, 1947
Domar E.D.
Essays in the Theory of Economic Growth, OUP, New York, 1957
Eichner A.S.
The Megacorp and Oligopoly, CUP, Cambridge, 1976
Eichner A.S.
A Guide to Post-Keynesian Economics, Sharpe, White Planes, 1990
Eindhoven, Philips
Jaarverslagen Philips—CFT 1974–1985

Einstein A.
Ideas and Opinions, Souvenir Press, New York, 1954
Einstein A.
The Evolution of Physics, 7th edition, Simon & Schuster, New York, 1967
Fisher R.A.
The Genetical Theory of Natural Selection, (1930) Dover, New York, 1958
Fodor J.A.
The Language of Thought, Harvard University Press, Cambridge Mass., 1975
Friedman M.
"The Quantity Theory of Money—A Restatement," in M. Friedman (ed) *Studies in the Quantity Theory of Money*, University of Chicago Press, Chicago, 1956
Friedman M.
"Inflation and Unemployment," *Journal of Political Economy*, Vol.85, Number 3, 1977
Galbraith J.K.
The New Industrial State, Signet Books, New York, 1967
Galbraith J.K.
The Affluent Society, Houghton Mifflin, Boston, 1967
Galbraith J.K.
"The Conservative Onslaught," in *The New York Review of Books*, New York, January 22, 1981
Garegnani P.
"Heterogeneous Capital, the Production Function and the Theory of Distribution," *Review of Economic Studies*, 37, 1970
Gellner E.
"Introduction," in Baechler J. et.al. (eds), *Europe and the Rise of Capitalism*, Blackwell, Oxford, 1988
George S. and F. Sabelli
Faith and Credit—The World Bank's Secular Empire, Penguin, Harmondsworth, 1994
Gillispie C.C.
"The Scientific Importance of Napoleon's Egyptian Campain," in *Scientific American*, September 1994
Ginzberg E.
"The Pluralistic Economy of the U.S.", *Scientific American*, December 1976
Ginzberg E.
"The Mechanization of Work," *Scientific American*, December 1982
Habermas J.
Technik und Wissenschaft als Ideologie, Suhrkamp, Frankfurt, 1968
Hansen A.
A Guide to Keynes, McGraw-Hill, New York, 1953
Harrod R.F.
"An essay in dynamic theory," *Economic Journal*, Vol.49, 1939
Harrod R.F.
Towards a Dynamic Economics, Macmillan, London 1948

Harrod R.F.
Essays in the Theory of Economic Growth, OUP, New York, 1957
Heisenberg W.
"The Philosophical Background of Modern Physics," Lecture notes from Dubrovnik seminar in 1975
Hicks J.R.
"Mr. Keynes and the Classics: A Suggested Reinterpretation," *Econometrica*, Vol.5, 1937
Hicks J.R.
The Crisis in Keynesian Economics, Basic Books, New York, 1974
Jaarverslagen Philips 1972–1984
Independent, The
February 4, 1995
Jacquemin A.
The New Industrial Organization, Market Forces and Strategic Behaviour, Clarandon Press, Oxford, 1987
Jaffé W.
"The normative bias," *Quarterly Journal of Economics*, Number 91, August 1979
James W.
The Principles of Psychology, Holt, New York, 1890
James W.
"Pragmatism's Conception of Truth," in *Pragmatism*, Longmans Green, New York, 1907
Jelinek M, J.A. Litterer and R.E. Miles
Organizations by Design. Theory and Practice, Business Publications Inc. Plano, Texas, 1986
Jevons W.S.
Theory of Political Economy, (1888) Penguin, Harmondsworth, 1970
Kahn R.F.
"The Relation of Home Investment to Unemployment," *Economic Journal*, June 1931
Kaldor N.
Essays on Value and Distribution, Free Press, London, 1960
Kaldor N.
"Alternative Studies of Distribution," *Review of Economic Studies*, Number 33, 1966
Kaldor N.
"The Irrelevance of Equilibrium Economics," *The Economic Journal*, 82, 1972
Kalecki M.
Studies in the Theory of Business Cycles 1933–1939, Augustus Kelley, New Jersey, 1966
Kalecki M.
Selected Essays on the Dynamics of the Capitalist Economy 1933–1970, CUP, Cambridge, 1971

Kant I.
Kritik der reinen Vernunft, (Riga 1781) Hamburg, Philosophische Bibliothek Bk 37a, 1976

Keynes J.M.
The General Theory of Employment Interest and Money, (1936) Macmillan, London, 1954

Keynes J.M.
"A Tract on Monetary Reform," *Collected Writings*, Macmillan, London, 1971

Kolakowski L.
Positivist Philosophy from Hume to the Vienna Circle, Penguin Books, Harmondsworth, 1972

Körner S.
Kant, Penguin Books, Harmondsworth, 1955

Koyre A. and R. Taton (eds)
A General History of Science, Vol.II, Thanes and Hudson, London, 1964

Kuhn T.S.
The Structure of Scientific Revolutions, University of Chicago Press, Chicago, 1970

Kuniyoshi Urabe et.al.
Innovation and Management; International Comparisons, Walter de Gruyter, Berlin New York, 1988

Lakatos I.
"Falsification and the Methodology of Scientific Research Programmes," in I. Lakatos and A. Musgrave, *Criticism and the Growth of Knowledge*, CUP, Cambridge, 1974

Lakatos I and A. Musgrave
Criticism and the Growth of Knowledge, CUP, Cambridge, 1974

Latour B. and S. Wooglar
Laboratory Life: The Social Construction of Scientific Facts, Sage, London, 1979

Latour B.
Science in Action, Harvard University Press, Mass., 1987

Latour B.
"Postmodern? No, Simply Amodern," *Studies in the History and Philosophy of Science*, 21, 1990

Leontief W.
"Exports, imports, domestic output and employment," *Quarterly Journal of Economics*, Vol.60, 1946

Leontief W.
"Introduction to a Theory of the Internal Structure of Functional Relationships," *Econometrica*, Vol.15, 1947

Leontief W.
The Structure of American Economy, 1919–29, New York, 1951

Leontief W.
"Econometrics," *A Survey of Contemporary Economics*, Philadelphia, 1948

Leontief W.
  Input-Output Economics, O.U.P., New York, 1966
Leontief W.
  "Academic Economics," *Science*, 217
Lerner A.
  "Functional Finance and the Federal Debt," *Social Research*, 10, 1943
Luxemburg R.
  "Leninism or Marxism," in *The Russian Revolution & Leninism or Marxism*, Michigan University Press, Ann Arbor, 1961
Malthus R.T.
  An Essay on the Principle of Population, (1789), Penguin, Harmondsworth, 1970
Manders A.J.C.
  Sturing van Produktie-Technologie, Kerckebosch, Zeist, 1990
Marcuse H.
  One Dimensional Man, Sphere Book Ltd., London, 1968
Marris R. and D.C. Mueller
  "The Corporation, Competition and the Invisible Hand," *Journal of Economic Literature*, 1980
Marx K.
  Critique of Gotha Programme, International Publishers, New York, 1938
Marx K.
  Das Kapital, Dietz Verlag, Berlin, 1972
Matthews R.C.O.
  The Trade Cycle, James Nisbet & CUP, Cambridge, 1959
Mitchell B.R.
  European Historical Statistics 1750–1970, Macmillan, London, 1975
McCloskey D.N.
  The Rhetoric of Economics, Harvester Press, Brighton, 1986
McCloskey D.N.
  If You're So Smart: The Narrative of Economic Expertise, University of Chicago Press, Chicago & London, 1990
Mill J.S.
  Principles of Political Economy, Augustus Kelley, New York, 1949
Mirowski P.
  More Heat than Light: Economics as Social Physics, Physics as Nature's Economics, CUP, Cambridge, 1989
Nossiter B.D.
  "Outcasts of the Islands," *New York Review of Books*, Number 14, April 1977
Ohmae Kenichi
  "Triad." De opkomst van mondiale konkurrentie, Veen, Utrecht-Antwerpen, 1985
Pareto V.D.
  Cours d'economie politique, 1895
Pareto V.D.
  Traité de sociologie générale, Payot, Lausanne, 1919

Pasinetti L.L.
"The rate of profit and Income Distribution in relation to the rate of economic growth," *Review of Economic Studies*, 29, October 1962

Pasinetti L.L.
Growth and Income Distribution: Essays in Economic Theory, CUP, Cambridge, 1974

Peirce C.
"The Fixation of Belief," in J. Buchler, *Philosophical Writings of Peirce*, Dover Publications, New York, 1955

Peirce C.
"How to Make Our Ideas Clear," in J. Buchler, *Philosophical Writings of Peirce*, Dover Publications, New York, 1955

Peirce C.
"Pragmatism in Retrospect: A Last Formulation," in J. Buchler, *Philosophical Writings of Peirce*, Dover Publications, New York, 1955

Phillips A.W.
"The Relation between Unemployment and the Rate of Change in Money Wage Rates in the United Kingdom 1862–1957," *Economica*, Vol.25, 1958

Pigou A.C.
Economics of Welfare, Macmillan, London, 1952

Popper K.
Conjectures and Refutations, Routledge & Kegan Paul, London, 1963

Popper K.
The Open Society and its Enemies, Harper & Row, New York, 1963

Popper K.
Objective Knowledge, Clarendon Press, Oxford, 1972

Popper K.
"Normal Science and its Dangers," in I. Lakatos and A. Musgrave, *Criticism and the Growth of Knowledge*, CUP, Cambridge, 1974

Quine W.O.
Methods of Logic, Routledge & Kegan Paul, London, 1970

Rawls J.
A Theory of Justice, Oxford University Press, 1972

Reijnders J.
Long Waves in Economic Development, Edward Elgar, Aldershot, 1990

Ricardo D.
On The Principles of Political Economy and Taxation, (1821) Penguin, Harmondsworth, 1971

Rorty R.
Consequences of Pragmatism, (Essays 1972–1980), Harvester Press, Brighton, 1982

Rorty R.
Contingency, Irony and Solidarity, CUP, Cambridge, 1989

Rossetti J.
"Deconstructing Robert Lucas," in W.J. Samuels (ed), *Economics as Discourse*, Kluwer Academic, Boston, 1990

Samuels W.J. (ed)
  Economics as Discourse, Kluwer Academic, Boston, 1990
Samuelson P.A.
  "Interaction between the Multiplier Analusis and the Principle of Accelaration," *Review of Economic Statistics*, 31, 1939
Samuelson P.A.
  Foundations of Economics, Atheneum, New York, 1965
Savigny on the Mythology of the Ibis, see Gillispie C.C.
Say J.-B.
  A Treatise on Political Economy or the Production, Distribution and Consumption of Wealth, (1803) Augustus Kelley, New York, 1964
Schumpeter J.A.
  Capitalism, Socialism and Democracy, Allen & Unwin, London, 1943
Segal P.T.
  Skinner's Philosophy, University press of America, New York, 1981
Shaikh A.
  "Laws of Production and Laws of Algebra," in E.J. Nell.(ed), *Growth of Profit and Property*, CUP, Cambridge, 1980
Smith A.
  The Theory of Moral Sentiments; or An Essay, Towards an Analysis of the Principles by which Men Naturally Judge Concerning the Conduct and Character, first of their Neighbours, and afterwards of Themselves, (1759) 2nd edition
Smith A.
  An inquiry into the nature and causes of the Wealth of Nations, (1776) The Modern Library, Random House inc., New York, 1937
Snels B.
  "Models of Politics and Economics: National Economic Policy in an Integrating Europe." Paper presented at 53rd annual meeting of the Association for Social Economics. January 8th, 1995, Washington DC
Solow R.M.
  "A Contribution to the Theory of Economic Growth," *Quarterly Journal of Economics*, Vol.70, 1956
Solow R.M. and P. Samuelson
  "Analytical Aspects of Anti-Inflation Policy," *American Economic Review, Papers and Proceedings*, Vol.I, 1960
Sombart W.
  "Capitalism," in the *Encyclopedia of Social Sciences*, Vol.III, Macmillan, New York, 1935
Spinoza B.
  Ethics, (1677), Dent and Sons, London, 1979
Spithoven A.H.G.M.
  Werkloosheid Tussen Markt en Regulering, Thesis, Amsterdam, 1988
Spithoven A.H.G.M. and Y.S. Brenner
  Mijlpalen in de Wordingsgeschiedenis van het Hedendaagse Economisch Denken, Utrecht University, Utrecht, 1995

Tarski A.
The Concept of Truth in Formalised Languages. Logic, Semantics and Metamathematics, Clarendon Press, Oxford, 1956
The Encyclopedia of Philosophy, Macmillan & Free Press, London, 1967
Tinbergen J.
"Over de mathematisch-statistische methoden voor konjunktuuronderzoek," *De Economist*, 76, 1927
Tinbergen J.
Econometrie, Noordduijn's Wetenschappelijke reeks, Gorinchem, 1949
Tinbergen J.
Economic Policy: Principles and Design, Amsterdam, 1956
Tinbergen J.
Central Planning, 1964
Toulmin S.E.
Cosmopolis: The Hidden Agenda of Modernity, The Free Press, New York, 1990
Walras L.
Elements of Pure Economics or the Theory of Social Wealth, (1874; 1877), English translation, Allen & Unwin, London
Walsteijn R.P.G.
Aggregate Demand, Income Distribution and Economic Growth, ISOR, Utrecht, 1994
Weinberg S.
"Life in the Universe," *Scientific American*, October 1994
Westwood A.R.C.
"R & D Linkages in a Multi-Industry Corporation," *Research Management*, jrg.27, No.3
Wittgenstein L.
Tractatus Logico Philosophicus, 1921
Wittgenstein L.
Philosophical Investigations, Basil Blackwell, Oxford, 1958

Index

Acceleration principle, 51–56, 209, 210
Aristotle, 89
Arrow K.J., 90, 227
Arrow's "Impossibility Theorem", 90
Arrow's axioms, 91
Atomic energy, 102, 176
Automation, 15, 23, 71, 190, 222, 228

Balzac de H., 158
Behavioral assumptions, 3, 12, 56, 91
Behaviorists, 136, 153
Blacks, 106, 160, 172
Blair D.H., 90, 91, 227
Bolshevism, 175
Boltzmann's theory of gases, 121
Bronowsky J., 66
Bukharin N.I., 43
Bureaucracy, x, 45, 73, 99, 180, 183–187
   bureaucratic insensitivity, 103
Business cycles, 32, 55, 56, 210, 230

Capital, viii, x, 1, 14, 15, 18, 28, 32, 33,
   39–43, 45, 51–56, 60, 61, 65, 76, 77,
   81, 86–88, 97–99, 195, 200, 209–
   211, 214, 228, 229
Capital/output ratio, 51–55
Capitalism, vii, ix, xiv, 4, 6, 10, 11, 16,
   21, 31, 35, 42, 48, 56, 57, 65, 69,
   72, 80, 89–92, 95, 100–105, 179,
   186, 187, 224, 227, 229, 234
Captains of industry, 8
Causality, 113, 123, 124, 210
Ceteris paribus, 2, 26, 65, 74
Chaplin's *Modern Times*, 71
Chase R.X., 60, 228
Chomsky N., 167, 223, 228
Christianity, 103, 200
Civil society, 176
Class, 7, 8, 17, 22, 25, 39–42, 44, 45,
   61, 62, 72, 73, 87, 89, 95, 95–97,
   102–105, 155, 160, 161, 162, 177,
   184, 186, 188, 189, 192, 195, 196,
   198–200, 204
Classical physics, 3
Clinton B., 205
Coalition–forming, 14, 15
Cognitive, 113, 116, 118, 119, 129, 154,
   160, 166, 215, 217, 221
Coherence theory of truth, 109–110,
   124, 147–149, 170, 212, 215
Communism, 45, 227
   communists, 45, 178, 210
Comparative advantages, 77, 211
Competition, vii, 4–9, 13, 15–17, 25, 29,
   33–36, 40–42, 47, 48, 56, 59, 60, 63–
   65, 67, 70–72, 76, 79–82, 89, 92, 96,
   98, 100, 102, 106, 177, 188, 190,
   191, 216, 218, 222, 227, 232
Comte A., 142, 143, 219, 228
Comte's project of positive science, 142, 143
Conceptual scheme, 118, 128
Condorcet's paradox of voting, 90
Confidence, vii, 10, 64, 77, 91, 92, 99,
   129, 154, 191–195, 199, 220
   self–confidence, 161
Consumption, 18, 25, 27, 31, 36, 39, 41–
   44, 47–51, 55, 56, 69–71, 80, 81, 92,
   98, 207, 210, 211, 213, 215, 219,
   222, 223, 225, 234
Contextualism, 110, 211
Copernicus N., 1, 66, 179, 209
Core activities, 13, 15–18, 34, 48, 98, 211
Correspondence Theory of truth, 109,
   147, 148, 170, 211, 212
Corruption, 10, 11, 83, 191, 195, 196
Crane W., 175
Crowe's list of foreign investors, 33
Cultural creation, 156, 170, 172

Darwin Ch. R., 120, 162, 228
Darwin's and Lamarcke's disagreement,
   120, 123

237

Printed in the United States
by Baker & Taylor Publisher Services